SYMBOLS
AND THEIR HIDDEN MEANINGS

SEVENOAKS

THIS IS A SEVENOAKS BOOK

This edition published in 2006 by SevenOaks
An imprint of the Carlton Publishing Group
20 Mortimer Street
London
W1T 3JW

A CIP catalogue for this book is available from the British Library.

ISBN-10 1-86200-405-6
ISBN-13 978-1-86200-405-4

Executive Editor: Amie McKee
Senior Art Editors: Zoë Dissell and Emma Wicks
Picture research: Steve Behan
Production: Lisa Moore

Printed in Dubai

SYMBOLS

AND THEIR HIDDEN MEANINGS

THE MYSTERIOUS SIGNIFICANCE AND FORGOTTEN ORIGINS
OF SIGNS AND SYMBOLS IN THE MODERN WORLD

T.A. KENNER

CONTENTS

HELLS ANGELS
MC
CALIFORNIA

AZA

INTRODUCTION

We are a very visual species. Sight is our most psychologically powerful sense, the one that we associate with the greatest richness and texture. Our ability to recognize patterns, even obscured ones, is incredible. For an example, just look up at broken clouds passing overhead – the myriad shapes and faces that appear and disappear are a powerful testament to our visual sorting instinct.

A symbol, literally, is something that represents something else by association, resemblance or convention. Whilst some objects are just symbols, tokens that have no inherent meaning other than that which they represent – some of the more abstract religious symbols fit into this category – in most cases, symbolic meaning is one layer of an item's or notion's overall purpose. A school tie-pin is still a tie-pin; a flashy red sports car is still a vehicle. Symbolism is usually a quality, rather than the be all and end all.

It is also important to remember that most symbols are also multilayered. They may have associations on several different levels, leading in radically different directions depending on which context you look at. A piece of Baroque art may be a beautiful pastoral scene on one level and a powerful statement on morality on another level – but on a third level, it is also a strong symbol of its owner's wealth, sensibility, taste and ideals.

To further compound the issue, symbolism is not an inherent structure of the human mind. It is a type of language, a way of conveying meaning, and like all languages, it requires that both participants in an exchange know what the words mean. Different cultures may have radically different understandings of a certain symbol, particularly where the symbol is fundamental, and broad-based. Some symbolic statements are nigh-on universal – bigger means stronger – but others may be restricted to a small subset of one culture. The number 42, for example, only symbolizes the answer to the great question of life, the universe and everything for fans of the late comedy sci-fi author Douglas Adams. Like codes, some symbols are meant only for certain eyes.

The use of symbols is more prevalent now than ever before. With every company, political party, product brand and good cause competing for your money and your attention, the clamour of desperation is often deafening. By incorporating as much powerful symbolism as possible into every moment of every message, the various competitors hope to sway you – and keep you – in their favour.

The people around you, the entertainments you enjoy, even the choices you make regarding your own basic lifestyle – all these things have strong symbolic associations. If you wear a tie, that is a symbolic noose representing ownership. If you have a red car, that is a symbolic statement that you are exciting; blue, that you are safe; brown, that you are reliable. Your hairstyle, the home you live in, the newspaper you read in the morning... our world is saturated with hidden meaning. Over the course of this book, we will explore some of the different types – languages – of symbolism which go to making up the landscapes of meaning in the world today. It is a rich and fascinating journey that will open your eyes to whole new levels of reality.

1 FOUNDATIONS

Symbols can convey their meaning to us on many different levels. Most of the time, a particular symbol is linked to one or more types of knowledge or experience. For example, only someone educated in European feudal heraldry would understand that a left-slanted bar across a coat of arms indicates a person born outside marriage. However, certain classes of symbol operate on a deeper, more primal level. They are part of the everyday experience of being human and provide a base that underlies all our other assumptions and symbolic understanding. While there may be some degree of cultural difference in the exact message that these foundation symbols convey, they still speak to all of us.

The three Fates symbolized the past, present and future. Here they are shown with Zeus, king of the Greek gods, measuring out a golden life of wonder and glory for Marie de' Medici in the 1625 painting by Peter Paul Rubens.

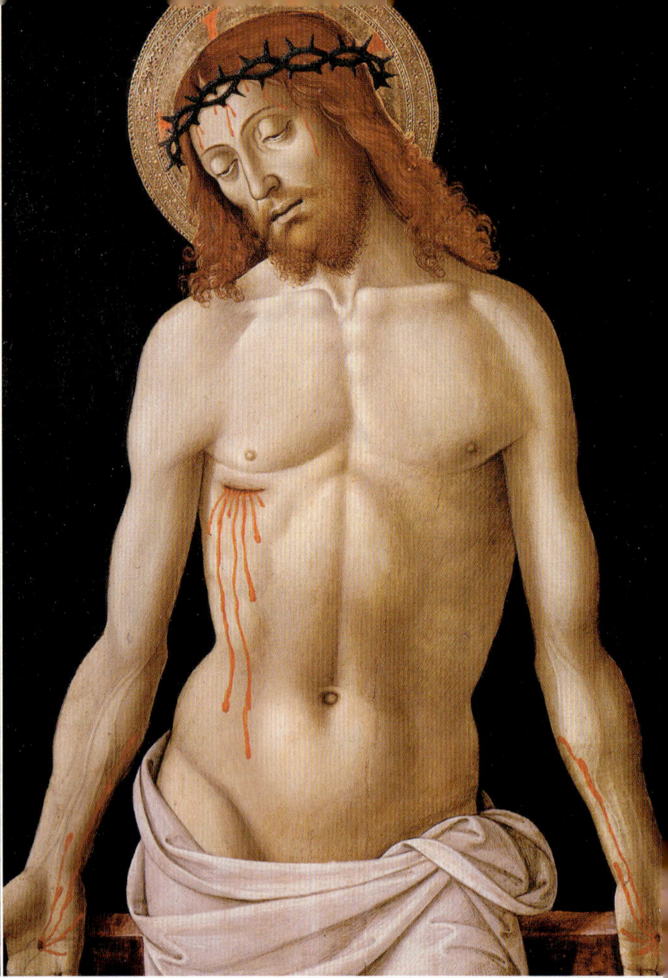

清洁即家珍
寻常无异味

As you explore the world of symbolism, you'll discover that foundation symbols crop up time and again, adding nuance and texture to more complicated images. In many cases, even the symbol's original creators may have incorporated foundations without ever truly realizing what they were doing – these elements are so fundamental to our experience of the world that we often use them implicitly. A person may be painted wearing a green shirt rather than a yellow or blue one – or holding three rods, rather than four or two – just because it feels right to the artist.

Foundation symbols help us to structure and order our lives in more ways than we can count. Once you look past the immediate, semi-conscious, automatic recognition of familiar sights, you'll find that the foundations apply almost everywhere, from traffic instructions to classic art. It's a fascinating glimpse into the human world's inner workings.

COLOUR

We become aware of colour even before we are able to recognize most shapes. It is the earliest of our visual cues and works its way into the deepest layers of our minds' symbolic language. We react to colour on an almost unconscious level; it influences our moods and reactions whether we know it or not. Our understanding of the language of colour comes from many sources: the natural world, our homes, the many different environments we experience, the ways certain objects affect us and, most powerfully of all, our own bodies.

CLOCKWISE FROM TOP LEFT:

THE PLANET MARS
The alien landscape of the red planet, Mars. Its colour in the night sky has given it a longstanding association with the colour red and its natural aspects in particular.

THE CRUCIFIXION
In Christian teaching and art, the blood of Christ is one of the most common symbolic associations with the colour red. This blood is a potent representation of power and force, the energy to transmute the Son into virtue. At the same time, it carries the associations of all blood, and the violence that shed it.

THE GOD MARS
The Roman god of war, Mars (right), is the exemplar of the colour red and its symbolic meanings. Powerful, excitable, passionate and short-tempered, he is a consummate warrior and enthusiastic, if jealous, lover. He is depicted here with Venus in a fresco by sixteenth-century artist Giulio Romano.

CHINESE BANNERS
For the Chinese, red is a powerfully fortunate colour. No important event or undertaking would be considered without making extensive used of the colour in time-honoured ways.

Red

Of all the colours, red is the one that has the strongest emotional effect on us. It is the colour that brings us into the world. We are born in blood, and quickly learn that it is the very stuff of life – it is blood that fills us, always ready to spring to the surface when we cut or graze ourselves. Blood is the nearest we can come to physically seeing our life-force – our birth, our existence and the awareness of our mortality, all wrapped up in one vivid hue.

Blood flushing to the skin can signal excitement, anger, sexual arousal, embarrassment and other moments of intense emotion – critically important signals to those around us. The presence of blood itself is a strong instinctive alert. It means that someone or something has been injured, possibly killed: the danger could still be present...or there might be vital food on a freshly-hunted carcass.

Although most individual flames shade across several colours, fire is red in our minds and in our symbolic languages. Like blood, it is both life-giving and lethal, a vital source of warmth and nurture, but also a clear reminder of pain and death. Harnessed fire is energy and power – light to live by, heat to cook and get warm by, and a weapon to drive off enemies with. It was the vital tool that allowed us to develop the society and intelligence that we have today.

From these critical foundations, red has taken on a complex web of meanings for us. Because of its strength, it represents power, force, leadership and courage. With the way that it colours our skins to reflect our emotions, it is also associated very strongly with sexuality, passion, excitement and love, and with defensive reactions such as anger, aggression, rage and shame. Through its links to fire, it carries meanings of energy, force and destruction, material security, stability and influence. Modern society has given it meanings that include debt (from the red ink used to mark ledger debits), left-wing politics and the instruction to stop. Blood gives the colour its deepest associations – with life and death, birth, menstruation, violence, danger, war and excitement. Above all, red is exciting, getting us ready for opportunity or threat, the joint thrills of pleasure and danger.

Across the world, culture-specific beliefs tend to reinforce the general human experience of the meaning of red. In classical times, the planet Mars, the brightest red light crossing the sky, was identified with (and named after) the Roman god of war. Heraldry used red to indicate boldness, ardent love and enthusiasm.

Around the World

For the Chinese, red is the colour of luck, because of its power over life and death. Across much of Africa, it is seen as one of the colours of sorcery, because of the power of blood. In Polynesia, it is the colour of the gods themselves. In India, it represents virginity and purity. Christian belief associates it with Christ's death, while Hindu thought attributes it to the power of Kundalini, the sacred life-force.

ABOVE: Exciting and adventurous without being threatening, orange represents everything that modern Halloween celebrations embody.

BELOW: The yellow smiley symbol.

Orange

Sunrise and sunset, the light from a fire, autumn leaves, "red" hair, carnelian and amber, and a whole range of good things to eat – orange is cheerful, stimulating, charming and productive. In the English language, the word "orange" dates to the introduction of the fruit that gave the colour its name. Before then, the colour had been known as "geoluhread", or yellow-red, and indeed many of orange's symbolic meanings today are a mixture of those belonging to red and yellow.

Although fire is considered red symbolically, individual flames are generally thought of as orange. The colour is warm without being aggressive, stimulating without causing alarm. It is exciting and engaging, but the edge and danger are missing; this is a colour for reflection, appetite and sociability. Many foods are orange, from squashes such as pumpkin, through roots such as carrot, sweet potato and ripe swede, to citrus fruits such as oranges and grapefruits. They lend the colour associations with wholesomeness, desirability, security, physical energy and success.

Precisely because it is simultaneously stimulating but wholesome, exciting but safe, orange has become associated with adventure, persuasion, eagerness, energy, vigour and confidence – the romantic notions of engaging in heroic pursuits. This gives it charm, seductiveness, wonder, and associations with both creativity and wholesome lust. In heraldry, it had the specific meanings of generosity, honour and strength.

The complementary colour to blue, orange shows up most clearly against an open sky, and so is widely used worldwide as the best colour for matters of safety and security. People engaged in dangerous work outdoors – builders, engineers, trackside train officials and so on – often wear orange. There are even officially described shades of orange known as "Safety Orange" and "International Orange", both used for signs, markers and safety equipment. Interestingly, the colour has also become associated internationally with political opposition and rebellion, possibly through its links to persuasion, adventure and success. Religiously, the colour is linked to Hinduism, some forms of Protestantism, and to Judaism in the Gaza Strip.

Yellow

The colour of sunshine, yellow is one of the most cheerful, uplifting hues. It is a warming, encouraging colour that brings hope and pleasure. With its overtones of ripe corn, sandy beaches and sunny weather, it is optimistic and easy-going, symbolizing desiderata such as harmony, peace, vitality, playfulness and idealism.

There is more to the colour than just sweetness and light, however. Because of the way the human eye works, yellow is the most visible of all the colours. That is why many American taxis and school buses are yellow – to catch the attention of potential passengers and other drivers on the road. Travel and movement are related. The colour stimulates the mind, giving it attributions of creativity, intelligence, philosophy, wisdom, knowledge, authority and personal power. It is supposed to denote the path to enlightenment, and so is also linked to divination, eloquence and communication.

Yellow is commonly found in situations that require attention or thought. Highlighter pens and sticky memo paper both started out yellow as a means of focusing attention quickly. Combined with black, it is a powerful signal of danger, as a wasp's stripes clearly show. In traffic lights, yellow (amber) indicates that the driver has to be prepared. Cheerful yellow walls in offices and study rooms have been found to stimulate productivity and personal effectiveness.

Yellow's associations with peace, harmony and playfulness have led to the colour being associated with pacifism and a reluctance to engage in warfare – and, by extension, with cowardice. But if having a yellow streak or yellow belly means being playful and creative rather than enraged and violent, maybe the term should be considered as a compliment rather than an insult. Heraldic devices used yellow as a token of knowledge, ability and wealth, through its closeness to gold. In the East, where rulers were assumed to be wise and enlightened, the colour

Father Christmas was traditionally dressed in green because of his links to the Green Man, the personification of nature's bounty. It was Coca-Cola who first dressed him in red and white in 1931.

has long associations with imperial power. Some cultures, such as ancient Egypt, associated the colour with death, perhaps because of postmortem skintone, or perhaps because of their hopes for a joyful afterlife.

Green

Green is above all else the colour of nature, and our relationship with nature has always been an ambivalent one. Right from humankind's earliest times, the green of forests, jungles, long grasses and other wild places has indicated a world that people depend on, but in which they are not entirely welcome. Despite its dangers, however, the natural world has been the only widely available source of resources for most of humankind's history. Green is therefore associated with wealth, currency, employment, good luck and fullness. The green colour of the American dollar has compounded this association.

Another aspect of nature's greenery that has been passed on to the colour is its lush fertility. Green represents all things that grow, namely the natural world – particularly where being "natural" is considered desirable – and by extension health, longevity, vitality and endurance. Rolling fields and tidy grasslands are signs of beauty and tamed nature, a great pleasure for most

Because of its associations with harmony, good luck and health, green has come to indicate that it is safe to proceed, particularly in the context of traffic signals.

of us, and in that aspect, as a harmonious, peaceful colour, green indicates stability, beauty, compassion, growth, transformation, unconditional love and sharing. This has been translated into permission to proceed in a number of important contexts, including traffic lights and most other transport-related situations. Similarly, business projects that have been given the go-ahead are said to have been green-lighted.

But there is a darker side to the natural world as well. In countries all over the globe, green has a history of representing danger and death. The natural world has long been a great source of menace to humankind. Dense woods and jungles – and long grass – can hide all sorts of dangers, from large predators to ankle-snapping holes to all manner of diseases and poisons.

In Western cultures, green is also commonly found as a sign of jealousy, inexperience, greed or nausea, particularly in its lighter shades. The Chinese use it as a sign of cuckoldry, particularly when linked to hats (worn by the cuckold). It is a sacred colour for Muslims and Catholics, and an indicator of growth in Christianity. Politically, it often represents ecological awareness. It is frequently used as a colour of light in electronic devices because it is physically the easiest colour for the eye to perceive, and the one in which we can distinguish the greatest number of shades.

The Green Man

Robin Hood, the legendary, green-clad outlaw, appears to have been at least partly related to Celtic ideas about death. His green outfit makes him an embodiment of nature – both a source of food and wealth for the hungry, and a lethal source of menace (although he is said to have killed only the unrighteous). The green of army camouflage and its automatic association with combat and death is an updated take on this sense of menace.

Calm, stable and comforting, blue is the colour most commonly associated with the ultimate mother, the Virgin Mary. She is depicted here with her infant son, the very soul of tranquillity, as saints look on in wonder.

Blue and Indigo

As above, so below. The colour of sea and sky, blue is deep, cool and calming. The second most emotionally powerful colour after red, blue is its counterpart, soothing and relaxing rather than energizing and intimidating. Like both sky and sea, blue is frequently distant, mysterious and evocative, provoking contemplation, meditation, thought and tranquillity. All over the world, blue is associated with understanding, protection, safety and peace, and, from a marketing perspective, it is considered the "safest" colour for use globally. It can help promote restful sleep, spiritual awareness and even, supposedly, intuitive powers.

Because of its associations, blue is often felt to convey an air of seriousness, importance and authority, particularly in its deeper shades. As such, it is frequently used by police forces, who traditionally wish to convey both power and safety to the public they watch over. It is also popular in the commercial world, where it is seen as conveying a calm, stable, authoritative air. Richer tones emphasize the colour's protective nature and are more common in religious and medical settings, or on signs that are designed to provide safety-related advice. Light shades of blue tend to hint at more sociable aspects of the colour, such as confidence, integrity, truth, independence, loyalty and unity.

BB King plays the blues, evoking the colour's tendency towards loneliness and depression. In extremes, blue can represent quite severe mental instabilities.

Marketing research has discovered that blue is the "safest" colour for use worldwide – in other words, it is the least likely to antagonize anyone, and the most likely to provoke a positive reaction.

On a more negative note, as red represents the excesses of energetic emotion, so blue represents the excesses of calm emotion. It is frequently considered synonymous with depression – as in "feeling blue", or having the "blues" – and can also represent withdrawal, isolation, loneliness and instability, even insanity. Lighter blues can be very cold, both physically and emotionally, while darker blues tend toward the obsessive; deep blue is said to be the colour of fanaticism. Blue also has associations with injuries, from the colour of bruises, and with vice – blue movies, for example – perhaps acquired from the colour's instabilities.

Nevertheless, blue is a very popular colour politically and with authorities of all kinds, particularly those that represent stability and conservatism. It carries connotations of nobility, quality and reliability that salespeople of all types have been quick to latch on to. Historically, a lot of cultures worldwide have not distinguished blue from green, and the colour was not used in artistic works until the time of dynastic Egypt. While this may have represented a global difficulty in acquiring blue pigments, it has also been suggested that the eye's ability easily to distinguish blue tones from greens and violets of a similar intensity may be a relatively recent development.

Possible reinforcement for this theory lies in the fact that the eye finds it particularly difficult to pick out the colour indigo – some people are still unable truly to distinguish it from the blue and violet that surround it. Indigo was named by Sir Isaac Newton in his definition of the seven visible colours of the spectrum. It has been suggested, however – even by the famous author and scientist Isaac Asimov – that Newton picked indigo out specifically to bring the number of colours up to seven, and that it should just be considered a shade of blue. Computer screens and (most) printing presses are unable actually to render indigo, which is best seen at dusk on a clear night. Symbolically, the colour is associated with psychic powers.

Purple is a powerful signifier of wisdom, authority, ceremony and prestige. That makes it a popular colour for high-ranking priests and clergy, including the much-loved South African cleric Desmond Tutu, seen here while still a bishop in 1987.

Violet and Purple

There is a great deal of confusion between violet, the final colour of the visible spectrum, and purple, which does not actually exist within it. Violet sees relatively little use in the day-to-day world, and is usually associated symbolically with spirituality and the divine – thanks primarily to its correspondence to the Hindu crown chakra, or spiritual energy point.

Symbolically, purple is by far the more important of the two colours. The deep, rich hue has traditionally been difficult and expensive to reproduce. As a result, the colour became firmly associated with rulers from around the world, both royal and imperial, who could afford these goods and also linked, by association, with the virtues that rulers typically wish their subjects to believe that they possess – wisdom, power, wealth and luxury. Other associations also come from this attribution, including ceremony, mystery, arrogance, transformation and cruelty. Linguistically, the colour has come to symbolize excess, as in "purple prose" or "purple haze".

The Vexed Question

While the two colours are similar, violet is distinctly bluer than purple, and also considerably less saturated. In practical terms, violet – which, like indigo, is almost impossible to reproduce truly in print or on screen – is light at a wavelength that marks the eye's threshold of perception, specifically around 380 to 420 nanometres, while purple is a mixture of blue light and red light, and contains light of two or more totally different wavelengths.

As a fusion of reds and blues, purple has often been used in recent years to indicate coalitions, compromises, blends and, by extension, homosexuality. In addition to its worldwide association with rulership, the colour also indicates penitence in Christian thought and widowhood in Thailand. Advertisers commonly focus on purple as a sign of wealth, luxury and prestige – a way of suggesting to potential customers that while spending money on, say, a particular chocolate or cigarette may not help you become emperor, it will still provide elements of the associated lifestyle.

Brown

If green is the active colour of nature, then brown is its passive counterpart. The natural colours of human hair and skin are all shades of brown, with a greater or lesser contribution from red – the colour of human existence. It is the colour of bare soil, from which we grow our food; it is the colour of wood, which we build so much out of; and it is the colour of decay, fallen leaves and faecal matter. It surrounds all stages of our existence at a very practical level. It is impossible to talk about it symbolically without referring back to these realities – the colour is grounded, down to earth, rooted.

Like purple, brown is a combination colour rather than a wavelength of light in its own right. Often considered a close hue to orange, brown is obtained by combining complementary colours – red and green, orange and blue, or yellow and purple. Brown is not a stimulating colour. In fact many people find it rather dull, even slightly depressing. It reminds us of our physical nature, brings us back down from heights of emotion, passion or fancy with the clear message that we live in the real world – the one in which we have to eat, sleep and wash.

Brown has plenty of positive associations, however. It is steadfast, reliable, comfortable and dependable. It conveys warmth and wholesome honesty, lacking the ambition, greed, coldness or excitability that other colours might convey. It is consistent and trustworthy specifically because it is a little dull. Excitability, inconsistency and imagination are not desirable traits when you are choosing an institution to look after your money, or someone to drive your

UPS Brown is a trademarked shade that the global package company uses to enhance its reputation for steadfast reliability and honesty.

school bus. It is essentially stable and restrained.

Internationally, brown does not see a lot of variation in its meaning. It is rarely used politically, not appearing often in logos or flags. For most advertising purposes, it is found to discourage sales. The colour is just not an aspirational one. Its most common application is in uniforms that are intended to indicate that the wearer is trustworthy, steady, reliable and unthreatening. As such, the colour is often found in service businesses worldwide. The international package delivery company UPS has even trademarked a specific shade of the colour as an important element of its corporate business, a hue now known officially as "UPS Brown". Not all uses have been so wholesome, of course. Symbolism can lie just as effectively as any other form of communication. The most reviled brown uniforms of recent memory are those of Hitler's *Sturmabteilung*, the stormtroopers who formed the paramilitary wing of the Nazi party.

Black

Technically the absence of light, rather than a colour itself, black is a complex symbol. In the Western world, it carries a lot of negative connotations, many of them centred around fear and the unknown. This is not necessarily the case in other regions, although almost all cultures recognize the duality and opposition between black and white.

One common theory regarding black's sinister associations is the obvious link to darkness and night-time. People are afraid of what the darkness hides; it is the time of thieves, nocturnal predators, malefactors and witches. If this is the main reason for black's negative connotations, then perhaps the Western world's particularly strong negative feelings toward black can be explained in terms of European weather. Unlike the arid regions in the Middle East, Africa and large parts of Russia and China, European skies are commonly cloudy. Night-time would have been genuinely pitch black, and therefore particularly intimidating. In countries where cloud cover was much less common, even moonless starlight provides a surprising amount of illumination, and night would have been much less blind. In other words, night just isn't as dark in the tropics and equatorial regions as it is in cloudy temperate zones.

Another possibility commonly put forth is that in any given area, people with the power and wealth not to have to work outdoors at menial tasks are going to be paler in skintone than those who are exposed to the sun all day. That is an inevitable biological fact. The implication then becomes that rulers and aristocrats are going to be paler than their poorest subjects. Taken to its extremes, these differences become symbolized as an antagonism between black and white, with black indicating meniality and inferiority.

Black lends an und eniable air of authority and power to a priest's influence, and if some of the colour's more intimidating aspects come with it, maybe that just helps to generate extra respect.

LEFT: A black armband serving as a badge of power rather than loss: in the football world, it is worn by the player who is team captain as displayed here by Manchester United's Rio Ferdinand.

RIGHT: One of the most powerful stereotypes associated with black is the image of the evil witch. Dressed all in black and skulking around in the middle of the night, witches were a genuine source of terror throughout medieval Europe.

As the greatest and most terrifying of life's mysteries, death is intimately linked with black in western culture. The Grim Reaper, as the personification of death, is hidden entirely by black cowled robes.

In the West, however, black's strongest associations are linked to the theme of evil. While these meanings may be retained to a certain extent outside the West, they tend to be significantly weaker. Backed up by religious imagery, black now symbolizes tragedy, sadness, loss, despair, fear, discord, lies, bad things, malevolence, sin, satanic works and rituals, the netherworld and – by extension of the theme of loss – mourning and bereavement. For the Chinese, by contrast, black is the colour of the element of water, and conveys stillness and passivity rather than badness.

Western popular culture's use of the colour has led to it being reclaimed, to an extent, by younger generations wishing to defy the orthodoxy, thumb their nose at authority, and generally irritate their parents. Accordingly, black now also symbolizes a whole swathe of interpretations on the theme of defiance and freedom, such as rebellion, independence, mystery, occult power, sexuality, anonymity, acceptance and anger. Politically, it is generally associated with anarchism.

Well before its uptake by youth culture, however, black attained a degree of respectability. It is a perennially fashionable colour for clothing – not only is it the most flattering and slimming colour to wear, it can also convey a degree of sophistication, elegance, seriousness and power. Authority figures have often used black to add weight to their influence – for example, priests, judges and the elite and secret police – particularly where blue's reassuring air of safety is not required. With black common to both establishment figures and rebels, the difference between them lies mainly in the style of clothing – but then, this year's rebels tend to become next year's authority anyway.

White

The opposite of black both literally and figuratively, white is the equal presence of light from all colours of the visible spectrum, brightness without hue. It is unblemished, and has become a strong metaphor for purity and perfection. Religious thought has further extended this image of purity into a whole range of different interpretations. These are dominated by the theme of goodness: virtue, sexual abstinence, innocence, obedience, truth, sincerity, reverence, cleanliness and humility. Other auxiliary associations include understanding and protection – peace, unity with God, wisdom, enlightenment and youth – and joy, happiness, glory, purpose and so on. In religious imagery, white dominates depictions of heaven, saints, angels and God Himself, because it is perfect and untainted.

However, it can be just as accurate to associate purity with sterility, coldness, withdrawal, isolation, arrogance, unworldliness, clinicalness, lack of compassion and emptiness. It is as empty of proper colour as black is; an extreme, and thus devoid of flavour or charm. Many atrocities throughout history have been perpetrated in the name of purity. In many cultures, white is the colour of death, misfortune and mourning, and even in the West it is associated with ghosts, the pallor of disease, and the impersonal formality of the medical world. In early Hollywood, white was used to depict heroes and black villains, but there has been a noticeable shift toward both black and white depicting extremism, and softer tones, such as earth colours, depicting moderation and sanity.

Politically, white has often been used historically to depict royalty and the current leadership. It is the sign of surrender and peaceful intention and, by association, pacifism. Inevitably, this has also led to some interpreting it as a sign of cowardice, and in Victorian England accusations of cowardice were delivered by presenting the target with a white feather.

Other Colours

There are of course a near-infinite variety of different precise colours, and many of them have their own specific interpretations. For example, the traditional associations of pink for young girls and powder blue for young boys still play a large part in Western culture, particularly in packaging for children's products. Grey is boring, predictable, old and reactionary. Silver represents the moon and witchiness. Gold symbolizes success. Many combinations have specific meaning, too. Red and pink together suggest sexuality, while red and green represent Christmas, particularly with a dash of white. Black and orange are autumnal, specifically Halloween; black and yellow, by contrast, as we have already mentioned, are a powerful danger sign. We only have room here to scratch the surface, but colour symbolism is a fascinating field of study in its own right, and the key to a much greater understanding of the coded messages that underlie our cultural experience.

ABOVE: The struggle of Good versus Evil – depicted here in the form of *Star Wars* characters Obi-Wan Kenobi and Darth Vader – is a universal concept of duality.

BELOW: The Yin-Yang symbol.

NUMBERS

As with colours, we all quickly build up a subconscious alphabet of associations related to numbers. The process with numbers is slightly more artificial than it is with colours, because it comes more from the assumptions that underlie our languages and cultures. This doesn't make it any less powerful, however. Our minds are designed to think in certain ways, and as we grow, we quickly absorb layers of meaning that we didn't really notice at the time. Of course, cultural acquisition of meaning like this provides the potential for great variation internationally in the symbolism of numbers – but despite this potential, numerical symbolism is actually quite consistent worldwide. This implies that the meanings we attach to numbers were probably first thought out a long time ago in our prehistory.

Zero

Just as black and white are not really colours, so zero is not really a number. It represents absence; it is a token that quite literally makes something out of nothing. It is a comparatively recent invention; the earliest use of true zero as a number is found among the Olmecs (the Central American forefathers of all the Mesoamerican civilizations) around 50BC, and it doesn't properly arise in the Old World until around AD300, in India. Even the ancient Greeks were uncertain of zero as a mathematical term, many arguing that the concept had no meaning.

Zero is actually a rather counter-intuitive idea if you think about it: if there is nothing there, then why have a symbol or name for it? Common sense says that if I have two apples and then eat one and give the other to you, then all the apples are gone, and there is no point talking about apples any more. Zero, on the other hand, introduces the alien idea that zero apples remain, as if somehow the ghost of their presence lingers on in a potential. It is a subtle but incredibly powerful difference, and a vital one for the development of truly sophisticated mathematics.

Symbolically, zero primarily represents absence, and by association loss, unimportance, irrelevance and low status. However, it can also represent the idea of the infinite void, and by extension anything that is omnipresent. It is endless, timeless, featureless and indistinguishable; zero apples is truly identical to zero cars or zero universes. In computing, zero also symbolizes the logical state of "False", roughly equivalent to answering "No" to a question that starts "Is…?"

Infinite Voids

In Islam and Kabbalistic Judaism, zero is the number of the perfect, infinite divinity. It therefore represents self-contained infinity – perfect, unblemished and entire.

One

The first true number, one is generally considered to represent the spark of life and the male principle. Almost invariably represented by a single stroke in cultures worldwide, the number has a strong visual association with the male phallus. Because it signifies a single item, it strongly symbolizes unity, solidarity and fellowship: "We stand as one." It is also the number of uniqueness, individuality, isolation, separation and loneliness – "the one and only". On its own, one is inherently sterile, unable to self-differentiate, develop meaningful self-awareness, or ever to open into any significant dialogue.

Being self-contained, one is seen in several cultures as the number of divinity. It is unable to procreate because of its isolation, so its ability to bring forth many must be an act of divine creation. Accordingly, one, like zero, has associations of completion and perfection, but unlike zero it lacks the implied sterility and emptiness. One represents the infinity of eternal presence, rather than the infinity of the empty void, and has overtones of power that zero lacks. Mathematically, one is seen as something of an exception, the odd one out, because it is a special case for so many rules. In computing, it represents logical "True", or the answer "Yes".

Two

The first number that has the potential for perception and interaction, two is the number of duality, possibility and the feminine principle. In duality, there is polar opposition, and two

The closest human embodiment of the number two, identical twins are seen as special throughout the world. Regarded as particularly lucky by the Chinese, and often as psychic in other areas, they embody the creative pulse of life.

is symbolic of conflict, opposition and diversity – good versus evil, dark versus light, hot versus cold, and so on. Furthermore, by deviating from the perfection of one, two can come to symbolize error, sin, deviance and corruption. Note that in the biblical account of the Great Flood, only the unclean animals went into Noah's Ark in twos.

The antagonism attached to the number two is not automatic of course, and two also represents stability, dependence, balance and reflection. As the blend of opposites, it is the Yin-Yang of Taoist philosophy, the dance of life that gives birth to all things. Indeed, the Chinese regard the number as lucky – "Good things come in pairs" is a well-known Chinese proverb. Two is the number of pregnancy, and it opens up the potential for creation. Two also symbolizes a straight path or linear direction, because the shortest distance between any two points is always a straight line. It is impossible to set a pattern with just two points of reference. Plato dismissed the number as meaningless, because he felt that its presence implied a relationship, which would automatically involve progressing to three.

Three

Three is the number of completion, the first number that earns the use of the word "all". The regular triangle, with three equal sides, is the most stable flat shape, more resistant to pressure and deformation than even a square is. If you are proving that a line is straight, three points are the least possible requirement to indicate that the pattern will hold. By contrast, if you want to indicate a pattern and then break it, three is again the least possible number of cases. Most jokes work in groups of three – the infamous Englishman, Irishman and Scotsman, for example – for exactly this reason: one to set the example, two to reinforce it, and three to turn it on its head, giving you the punchline.

Three is also the number of fertile sexual union, one and two, male and female, joined together to produce a third. By extension to the concept of fertility and birth, three is also the number of manifestation, of making something happen. It indicates creative power, moving energy, resolving the conflict of duality, growing and developing. Wishes, petty misfortunes, witches and many more things are all said to come in threes.

Linking back toward completeness, three is the number of the cycle of life: beginning, middle and end; past, present and future. By association, it is often thought of as magical or divine. The Trinity of Father, Son and Holy Spirit is a powerful symbol of tripartite completeness. So, too, historically, are the three Fates (or Moirai) of Greek mythology – the triple-goddess of Maiden, Mother and Crone (found also as the three Norns of Norse myth) who spin a life-thread for each person, measure it, and then cut it. Similarly, the moon is often seen as tripartite, waxing, full and waning, and moon deities (such as Hecate) often had three faces; lunar animals were commonly supposed to have three legs.

LEFT AND RIGHT: Stable, perfect, complete: the triad is the strongest arrangement of elements, the first number to introduce the idea of depth, and the symbol of creative power. It is a strongly divine number, as embodied by the Father, Son and Holy Spirit in this 1636 painting by Ribera.

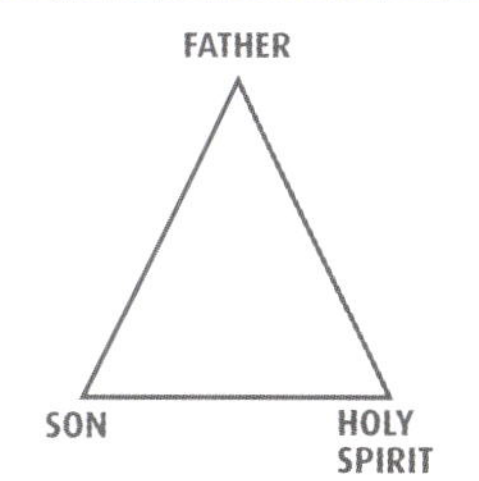

Four

If three is the number of creative potential and manifestation, then four is the number of stability, of the manifest world brought into existence. It is the first number that contains the potential for solid, three-dimensional reality – the tetrahedron, a pyramid shape with a triangular base, has four corners. Many elements of the outside world are broken down into groups of four: the four classical elements of air, earth, water and fire; the four cardinal directions of north, south, east and west; the four seasons of spring, summer, autumn/fall and winter. Many management (and military) theorists suggest that four is the most stable nodal structure in an organization – that no person should have more than four people reporting *directly* to him, so as to avoid overcomplication and chaos.

Perhaps because of its role as such an earth-centred number, four often has unfortunate religious overtones. It is said to be the number of Lucifer the fallen, the banished fourth who came after the Trinity. The last Apocalypse will be heralded by four horsemen, Death, War, Plague and Famine. In China, Korea and Japan, the word for four sounds very similar to the word for death, so it is often considered highly unlucky right across the East, where some buildings are numbered without a fourth floor. Some numerically named product lines with a strong Far-Eastern market presence entirely omit the four-series for the same reason – Nokia mobile phones, for example. Of course, four also has plenty of religious significance attached to its symbolism of stability and completion: in Christianity, for example, there are four archangels, four cardinal virtues and four rivers of paradise. There are also the four boundless wishes of Buddhism, the Islamic four Principles which make up the divine, the four worlds of the Hebrew Kabbalah, the four faces of Brahma in Hinduism, and so on.

Five

Five is the number of life and of human experience. In classical Greek and Hindu theory, it represents the four elements, which were seen as the building blocks of matter, fused with the animating force of spirit. For the Chinese, spiritual energy was inherent in each element, and didn't need a separate designation – but they defined five elements, rather than four, having

ABOVE: The four cardinal directions of north, south, east and west are encapsulated by the compass, which takes in the entire scope of the manifest world.

LEFT: The Four Horsemen of the Apocalypse, due to be let loose by Lucifer for the Last Battle, may have contributed to the number's unfortunate connotations.

wood and metal in place of the more abstract classical element of air. Five is the most fundamental number of human existence: we have five fingers; five senses (sight, hearing, smell, taste and touch); five tastes (sweet, sour, salty, bitter and savoury); five sets of openings into the body (ears, nostrils, mouth, nipples and sexual/eliminatory organs); and, when we stretch out, five points of the body (the four limbs plus the head). The magical symbol of the pentagram, the five-pointed star, is thought to suggest a person with arms and legs spread wide, and as such to represent individuality, spiritual aspiration, and protection.

The Star of David, which looks like two interlocking triangles pointing in opposite directions (for a total of six points), is a powerful symbol of mankind bathing in God's love, with heaven and earth in accord.

With such an intimate personal connection to the number five, it is no surprise that it feels like an automatically natural value for a set of objects. Most mathematical systems around the world operate on groups (i.e. "base") of ten, the number we can get to counting by counting on the fingers of both hands. The few cultures that do not work in groups of ten, such as the Ikwaye of New Guinea, tend to work in groups of twenty instead, using both fingers and toes. As befits such a visceral number, five crops up repeatedly in religious imagery across the world, particularly with reference to human experience: the five wounds of Christ; the feeding of the five thousand; the five Dhyani Buddhas guarding the five directions ("centre" is also a direction); the five faces of Shiva in Hinduism; the sacred role of five in the modern US Discordian movement; and the Five Pillars of Islam and their five fundamental dogmas.

Six

Mathematically perfect and triangular, six is the number of equilibrium, harmony and balance. Its two visual equivalents, the six-sided regular hexagon and the six-pointed Star of David, both represent this completion. The hexagon is the first complex solid (triangles and squares are considered trivial cases) that can fit in an infinite field of itself and leave no gaps. It is the number of heaven and earth in unity and, as the sum of five and one, it represents humankind in the state of grace with God.

As the number of sides on a cube, six is associated with dice, and therefore with luck, chance, victory and health. It is also linked to creation, as the number of days required to make the world in several traditions, and to humankind because in the Bible humans were created on the sixth day. The Great Beast of the Book of Revelation is said to have the number 666 as a trinity of earthly, human influences, simultaneously mocking and lacking the true heavenly Trinity.

As the number of human creation and harmonious balance, a trinity of sixes – famously described in the bible as a "human" number – is associated with the Devil's son, the Antichrist, appropriately titled lord of this world.

Seven

A highly mystical number, seven represents humankind's connection to the divine. It is the union of four with three, the manifest world joined to the Holy Trinity, and therefore the path to God. This has made the number considerably important to mages, alchemists and would-be wizards throughout history. Seven is often found underlying grand schemes of existence – days of the week, wonders of the ancient world, pillars of wisdom, deadly sins, rays of creation, levels of hell, colours of the rainbow, musical notes, even Shakespeare's ages of man. It is internationally associated with integration, synthesis and the larger scheme of the universe. In Buddhism, the seven steps correspond to mastering time and space; in Hinduism, the seven primary chakras mark the ascent from the earthly to the divine.

Shown here are four of the nine Worthies, historical defenders of truth and righteousness, known as the Knights Valiant – Arthur, Charlemagne, Hector and Judas Maccabeus.

Eight

Eight is the number of regeneration and rebirth. The baptismal font is eight-sided, being the basin in which the young are reborn free of sin. There are eight beatitudes in Christ's Sermon on the Mount; eight Auspicious Symbols in Buddhism; eight trigrams of the Taoist Ba'gua (and eight immortals who have mastered the Way); and eight divisions in Islam. In several mystical doctrines, personal transformation can be obtained on the eighth day, after seven days of fasting and meditation. Eight is the number of corners on a cube, and as such it is also seen as representing solidity, physical perfection and the scope of reality. The Chinese consider the number to be lucky, because their word for it sounds like the word for "prosper".

Nine

If seven is the number of mystical connection, nine is the number of magical power. As three times three, it is the ultimate expression of creative power fulfilled, of energy directed and divine will channelled. Its potential is highlighted in the Magic Square, a square divided into three by three cells in which each line, column and diagonal add up to the same number – fifteen in the case of the three-times-three square that uses each digit once.

A potent symbol of rebirth in God's grace, the baptismal font is typically eight-sided. This beautiful example from the area around Milan in northeastern Italy is from the sixth century AD.

8	1	6
3	5	7
4	9	2

Many cultures around the world have considered the number nine to be representative of spiritual and divine power. In European myth, it was associated with the Nine Worthies, three sets of three mighty heroes and defenders of truth from pagan, early Christian and later Christian times. In Buddhism, nine is the celestial number of supreme spirituality. In China, it is the most auspicious of all numbers, as it represents the eight directions plus the Hall of the Heavenly Emperor. In Hindu legend, it is the number of the fire that leads to the square that encloses the universe.

Ten

As the first double-digit number in our modern mathematical system, ten carries a sense of wholeness and completeness. The Ten Commandments of Mosaic law were God's complete pronouncement. We describe ten as a "round" number, meaning that it is satisfying. It also has implications of maximum quality, of being as good as it is possible to be – ten out of ten, a "perfect" ten. By implication ten contains all the digits from zero through to nine, which emphasizes its completion – and thus it can by extension represent the whole of

The twelve signs of the zodiac represent a complete model of human psychology, no matter how idiosyncratic. This is symptomatic of the number's association with cycles, systems and numerical completion.

creation. Note that in the distant past, the number twelve more commonly served this role, and ancient symbolic uses of the number ten may not carry quite the same implications.

Eleven

Represented by the figures 1 and 1 set next to each other, eleven is something of an analogue to two – a higher octave, according to numerologists; but as it represents two individuals rather than a pair, it is necessarily somewhat more isolated. It is considered neutral in many ways – a middle ground between oppositions. It has connotations of being almost, but not quite too late – as in the "eleventh hour".

Twelve

Historically, twelve is the natural number of measurement, a position that ten has usurped to a certain extent. This is thought to be because twelve is so easy to divide – into halves (by six), thirds (by four), quarters (by three), sixths (by two), and even eighths (by one and a half). This made it very useful for any system that required frequent division by the uneducated masses, such as time, distance and currency.

Because of its clear associations with circular notions of time – twelve months in a year, twice twelve hours in a day, five times twelve minutes in an hour, twelve signs of the zodiac, and also twelve inches to a foot – twelve is associated with cycles and closed systems. It is also seen as a good number for a complete set of objects, one that covers all the bases. So there are twelve tribes of Israel; twelve labours of Hercules; twelve gates to New Jerusalem; twelve days of Christmas; twelve gods of Olympus; twelve sons for Jacob and for Ali; and twelve disciples or companions for Jesus, the Dalai Lama, King Arthur, Charlemagne and Mithras.

The long, straight, inflexible train thundering into the open circular tunnel in front of it is an almost stereotypical Freudian symbol for the sexual act.

Further Numbers

Many other numbers have significant symbolic value, of course. Thirteen is famously unlucky; sixteen, eighteen and twenty-one all involve coming of age; twenty-three is associated with creative chaos; twenty-five with silver anniversaries; forty-two with life, the universe and everything; fifty with golden anniversaries; sixty-nine with sexual activity; and so on – and that is just whole numbers. The most important symbolic associations, however, lie within the numbers from zero to nine.

PSYCHOLOGICAL SYMBOLISM

There are two main branches of psychological theory, Freudian and Jungian, that deal with inherent symbolism in the mind. These symbols are seen as being a result of the way the mind is structured, as automatic and natural as knowing how to breathe. Both branches agree that certain symbolic meanings are automatically acquired, like instincts; however, the two diverge significantly on exactly what sorts of symbols are involved. It is important to note that orthodox science tends to reject both schools out of hand. Whether either or both are true doesn't actually matter much, however. The fact is that both schools have their followers in and out of the arts, and the symbolic languages they describe find frequent deliberate use in the real world. In other words, the original research has become self-fulfilling in that the symbols they describe are now a common part of our psychological landscape.

Freudian Symbols

Primarily concerned with sexual expression, Freudian symbolism provides a model in which the libido is fixated entirely on sexual gratification. One way or another, the mind's unconscious vocabulary becomes connected entirely to sexual matters and desires.

The most important associations in Freudian theory relate to the shape of the symbolic object. To boil it down to basics, according to Freud, a long, straight object – a pen, a cigar, a sword – represents an erect penis, particularly if the object is capable of thrusting or penetrating; while a round or oval object – a cave, a shield, a plate – represents a vagina, particularly if it can be receptive. Juxtapositions of assorted items were indicative of personal inclinations for sexual activity. Thus a doodle of crossed swords might indicate male homosexuality, while a miner with a pick entering a coal mine demonstrated a desire to be utterly consumed by sexual experience, and a train entering a tunnel was

LEFT AND RIGHT: Jung's theories proposed a wide range of recurrent Archetypes that were fundamental to the experience of being human, and that therefore would crop up time and again across the world, in all times and locations. These Archetypes are familiar to us precisely because of their ubiquity. Thus the Wise Old Man (Left) and the Innocent Child (Right) are immediately recognizable to us. The Archetypes share a sense of enlightenment and power for us, but from totally opposed sources – the Wisdom of experience and understanding against the unprejudiced Perception of true innocence.

a depiction of sexual union. Challenged on this point while smoking a long, thick cigar, Freud is famously said to have pronounced: "Sometimes a cigar is just a cigar."

Freud also maintained that part of growing up involved wanting to murder the same-sex parent so as to sexually possess the alternate-sex parent; that masturbation reduced the mind to a state of bestial ignorance; and that women felt massively inferior to men because they lacked penises. Some believe his theories set back women's rights by decades, and they are still often trotted out to justify sexual bigotry.

Jungian Symbols

In contrast to Freud's ideas, Jungian symbolism is predicated on the notion that there is an objectively real common pool of symbolic meaning. This pool, the so-called "mass mind", exists outside any one individual, although all unconscious minds can tap into it. Within the mass mind, a set of symbolic blueprints that Jung called Archetypes act like the building blocks of our personal mental landscape, just like our DNA directs the building of our bodies. The mass mind is usually conceived of as some kind of low-grade, vast group telepathy that all humans share at a deep unconscious level, so that all our minds are interlinked and provide a sort of landscape for the Archetypes to exist in.

Some of these Archetypes are rooted in our own minds. The Animus and Anima are respectively the male and female aspects of the personality. A healthy person's personality is developed within the aspect of their own sex, but remains in balanced contact with the aspect of the opposite sex. There is also the antithesis of the personality known as the Shadow, which gathers up all the person's negativity and ill will, and seeks the exact opposite to whatever the core personality desires.

In wider terms, any symbolic image that seems to recur across human experience and culture could be a Jungian Archetype manifesting from the mass mind. Thus common symbolic clichés such as the Wise Old Man, the Innocent Child, the Resolute Hero and the Dark Stranger are all examples of Archetypes – clichéd specifically because they are common to human experience.

Jung was particularly interested in the way Archetypes manifested through dream and artwork, and sought to explore the possibility that such things had important life messages to convey. Jung's detractors suggest that clichéd images became widespread for more obvious reasons – namely that they simply held elements of truth about human life – and that Jung's idea of dream messages was just a tendency toward shamanic mysticism painted over with a veneer of scientific thought to disguise it.

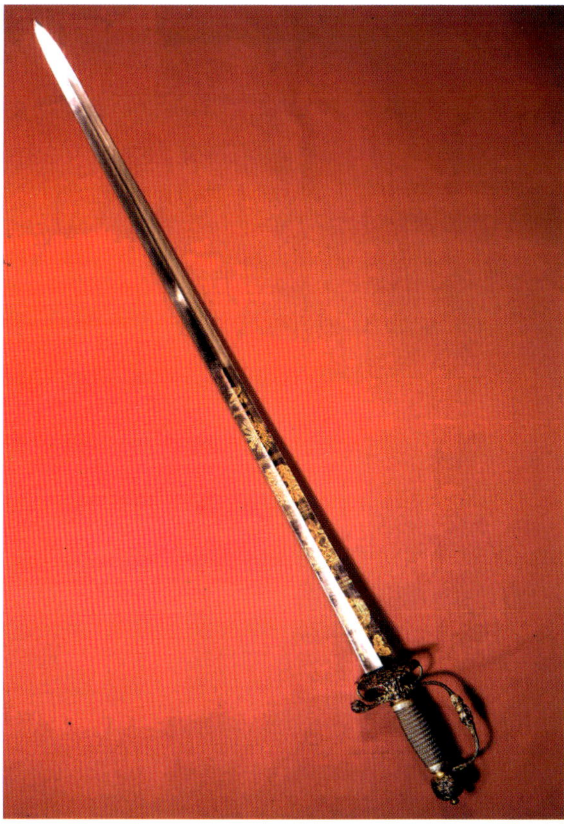

Long, strong, rigid and well-suited for thrusting and penetrating, the sword was a straightforward representation of the penis for Freud.

2 ENVIRONMENT

We live on a ball-shaped planet, spinning through space at more than 110,000 kph (70,000 mph). With the exception of a few fundamentalist religious thinkers, we all know and accept this... but it is not the way that we perceive the Earth around us. To the unconscious mind – which pays far more attention to our senses and experiences than it does to our conscious awareness – the world is the totality of existence, vast and flat, the dramatic screen upon which our lives are played out. The language of symbolism doesn't translate into environmental crises and invisible pollutants, it speaks of sweeping plains, endless deserts and sheltered coves. The settings in which we live our lives have strong symbolic meanings, and it can be difficult to understand the intent behind art and literature, myth, architecture and even sometimes music without some knowledge of the language of environment.

Timeless, dominant and spiritually stark, mountains are extremely powerful landscape features. Often considered the centre of the world – and/or the home of the gods – by earlier cultures, they are a potent symbol of the environment's might.

EARTH

Our relationship with the planet has always been a troubled one. There is a tendency in modern times to romanticize the natural world, but in fact humanity's history is all about the struggle to escape it as much as possible. This means that the very ground we stand on has a complicated set of meanings for us that can easily leave us feeling confused and uncertain about our place in the world.

On the one hand, the Earth is quite literally where all of our resources come from. It feeds us, clothes us, shelters us and warms us. Even in the modern, urban world, it is impossible to escape the symbolic association between land and life. The ground is nurturing, providing, maternal and caring. It can be a thing of great beauty, warmth and comfort. Travellers by air and sea are often struck by how alien those environments become, and how much returning to dry land feels like coming home. Particularly in the sterile settings of modern life, this caring warmth is a great draw, and many of us feel a strong attraction to the outside.

On the other hand, the Earth is also the home of all that threatens us. Historically, it is the source of wild beasts, poisonous plants and creatures, dangerous terrain, threatening weather and everything else that bedevils us, including other people. It is as likely to be dark and scary as it is to be light and lovely. Nature is not kind, it is ruthless. All those deadly dangers remain in the back of our minds, as anyone who has managed to spend the night alone in deep woods can attest.

Even more powerfully, the ground is where we are laid to rest. Dust to dust: when we die, the Earth opens up and swallows us, and makes us part of itself. It is the cold of the grave, a hungry monster devouring all flesh. To our symbolic thoughts, all ground is teeming with ancient carcasses, every drop of soil the broken-down remains of some poor soul. Bare earth, in particular – ploughed fields, empty flowerbeds and so on – carries this strong association with mortality, inevitability, death and decay. No matter how beautiful the Earth may be, it always carries with it the charnel whiff of the grave – and underneath our modern romantic longing for nature, there is always a pang of fear.

Direction

The cardinal directions of the compass carry symbolic meaning gained from the experience of life. The most universal, unsurprisingly, are east and west, following the daily rising and setting of the sun. All cultures share the experience of the sun rising in the east. The sun is universally regarded as a source of hope and life; even in the harshest climates, it seems, day is preferable to night.

East is the direction of birth and rebirth, childhood, youth, happiness and energy. Many religious ceremonies, historically, have been conducted facing east – certainly all solar gods and religions have laid a great emphasis on the eastern horizon. By extension from the idea of birth, childhood and youth, the east is also the direction in which home lies. Taken as a cultural metaphor, the east becomes the cradle of civilization, the direction of ancient knowledge and wisdom. East is the direction of origins, mysteries and wonders, the home of the light, the source of life, eternal youth, immortality and divinity.

West, by contrast, is the universal direction of death. The sun dies in the west every night, bringing darkness and danger. Evil and misfortune are associated with westerly directions, along with autumn, old age, sickness and the lands of the dead. In ancient Greece, the entry to Hades was said to be near the western edge of the country; in Egypt, the souls of the dead had to make a dangerous pilgrimage to the lands of the west in order to find their eternal reward – a myth paralleled almost exactly by Tolkien's elves in the *Lord of the Rings* cycle. In modern American mythology, the Wild West is a byword for lawless violence and sudden murder. Not all of the western associations are so negative, however. Modern cultural patterns are giving it an association with progress and scientific advancement, and traditionally it has been the direction associated with explorers, new frontiers and discoveries.

Drawing more on the geopolitics of the last five hundred years than on any particular facet of the natural world, north has come to represent modernity, materialism, advance, industrialization and thought in general. It is masculine, aggressive and dynamic. The south, by contrast, is considerably more innocent. Viewed as relaxed, it symbolizes feeling and intuition. It has a holistic nature lost to the north, and represents older, less sophisticated, values.

Cerberus, the terrifying three-headed monster dog, is shown here guarding the entrance to Hades, the Greek underworld. Located in the far west, the entrance to Hades marked the boundary of the real world.

When he needed to gain spiritual clarity and understanding, Christ took himself off into the wilderness of the desert for forty days and forty nights, as depicted here by Ivan Kramskoi in 1872.

Tarzan is a potent symbol of the jungle's lush fertility and uncontrolled sexuality. Exciting, dangerous and untamed, Tarzan's adventures are a popular way into the mystery and excitement of jungles for people worldwide.

TERRAIN

Individual landscapes and settings play a major part in shaping life for their inhabitants. Each type of terrain provides its own set of opportunities and challenges, and it rewards certain types of behaviour and punishes others. Accordingly, landscapes have acquired a powerful symbolic meaning for us that reflects their nature, and the nature of the life that is lived in such places. As with the cardinal directions, these meanings tend to be broadly similar for all races and cultures.

Desert

Arid landscapes with little or no vegetation, deserts are hard places to survive in. Although the stereotype of a desert is a rolling sea of sand, they can be cold as well as hot, and consist of rocks or bare earth as well as sand. Both visually and symbolically, the desert is free of confusion; they are free of doubt. Because they are wide, open vistas without any covering vegetation, they represent brutal honesty, impersonal struggle and the harsh realities of survival. Human beings are poorly tolerated in these areas, largely occasional visitors who stand out clearly.

There are no distractions in deserts, and this gives them an association with clarity, revelation and purity. Because it is such a difficult, threatening terrain type, desert represents barriers, obstacles and challenges. There are strong overtones of spirituality and religion bound up symbolically with desert landscapes. These areas are brutal, but they call upon the deepest reserves of a traveller's will. In these struggles, there are no barriers to the heavens, no distractions or comforts to distract the soul from its communion with the divine.

Accordingly, the desert can be a source of wisdom and enlightenment, of trial but also of reward. It is so beyond normal existence that only the spiritual and divine can touch and influence it. We assume a fundamental antagonism between the physical and the spiritual, feeling that gluttony and excess obscure the divine. Thus the desert – the ultimate site of physical scourging – becomes the holiest territory available. It is no accident that prophets, visionaries and hermits throughout history have been strongly associated with these barren lands.

Jungle

Representing everything that deserts are not, both literally and figuratively, jungles are the densest source of living things on the planet. They are hot, noisy, smelly, damp, and just about as dangerous as the desert sands, particularly to the casual visitor. If the desert is nature at its hardest, the jungle is nature at it most frenetic.

The overriding symbolic impression of jungle is of lush fertility. This is not the ordered fertility of farmland, though; it is wild, uncontrollable, threatening – fertility (and, by extension, sexuality) run rampant. Another important symbolic aspect is chaos. The jungle is full of confusion, noise, movement and danger. It is exciting and crammed with possibility, but even a small misstep can prove disastrous. As such, it is often used as a metaphor for teeming city sprawls, particularly unfamiliar territory ("It's a jungle out there!").

As the home territory of many native tribes and lost civilizations, jungle also has powerful associations with primitive culture, hidden secrets and mysteries, buried threats, treasures and adventures. In among all this mystery and confusion, it is easy to believe in just about anything; jungle is symbolically pregnant with possibilities and enigmas. It is a link to a long-lost past, one in which anything could happen.

George Morland's 1793 image *Gathering Wood* shows Hansel and Gretel in the dangerous place where the forest switches from kind nurturer to cruel heart of darkness.

Forest

For centuries, forest has marked the edges of humankind's domain. Across Europe, North America and the Far East, people have had to carve living space out of the great temperate forests. Much of the world has a long history of being in close proximity to these green wildernesses. Forests are strongly symbolic of the cycle of life, from the growth of spring and the flowering of summer to the decay of autumn and the barren emptiness of winter. Frequently trackless, inhabited by potentially dangerous animals, forests are places of danger and trickery.

Where the jungle is an unsubtle, all-out attack, forests are subtler – a familiar presence, outwardly calm and tranquil, but firmly marking the boundary of people's authority. Where the desert is stark and revelatory, forests seemingly take joy in shading and dappling, defeating the sun, blurring and softening everything into uncertainty. Vegetation is in control here, unregulated; it is the domain of the earth mother, the feminine principle. The heavens – and Heaven itself – are hidden in forest, out of sight, out of control.

Accordingly, there is a long association between forestry and the unconscious mind, which is often seen as feminine – forests are home to fairy tales, legendary bandits and monsters, witches and wizards, and all manner of magical presences. The trees themselves are reminiscent of temple columns – but what terrifying god or goddess could need such a vast church? Children's stories are full of forest dangers, from the Big Bad Wolf on downward, which represent a symbolic journey into the frightening subconscious.

As a marked boundary, forests symbolize the frontier, thresholds, the unknown. Journeys into them are seen as initiations, tests and challenges; to return is to be reborn, the uncertainty of the unconscious laid to rest. Forests are the fringe of darkness that lurks on the edge of civilization, a space where we can project our deepest anxieties and fears.

The most famous embodiment of the sea's random malice and lethality, the great white whale Moby Dick takes its spite out on half-mad Captain Ahab in Melville's classic story.

Ocean

Water is life. The planet's surface is mostly water, and so is living matter. At the very beginning of the world, water was where life began, where we all came from, back in the ultimate creation. To a certain extent, therefore, the ocean is symbolically the world's womb, the source of all. As mentioned earlier, Freudian symbolists would take this image further, to symbolize all sexuality and procreation.

The oceans, however, are not hospitable or nourishing. If they once gave us birth, they are now closed off to us forever. In terms of hostility, the ocean is even less forgiving than the desert. Its water is poisonous to us, its moods fickle, its storms lethal. If we attempt to traverse it without a boat or raft of some sort, it is a constant fight just to stay floating. The sea is a byword for cruelty, changeability and lack of sympathy. Historically, many sailors never bothered learning to swim, because being lost overboard generally meant death – whether you could keep afloat for a little while or not.

The ocean is a place apart. It has no up or down, no heights or valleys. It is separate from all solid experience,

Rabelais' famous sea monster, Gargantua, depicted here by Gustav Doré, is a mighty terror of the oceans, a vast, monolithic atrocity that devours sailors by the boat-load. It is also a metaphor for the French aristocracy.

Shoreline

Seashores are inextricably bound up with notions of romance, peace and beauty. They present the very best of the sea, mysterious and evocative, with the theoretical possibility of allowing a journey to anywhere in the world (or out of it, for the whimsical), but safe, tamed, a source of beauty and bounty rather than hardship. Even on the wildest shores, the sea is safely at arm's length. At the same time, shores tend to be away from the bustle and aggressive drive of the rest of the world. They are not on the way to anywhere else; they are a dead end for the land-based. That means that the stream of urgent business passes them by. Symbolically, they are small oases of calm and evocative possibility, beautiful places for retreat, contemplation and romance.

unmarkable, featureless, timeless. Symbolically eternal and infinite, it is a place where identity dissolves and differentiation has no meaning. To the ocean, the only direction is depth. Its surface is a tiny skin of light stretched tight over vast, invisible, crushing black depths that symbolize gigantic monsters, hideous revenants, even hell itself. Like the desert, the ocean is a barrier that can only be crossed; unlike the desert though, even the slightest mistake here can prove fatal.

Rivers

The flow of a river is the flow of time. Home to all manner of plants, fish, insects and even birds, merrily churning away, rivers are a model of life itself. At the same time, they seem unchanging, eternally refreshed, yet any given drop of water is immediately whisked away from in front of your eyes, never to be seen again. They are a constantly renewed stream of instants, each one gone almost before it can be imagined, yet simultaneously the whole is not only habitable and alive, it is positively inviting. The similarity to the passage of seconds and years is incredible – it is no wonder that we talk about time streams. Furthermore, rivers are strongly symbolic of roads; they can provide passage through all sorts of territory. Heading upstream is symbolic of adventure, entering mysterious territory, the "dark heart" of the land; downstream, by contrast, represents escape from a situation, fleeing toward the sea and new life.

Rivers also represent controlled, agricultural fertility, irrigation and the growth of crops. They enable concentrations of people to live in proximity, and help give birth to towns and cities. It is a rare city that does not boast at least one river or stretch of coast. There is power in rivers, however. Like the rest of nature, they cannot be assumed to be tame. Floods, drownings and disease are the price that has to be paid for the river's bounty. Over the millennia, the power of rivers can be awesome, the creation of the Grand Canyon being a spectacular example. They therefore represent the power inherent in nature to defy all else. This is why magic is said to be nullified by moving water, and why vampires cannot cross rivers and streams. Fugitives defeating tracker dogs are a similar symbolic image. Fiercely independent, the river is a sleeping giant, woken at everyone's peril.

Mountains

Symbolizing resilience, constancy, dominance and the utter refusal to yield, mountains dominate any landscape that they overlook. They are frequently considered to be the centre of the world by the people who live near them. They catch clouds and storms, often retain snow, and represent the earth's magnificence and power, hence they are frequently associated with elemental gods and goddesses and their spirits. There is a purity and clarity associated with them too – a defiance of all the world's distractions and pettiness.

Mountains also symbolize sanctity. They reach up toward the heavens, the closest that we can get to divinity. The provide us with the vision of perspective, the long-range view. To reach the top of a mountain is to become fully conscious, symbolically. They link objective presence with massive height, which gives them indisputable presence and majesty. To journey up a mountain, particularly a sacred one, is to put aside the world in favour of determination and dream, and a lingering desire to touch the divine as fully as possible.

TOP LEFT: As the embodiment of time's passing, it is only natural that the passage to the lands of the dead in Greek mythology should have been represented by a mighty river, the Styx. Again like time, the journey down the river was strictly one-way.

LEFT: Anuket was the Egyptian goddess of the Nile. By far the most important source of the country's fertility, agriculture and irrigation, the river – like the goddess – was untamed, often lethal, but always loved and respected. The Nile Valley around was the cradle of Egypt's civilization.

Valleys

Fertile, sheltered, hospitable, valleys have been associated with the earliest beginnings of civilized life for millennia. Protected from the extremes of local weather by their surrounding hills and mountains, valleys are places of peace and plenty. The resources that they offer are vital for larger-scale settlements, which is why most early development of civilization took place in them – the Nile River Valley in particular. The memory of their historical value remains in the symbolism we attach to them – not just cultivated ground or herds of farmed animals, but life, new beginnings and stable development.

Caves

Truly liminal spaces, caves symbolically exist entirely outside of reality. They are windows into the dark spaces behind the world, places outside time and space in which anything can happen. They are the sites where people have always gone to step beyond mundane reality, to unlock their perceptions and seek communion with the divine, the dead and the unreal. Often dangerous and frightening, always dark and dank, caves strongly symbolize the underworld, the hidden power of the mind, lost secrets, initiations, death and rebirth. Caves also represent the womb of the Earth and are linked to the fertility of nature, and this helps to emphasize the death-and-rebirth associations of passing beneath the ground.

ARTIFICIAL ENVIRONMENTS

We now live in a highly self-created world. The social use of space, on this crowded planet, carries its own symbolic language and meaning quite apart from our experiences with – and our social memory of – the natural world.

City

Originally, cities took shape around unusually desirable resources, such as the final object of an important pilgrimage, the seat of power of a king, the security offered by a strong local leader and his military force, and/or a particularly valuable resource for learning. These various factors drew travellers, both visiting and migrating, and they then drew others who could offer them a service. In this way, layer upon layer, the city accreted, like layers of nacre transforming a mote of dirt into a pearl. So right from the beginning, the city has symbolized opportunity, availability, divinity, power, security and knowledge, and this remains a powerful strand of its symbolic meaning.

The city also exists in direct contrast to the countryside; in place of peace, innocence, limitation, virtue and ignorance, it offers communication, opportunity, noise, ambition, cynicism, vice and experience.

In addition, cities have come to symbolize the mystery, danger, adventure and romance of the noir

LEFT: Far outside the normal realms of experience and everyday reality, caves are special spaces where mankind has long ventured to seek communion with the divine. The purpose of these enigmatic Norwegian cave paintings remains obscure, however.

BELOW: The product of centuries of living in deep caverns, gnawing over old bitterness and searching for non-existent secrets, Gollum from JRR Tolkien's Lord of the Rings embodies the darkest side of the cave's symbolic meaning.

LEFT: The Pilgrim's Progress from the City of Destruction to the Celestial City is a winding path allegorical of the opportunities, perils, adventures and mysteries of the modern city.

BELOW: In Chinese teaching, Feng Shui is used to map the walls and spaces of the house to various beneficial aspects of life. The Trigram wheel orients to north to identify which area of the house or room has which qualities, complicated by the fact that the front door and the room's door can also stand in for north in certain circumstances.

genre. Through countless crime stories, the city has been transformed from a place of industrial productivity into an almost mystic representation of the otherworld – a glittering backdrop of unknown places, strangers and dazzling lights, dangerous but seductive, where all types of person from all sorts of cultures blend together in a welter of corruption, death and intrigue. The city has acquired the symbolism of the modern land of the Fae – enchanting, mysterious, lethal. It is no surprise that vampire stories have moved from distant villages to urban settings – the city is where all the modern monsters are to be found.

The City as Macrocosm

Any particular city also symbolizes and enshrines the culture that gave it birth. London, Washington, Damascus and Hong Kong – to pick a selection of four cities more or less at random – could not be more different from each other in symbolic tone.

House

A house is a boundary, a space that walls out the outside world and provides much-needed privacy in a public world. It symbolizes early home, the feeling of being secure and protected within a family environment. Enclosed, protected and private, a house has symbolic similarities with the womb and remains the most important space in a person's life. It is our arena of symbolic power, the place where we can define our own reality, where we can dream our lives without interruption or persecution. As our continuing personal commodification progresses, it is the stronghold where we can stash the items that define us. Each house therefore also symbolizes its inhabitants, or at least their lifestyles. Telemarketers and junk post infuriate us precisely because they intrude on our space, reminding us that even our most private sanctums are not actually all that private any more. There is no escape from the world.

But if houses are not as private as they once were, what of those who don't even have that small retreat? It is becoming increasingly difficult for the poorer sections of society to afford a home. Housing projects, tower blocks, apartments, condos, flats, even dorms… the closer our personal space gets squeezed together, the less power it has to protect us from the outside. A house, set in grounds that divide it from neighbours – even if just by a few inches – remains a powerful draw for people worldwide. Without this recourse to privacy, study after study has found evidence of increasing frustration and unhappiness. What use is a boundary whose walls are breached?

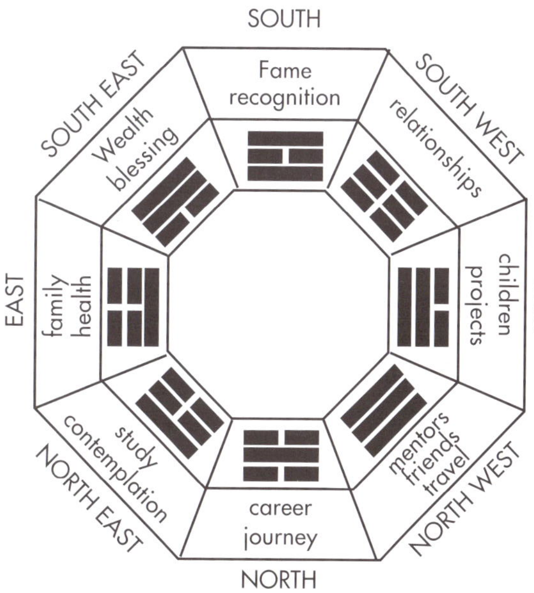

3 ART

Of all our modes of human expression, art is the most symbolic. There is an understanding that even at its most literal, an artistic image is a representation rather than a depiction of reality. A colour photograph can be as realistic as an artistic depiction can get, but even that conveys only how something or someone looked from one specific angle, for one moment, and under one certain set of lighting conditions. It does not capture the whole subject, nor can it ever do. For artistic modes that are less interested in realism, every element of a composition can become a multifaceted symbol. Whole books could be written analysing the symbolism behind any piece of art – and often are, frequently disagreeing with each other – but over the next few pages, we'll look at a range of works from various artistic periods and styles, and the major symbolic representations they involved.

The art world is one of the most important treasuries of symbolism and symbolic meaning. Artists often take great pains to encode a wide range of deep, subtle symbols into their work, offering us valuable insight into their lives and times.

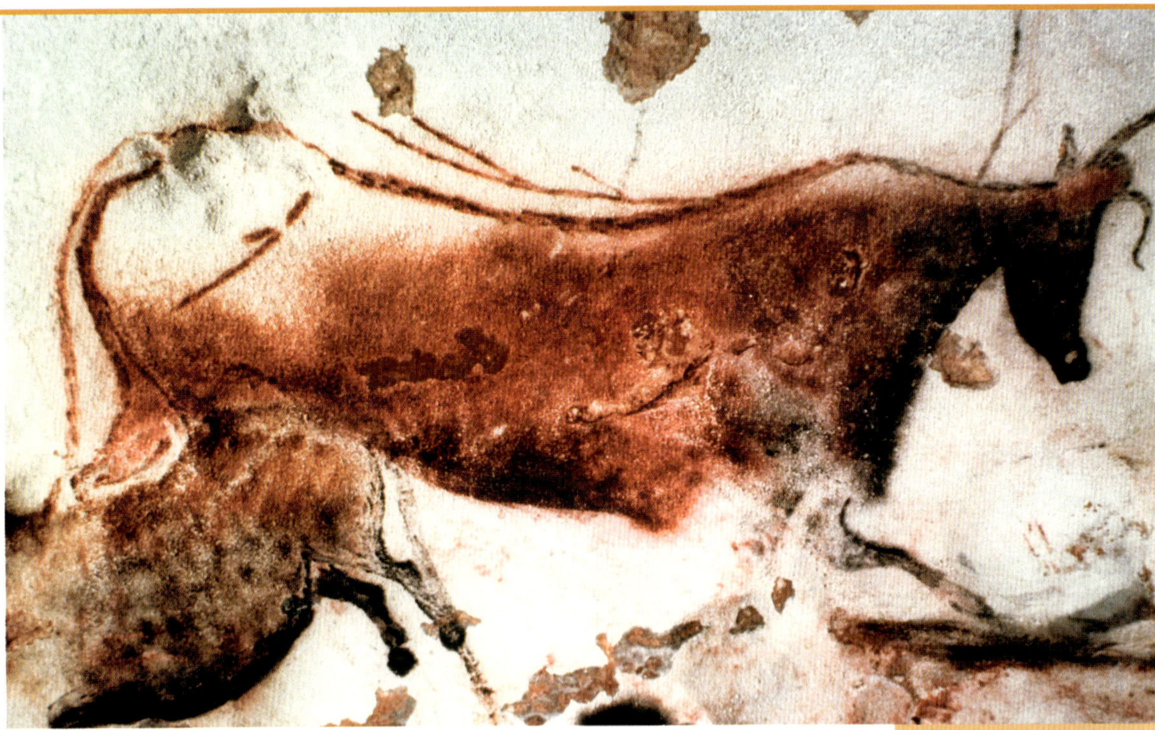

Cave paintings are one of the most enigmatic remainders of the Paleolithic culture that predated modern humanity. The simple truth is that we still have no idea what the images meant.

EARLY BEGINNINGS TO THE MIDDLE AGES

Art as a means of self-expression, art that is for the artist's satisfaction, is actually a comparatively modern phenomenon. As late as the 16th century in Europe, art was seen as a purely devotional activity, a way of glorifying God. It was so bound up with church and ritual that the idea of an artist painting to communicate his or her personal vision was unthinkable. Right from its earliest times, art has been closely associated with religion and magic.

Paleolithic Art

Dating as far back as 30,000BC, Paleolithic, or Stone Age, art is most commonly found in the form of enigmatic paintings on the walls of deep caves, primarily in Spain and southern France. In addition, but less common, some small carved objects have been discovered, and there are also a few examples of external rocks bearing markings. Paleolithic art was unknown until near the end of the 19th century, and it was only accepted as genuine by archaeologists after the turn of the 20th century.

The most common images depicted in cave art are horses and bison, typically accompanied or surrounded by human stick figures, often carrying weapons. Mammoths, deer, fish, ibex and birds are also found, and there is even one known example of a unicorn. Exaggerated female statuettes that have been dubbed "Venus figurines" are also relatively common.

Theories still abound regarding the purpose of cave art. It is too ritualistic to be just decorative. Early theories suggested that all cave art was magical, an attempt to sway hunts in the hunters' favour, but no scenes showing a successful hunt – i.e. animals killed by hunters – have been found. Others proposed that the purpose of the art was to capture the fertility of the animals, but another striking fact is the absence of genitals in the pictures. One theory, popular in the 1950s, suggested that horses and bison represented a male/female duality; however, without some sort of corroboration, it is impossible to say. There are still many theories, but only one point of agreement – that the images were symbolic of something.

The Language of Cave Art

Without some sort of interpretive "Rosetta Stone", the symbolic language of Paleolithic cave art may be lost to us for good. It serves as a salutary illustration of the danger of using symbolism to convey meaning: it can be understood only by people who are already well versed in the same code of meanings.

Classical Art

From the beginnings of early modern culture around 5000BC, art found a place providing the links between the more impersonal aspects of life and the various gods who, likewise, remained broadly impersonal. Deities were believed to be concerned with their own business and affairs, and to use the mortal world whimsically,

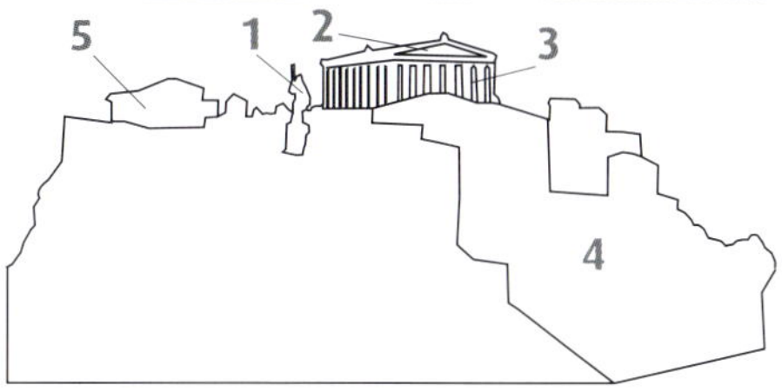

The mighty Acropolis complex, guarded by the grand Northwest Stair (4), was one of the most sacred spots in Greece, and housed not just the Parthenon, but many other sites including the famed Erechtheum (5).

often cruelly. This perception first started to change around 500BC, during the classical period of ancient Greece. The so-called "geometric" period of Greek art, which was characterized by a literal and impersonal style, had gained a lot of popularity. Gradually, this tendency gave way to the idea that artistic representation could be personal and could demonstrate to the viewer that artistic images were relevant to their own lives, and were not just abstract lessons about history, war or farming.

This new approach to art marked a major shift in thinking. It is clearly illustrated by the different styles of the figures carved on the east and west pediments of the Temple of Aphaia on Aegina, an island near Athens. Built around 500BC, the temple's east pediment shows a dying soldier collapsing like a puppet, but dispassionate, unaware – uninvolved. The west pediment, renewed just 20 years later after an attack, shows the new style of art – a dying soldier is depicted in an agonized pose, clearly suffering, properly involved in his fate. In the old style, it is the existence of the art itself that is a symbolic statement – more so than the content. In the new style, however, the art is attempting to reach out to its audience, the content itself having symbolic meaning.

The highlight of classical Greek artistry was the Parthenon (3), the iconic temple to Athens's patron goddess, Athena Parthenos, that still stands on the Acropolis, looking over the city. Although it was accidentally blown up in the 17th century by Turkish occupiers – who were using it for gunpowder storage – and then grossly vandalized by Lord Elgin, who removed most of the carvings (2) and sold them piece by piece to the British Museum in the 19th century, the Parthenon remains the national symbol of Greece. As such, it stands for all of the country's ancient heritage, the foundations of philosophy and rationality, and the first beginnings of modern democracy.

At its zenith, the temple was richly decorated with carvings and friezes depicting all sorts of mytho-historical scenes from Greek history and tradition, and the compound housed the famous gold and ivory statue of Athena (which no longer exists). Standing 12 metres (39 feet) high, the statue showed Athena (1) in full armour, with a helmet bearing the figures of a sphinx and a griffon, and with Medusa's head at her breast. She carried a statue of Nike, Goddess of Victory, in one hand, and a spear in the other, and she had a shield and serpent by her feet.

All of Athena's outfit was symbolic, of course. The helmet was her defining symbol – she was the only goddess to wear one – and signified her wisdom and prowess in battle. It granted her the power of moving unseen, symbolically implying a degree of omnipresence on her part – she could be anywhere, unnoticed. The helmet's royal sphinx decoration represented mystery, enigmas, vigilance, strength and power. Her spear symbolized the power of lightning – she was the holder of Zeus's thunderbolt – and indicated the force of her nature. The snake at her feet was, interestingly, a symbol of the divine child and, like the owl, another of her symbols, a protector of human interests. Taken as a composite, Athena was a wise, royal protector, the guardian of Athens and by association the entire Greek culture.

Medieval Art

Art really began to flourish as a means of expression in Europe during the Gothic period of the Middle Ages, from approximately the 13th to the 15th centuries. Drawing on the Romanesque architectural style of the 11th to 13th centuries, which had attempted to incorporate classical themes into the architecture and decoration of the time, Gothic marked a desire to convey a stronger sense of the glory of God in church architecture. In fact, the Gothic period received its name only at a later age – from Italian Renaissance artists who wished to portray the entire movement as primitive, crude and valueless. The term "Gothic" at that time still only really applied to savage Germanic tribes that had damaged Italy so badly over the centuries.

Typical Gothic buildings were tall and quite sparse with their stone, making way for huge vaults and wide areas of decorative glass. The stonework was often highly decorated. The overall effect was more ethereal than the comparatively sombre Romanesque, yet powerfully charged with emotion. A Gothic artistic movement followed in the wake of architecture, spreading across Europe by 1300. However, like much religious art, it was mostly concentrated around painted wooden panels, along with frescoes, stained glass windows and illuminated manuscripts. Its dominant expressive mode was narrative – it told stories, rather than evoking instants or perceptions.

FROM THE RENAISSANCE TO THE MODERN WORLD

As wealth gradually spread from church and state to private institutions and even individuals during the 14th and 15th centuries, the notion of secular art became increasingly acceptable, even popular. The shift toward a money-based economy, complete with cities, universities, better literacy rates and even an active bourgeoisie provided opportunities for artistic commissions. Greater emphasis on popularization and accessibility rather than remote preaching marked the end of the Gothic period – and laid the foundations of the modern world in the Renaissance.

The Renaissance represented a strong period of reconnection between European culture and the collected knowledge, philosophy and scientific spirit of inquiry of classical Greece. It also included the absorption of a lot of Arabic and Jewish knowledge (especially mathematics), a more humanistic emphasis on living life as a potentially pleasurable experience, and the fusion of all these influences and developments in a wealth of new artistic, architectural and poetic styles. The invention of the printing press gave this new cultural wave the power to spread and finally to bring Europe out of the doldrums of the Dark Ages – the centuries that followed the collapse of the Roman Empire.

Early Renaissance

Giotto di Bondone, the son of a Florentine peasant – and himself a shepherd – was the artist who provided the first part of a bridge from the medieval period's Byzantine artistic culture to the humanism and realism of the Renaissance. His great innovation was the introduction

Giotto's *Lamentation of Christ*. Note the characteristic depth and perspective in this portrait. His work marks a major departure from the flat, iconographic depictions of Byzantine art.

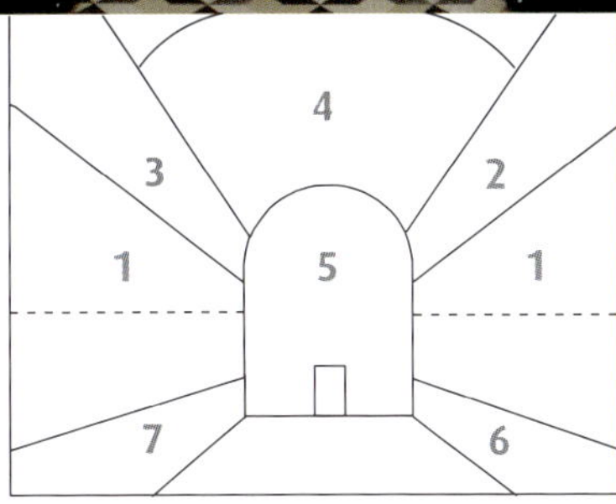

Giotto's Arena Chapel depicts various groups of scenes from the lives of Joachim (2) and Mary (3), a double-row of scenes from the life of Jesus (1), warnings about the virtues (6) and vices (7), and, at the end of all, the Last Judgement (5). Various saints watch on from the heavens (4).

of three-dimensional space in his art. The Byzantine style of images depicted people as flat, without perspective and out of proportion; Giotto painted people in a way that made them appear solid and tangible. It was a vast leap in humanizing art. Coupled to this, he also had a tendency to invest his subjects with clear, visible emotion – real people, in real situations – where, again, the Byzantine technique centred on complete emotional absence.

Giotto's masterwork was the set of devotional images in the so-called Arena Chapel, built by a rich merchant named Enrico Scrovegni on the former site of a Roman arena as a way of making restitution for the wealth his father had accumulated while lending money. Giotto's frescoes inside the chapel explored the lives of Mary and Jesus, with a certain pointed emphasis on scenes of usury, the sin of money-lending. The frescoes themselves were engaging and immediately recognizable, literal rather than laden with symbolism – but it is their very existence that makes them such important symbols. Even today, they represent an anti-authoritarian mindset, the idea that God is for the people, not just for the priests.

About a century after the death of Giotto in 1337, one of the most influential works of art of the early Renaissance was created: the statue of David cast by the Florentine sculptor Donatello in 1430. To start with, it was the first freestanding nude statue that had been produced since the classical period, well over a millennium before; as such, it was a powerful symbolic act of reclamation against earlier cultural and religious restrictions. The proportions and details are all powerfully realist – again, unheard of at the time. Symbolically,

One of the great Renaissance sculptures, Donatello's *David* was very much a product of its time, impossible even fifty years before. It remains an iconic and aspirational image for many modern gay and transvestite movements.

realistic depiction implies accuracy – that is, the artwork does not simply appear plausible, but actually depicts events and people as they really were.

Donatello's David is wearing a laurel-wreath on his head and a pair of boots, and his posture, appearance and physique are markedly effeminate. He is obviously a boy rather than a man, and the statue has become something of an iconic and aspirational image for transvestites worldwide. Goliath's tortured head is at David's feet, but David's expression is one of total self-absorption rather than triumph, devotion or relief. Symbolically, the nudity and vulnerability make it clear that it is God's protection that has vanquished the giant. It has been suggested that even a hundred years before it was created, the statue would have led to Donatello being burnt at the stake. To the people of Florence, the statue symbolized the smaller town's independence from monolithic Rome to the south, and the boy's depiction merely affirmed his – and by extension, the town's – artistic sensibilities.

Donatello's statue played a large part in influencing the sculptor Lorenzo Ghiberti. His masterworks were the northern and eastern doors of the Baptistery of San Giovanni in Florence, the city's oldest building, which dates back to the sixth century. In 1401 the authorities held a competition to select a sculptor for the baptistery's north-facing doors. Ghiberti won the competition, and spent the next 21 years working on the gilded bronze doors. These have 28 panels, each one depicting a scene from the New Testament, and their completion was lauded as the most important event in Florentine art in the first quarter of the 15th century.

Undaunted, Ghiberti followed this incredible undertaking with a second set of doors for the baptistery, this time to face east. He and his workshop spent almost 30 years on the eastern doors, creating 10 magnificent panels with further biblical scenes. It was Michelangelo who said that they were so perfect, they were fit to be the Gates of Paradise itself – the name by which they have been known ever since. Even a century later, fellow artists were still praising them as the most perfect creation ever made.

The Gates illustrate stories from the Old Testament, each one depicting several aspects. The Temptation of Adam and Eve (1) is famous for Eve's heart-wrenching backward glance on leaving Eden. Cain's Murder of Abel (2) is contrasted powerfully with scenes of the brothers' earlier life. Noah's Ark (3) is shown as a mighty pyramid, following the early theologian Origen's theories.

Abraham and Isaac (4) tells Abraham's tale, from God's disguised visit to his ultimate test of faith. Jacob and Esau (5), Isaac's children, commemorates Jacob's usurpation of his older brother's inheritance. The Fall and Rise of Joseph (6) shows the famous favourite son's progress from multicoloured-coat wearer to slave to governor of Egypt.

Moses on Mount Sinai (7) is a single scene – God imparting the Ten Commandments. The Life of Joshua

(8) shows the Israelite tribes entering the promised land and conquering Jericho. David and Goliath (9) is a stark battle scene; the background Jerusalem is clearly inspired by Florence. Solomon's Temple (10), finally, shows the wise King meeting the lovely Queen of Sheba.

By the last quarter of the 15th century, artists were starting to feel comfortable pushing artistic boundaries, and loading paintings with symbolism. When themes were controversial, the symbolic content had to be particularly enigmatic. One of the most famously symbolically-loaded paintings to come out of the entire 15th century is Sandro Botticelli's *Primavera* (Spring) (see page 42). It depicts a spring garden inhabited by an "ennead" of figures – three groups of three – who give the image its true content. In the rightmost group, Zephyrus (1), the spring breeze, is caressing the reluctant earth nymph Chloris (2) and transforming her into Flora (3), the flower-decked herald of spring. This is a fairly straightforward allegory of winter giving way to the new season.

In the centre of the painting, Venus (4) stands at the heart of the composition as the ruler of the second triad. She is joined by Cupid (5), above, and Mercury (6), at the far right of the painting. The third group, to the left of Venus, contains three of the graces. Haughty Beauty (7) and languid Pleasure (8) bracket a shy-looking Chastity (9). The women are clasping hands in two knots, above and below. While Pleasure looks at her knowingly, Chastity is gazing across at the very masculine Mercury on the edge of the picture, and her dress is slipping off her shoulder. Cupid's arrow is aiming straight at her.

Symbolically, it seems that beauty and pleasure have overturned Chastity, awakening her to desire. Cupid's arrow is ready to spear her, awakening her fully to the meaning of love, with Mercury waiting, in a pose that suggests he is pulling back an unseen veil from the world. With Chloris's transformation to the right, and Venus presiding over all, it is not difficult to read the whole composition as a sexual awakening: after the winter of maidenhood, Chastity has been overcome by Pleasure and Beauty, and is about to awaken to a blossoming springtime of sensuality and delight. It was a revolutionary message for the time, and *Primavera* is widely considered the greatest depiction of the new Renaissance attitude toward love, sex and eroticism.

One of the most incredible pieces of art ever created, Ghiberti's so-called Gates of Paradise took 30 years to complete, every inch lavishly detailed with the most exquisite and symbolically laden carvings. It is a true masterwork, from an age when the term denoted genuine life-long striving.

Opening the Gates

While the north doors of the Baptistery symbolized the life of Christ, and the east doors depicted 10 of the most famous stories and characters from the Old Testament, the real symbolic power of Ghiberti's work lies in his style, particularly with respect to the Gates of Paradise. Using revolutionary techniques such as changing the elevation of the relief to show depth, and the scientific angle of one-point perspective, Ghiberti made the doors a powerful statement about the artistic and philosophical changes that were brewing at the time; they were a symbolic move away from the anti-rationalism of the medieval period toward a more realistic world-view.

High Renaissance

Botticelli's *Primavera* appears tranquil and genteel, and perhaps it is in the light of modern aesthetics, but when created, its message of the natural beauty of sensual pleasure was dangerously revolutionary.

A very different message lies within Leonardo da Vinci's sketch for *The Virgin and Child with St Anne.* A true embodiment of the Renaissance, Leonardo da Vinci remains possibly the greatest genius that the world has ever seen. He could write in perfect inverted mirror script, draw perfect circles freehand, and had an accurate knowledge of bodily form that has rarely been equalled. He was famous even in his own time as a master of painting, sculpture, architecture, engineering and science, and his work proved innovative in many fields for centuries after his death. Scientifically, his work in anatomy, optics, hydraulics, mathematics, aerodynamics and several other areas has often closely foreshadowed even the most modern developments. Unfortunately, bad luck or poor timing meant that much of his work went unfinished, and of the commissions he did execute, many did not survive.

Although the final artwork is fairly standard symbolically, da Vinci's cartoon of *The Virgin and Child with St Anne* at first glance shows Mary talking with her mother Anne, both smiling, with Mary holding the baby Jesus while a second child plays at Anne's feet. However, even a quick second glance shows that something is not right. To start with, Anne does not seem to have a body of her own. Her shoulder blends seamlessly into Mary. From da Vinci, the consummate master of anatomical depiction, the impression must be deliberate. Furthermore, the two women's heads are on the same level, whereas if Anne was truly behind Mary, her perspective should be slightly above and/or behind. Biologically, Anne has to be at least fifteen years older than Mary, but the two women are clearly the same age, and almost identical in their features. Similarly, the two children are so similar that they could be twins, except that the one on the right has thicker hair, a slumped pose, and a moody expression. Between the two children, a ghostly hand – perhaps supposed to be Anne's – points to the heavens.

The real key to the sketch, though, is in the women's faces. Mary, as is to be expected, is a study in sweetness and light. Beautiful, happy and innocent, she is gazing down at the child in her arms with adoration. The other face, however, is exactly the opposite. While Mary is rendered in

tones of light, Anne is shown through contrasts of darkness. Her eyes are sunken pits of shadow, her cheeks skeletally hollow, and her smile is actively threatening, predatory even. It is as if she is about to strike the good head down.

The symbolism of the juxtaposition between good and evil is inescapable. The women appear to be sharing a body because they *are* sharing it. The figure can be seen as the creator-destroyer, nature herself, all-bountiful yet also lethal. The children, too, seem to represent poles – the good child is Apollo, light, reason and understanding, and the dark child is Dionysus, passion, madness and frenzy. The Christ child is blessing his companion, accepting and embracing the evil side of his nature. The hand between them shows the source of this duality, that the heavens themselves are the source of both good and evil, reason and madness, life and death.

Da Vinci's sketch is a terrifying vision of good and evil united in heavenly mandate. Had it been distributed – and understood – during the genius's life, it could well have led to his execution. Its implications would still upset many religious organizations even today.

The palatable face of dualism. By considering the subject from the viewpoint of the debate between the abstract and the practical – almost Yin and Yang, in fact – Raphael highlights the discourse required for progress while steering well clear of any theological implications.

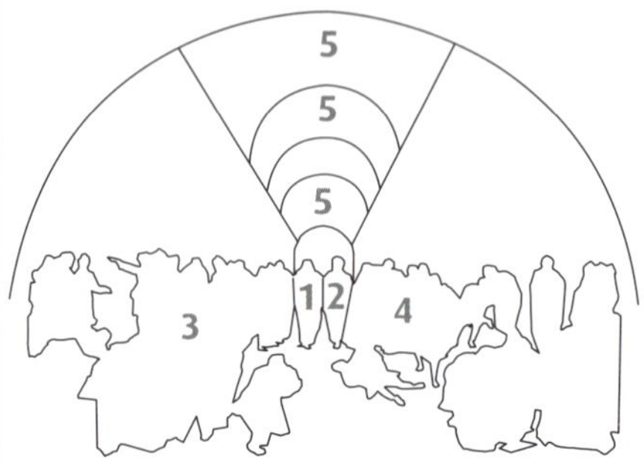

A more positive version of the same basic message is conveyed in Raphael's *School of Athens* (begun in 1509). A piece of technical mastery that incorporated many classical techniques – including pyramidal composition, a definite vanishing point, and pose-related details such as weight-shift, drapery and chiaroscuro – the picture depicts Plato and Aristotle among a gathering of mathematicians both Platonic (3) and Aristotelian (4). The two philosophers are the founders of the two main threads of Western thought. Plato (1) is carrying his book *Timaeus*, on the origin of the universe; Aristotle (2) is carrying his *Ethics*. Plato is on the left and gesturing to the heavens, symbolizing contemplation, withdrawal, theoretical philosophy and the feminine principle. Aristotle is gesturing forward, symbolizing activity, engagement, practical philosophy and the masculine principle. Three half-circular arches (5) span the space above them, symbolic of the circle of eternity. The two men are engaged in conversation – indicating that the two traditions they represent are both necessary. Symbolically, the picture is a vivid call for duality of thought, research and life itself.

The third artistic giant of the High Renaissance was Michelangelo Buonarotti, the celebrated artist who painted the ceiling of the Sistine Chapel – the papacy's own place of worship in the Vatican. In fact, Michelangelo was primarily a sculptor. His statue of David – a much more kingly version than Donatello's – and his *Pietà* (Pity), showing Mary holding Christ's

The *Pietà* shocked Italy with its uncharacteristic depiction of Mary holding Christ's body as he would have been after his death – adult, rather than baby – but Michelangelo's logic was flawless, and once the surprise wore off the piece received the accolades it deserved.

body after the crucifixion, are widely regarded as two of the most masterful sculptures in existence. As a sculptor, Michelangelo was reluctant to take on the Sistine frescoes, but Pope Julius II insisted, and his confidence proved well placed. The result, completed in 1512, was, and still is, stunningly beautiful, rife with appropriately religious scenes.

The most famous section of the chapel's ceiling is the Creation of Adam, in which God passes on the divine spark to his languid, newly-made creation.

The image has always been taken as representational until very recently, when Dr Frank Meshberger of St John's Medical Center in Anderson, Indiana, pointed out that the depiction of God and his surrounding angels looks, intriguingly, almost exactly like a cross-section of a human brain.

Michelangelo, who had a dissection table in his studio, where he performed autopsies to study anatomy, was well known as a visual joker. Whether the Creation of Adam is actually symbolic of God bestowing intellect rather than life, as Dr Meshberger believes – or even a well-hidden suggestion that God is a creation of the intellect, which would be a joke of epic proportions on the ceiling of the Pope's chapel – will remain unknown, of course. A great deal of symbolism remains obscure.

The Creation of Adam. God's cloud does depict several brain structures, including (but not limited to) the Sulcus (1), Pituitary Gland (2), Pons (3), Spinal Cord (4), Cerebellum (5), Limbic Cortex (6), the Fissure of Silvius (7), the Optic Tract (8) and the Frontal Lobe (9). But is Adam being created... or creating?

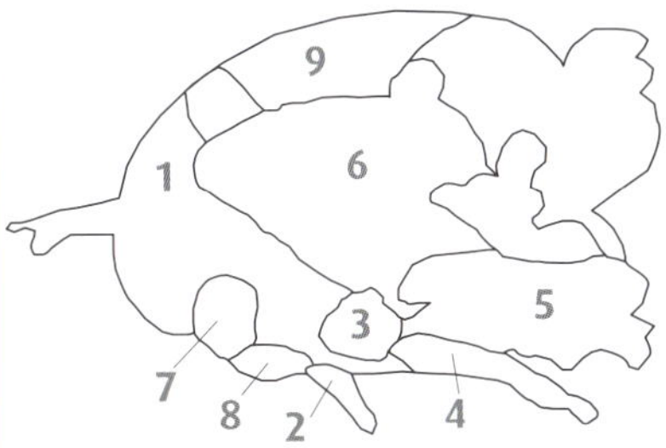

Baroque

As the 16th century gave way to the 17th, the characteristic art of the Renaissance developed into the Baroque movement. This differed chiefly from the earlier style in the incorporation of surroundings into the composition of the artwork or

sculpture. During the Renaissance, the emphasis had all been on dramatic figure play and reclaiming humanity of form and depiction. The art of the Baroque period added an interplay with backdrop and external form. Thus the space around the figures became an important resource for the design and the artist. There was also an explicit understanding that the art should try to reach out to everyone, regardless of educational level – to do with paint what could not always be done with print.

Michelangelo Merisi da Caravaggio was one of the leading forerunners of the Baroque. He is famous for depicting religious figures in everyday situations, which earned him a certain controversial reputation with the church, but also helped cement his popularity with wealthy individuals. At the time, he was almost as famous for his frequent drunken rages and brawls, and it is recorded that he died young under ambiguous circumstances in southern Italy, before a papal pardon undoing his exile from Rome could reach him. He painted several masterpieces, but one of the most talked-about, even now, is *Amor Victorious*. The painting depicts a gleeful Eros clutching a handful of arrows and surrounded by the clutter of all other major human endeavours: music, science, war, government.

The symbolism of the painting appears clear enough – music (1) is represented by a violin, a lute and some sheet music. Learning and knowledge are indicated by a book and inkpen (2), and architecture and design by a set square and compass (3). The arts of war are there, too – martial prowess in the form of armour (4) and strategy as the sceptre (5) – as are the tokens of authority to indulge in it, with nobility represented by a crown (6), authority by an imperial laurel wreath (7) and so on – but it is possible to interpret it in other ways. Some have suggested that the symbols divide into representations of the feminine and the masculine, and that love is the

Amor Celebrative?

Further justification for the theory that Caravaggio's painting is a tribute to his patron is that the items chosen are specifically representative of Vincenzo de Genovese. The musical score at Eros's feet clearly shows the letter V. The Marquis was famed for his military prowess and astronomical knowledge, wrote about music and art, and was an accomplished architect. In fact, there isn't one item scattered at Eros's feet that doesn't fit with Vincenzo's famed attributes.

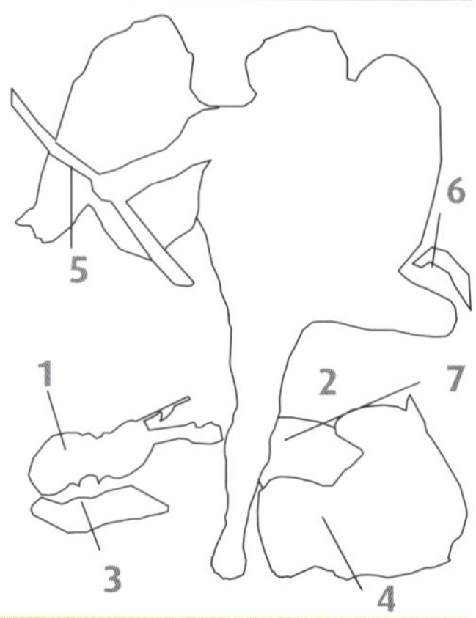

A violent and unhappy man despite his artistic genius, it has long been suspected that Caravaggio painted Amor Victorious to celebrate the achievements of his patron and presumed lover, the Marquis de Genovese.

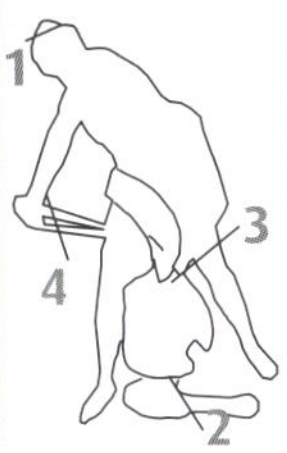

Bernini's *David* is the only one of the great classical statues of the biblical hero to truly suggest a man fighting an enemy, rather than just depicting a study of a boy.

the uniting principle, greater than both, that makes the separate halves whole. It is also thought to allude to Caravaggio's patron and likely lover, the Marquis Vincenzo Guistiniani de Genovese.

Given that one of the Baroque's common features was the multi-dimensional use of symbols involving layers of meaning, the association seems likely. If Eros and Genovese are to be considered conflated symbolically, then it is also the possible that Caravaggio was expressing more than just admiration for his patron.

The foremost artist of the Baroque period was the sculptor, architect, set designer, painter and pyrotechnician Gian Lorenzo Bernini. Bernini's father was not only a prodigious artist but a well-known sculptor in his own right, and Gian Lorenzo was producing interesting works even before reaching maturity. His work – statues, fountains, tombs, roofs, whole churches and chapels – still covers Rome. Bernini's statue of David couldn't be more different to the versions by Donatello and Michelangelo; Bernini's work is a masterpiece of furious action and vengeance. The figure is frozen in the instant before he releases his missile, coiled like a spring. His face (1) is a study in furious intent and righteous confidence; the statue's stare is, frankly, intimidating. David's total focus is represented by the discarded harp (2) at his feet – even his beloved music is being trampled without a second thought – and his armour (3) is down there with it, because of his absolute faith that God will protect him. Meanwhile, the slingshot (4) is the focal point of all the torque and energy of his s-curved body; as he unwinds, every muscle will pour its power into the stone. Looking at Bernini's statue, it is almost possible to feel momentary pity for the poor fool giant on the receiving end of David's wrath.

Bernini's work, however, is famous for hidden symbolism and in-jokes. Quite late in life, he was commissioned to provide a base for an Egyptian obelisk. The elephant he devised has often been noted for its mysterious smile. Looking at the rear end indicates why – with muscles tensed, and tail shifted away, the elephant is in the middle of defecating. It is no coincidence that the rear is pointed directly at the office window of Domenico Paglia, an anti-artistic Dominican friar who was one of Bernini's harshest critics.

Nowadays, possibly the most famous of Bernini's works worldwide is his sculpture *The Ecstasy of St Theresa.* Depicting a scene from the Spanish mystic's life, in which she was filled with divine joy during a vision, Bernini's work has Theresa lying back, tousled and dishevelled, her face in the throes of ecstasy. An angel stands over her, arrow pointed straight at her groin. From a modern sensibility, the symbolism does seem to suggest that, to Bernini at least, Theresa's experience is sexually

In *The Ecstasy of St Theresa,* Bernini walked a fine line between piety and heresy. It is a testament to his political genius that the sculpture ever made it on to display.

charged. While orgasm as a route to the divine may fit certain mystic notions, it would have been a lethally heretical suggestion to make at the time.

Bernini was certainly no stranger to heresy, of course. Although he always managed to stay on the right side of the Church with the help of clever manoeuvring and powerful allies, he came close to crossing the line. Several of his works include symbolic codings in support of his friend Galileo's teachings. Galileo espoused the Copernican theory of astronomy, namely that the Earth revolves around the Sun, and he was almost burnt at the stake for his pains. Even so, Bernini's exact intentions regarding *The Ecstasy of St Theresa* remain unsure, and probably always will. (As an aside, it is worth noting briefly that the Dan Brown novel *Angels and Demons* took significant amounts of artistic licence with the structure of Rome in general and Bernini in particular, and there is no "Path of the Illuminati".)

The great heroine of the Baroque was Artemisia Gentileschi, who overcame horrendous circumstances and events to become one of the movement's finest painters. The daughter of a successful artist, she was already guaranteed a hard time simply by wanting, as a woman, to be creative in such a repressive age. As a young student, she was raped by her teacher, Agostino Tassi, in her father's studio. However, she refused to submit to his blackmail threats, and the matter was eventually brought to trial. Artemisia had to endure repeated slander, character defamation and even court-imposed torture before winning her case. To then fight her way out of the shadow of her famous artist father and become respected in her own right – while bringing up a child (not the product of the rape) as a single parent – was a genuinely heroic achievement.

Her trials naturally illuminated her work, which became famed for its unflinching determination to tackle potentially distasteful subjects honestly. Much art at the time was rather coy; Artemisia's refusal to pander to social niceties eventually earned her a lot of respect. Her most famous painting, *Judith Slaying Holofernes*, is a depiction of the biblical story in which the Jewish heroine, a widow in a small town under attack by the Assyrians, crosses over to the enemy lines and gets the Assyrian general Holofernes drunk while he attempts to seduce her. When his strength is sapped, Judith has her maid hold him down while she saws off his head with his own sword. With their leader gone, the Assyrians fall apart in confusion and are subsequently defeated by the local army.

Artemisia's picture shows Judith in the midst of killing the enemy commander. The general is pinned

Judith Slaying Holofernes is remarkable for its boldly matter-of-fact depiction of the heroine and her maid hacking up the drunken warlord. It has given many men pause for thought over the years.

down, his hairy, bestial face contorted in terror. Judith is intent on her work, unflinching as gouts of blood stain her dress. There is no pity or anger in her expression, just concentration. The maid, Abra, is equally impassive. Judith is obviously physically strong herself, with an intelligent face rather than a lovely one – it is often said that there is a fair amount of self-portraiture in the figure. Symbolically, the painting is often seen as Artemisia reclaiming her power over Tassi, the man who raped her, and the masculine world in general. The very soul of necessary practicality, Judith has a businesslike demeanour that stands in powerful contrast to the horror of the brutish general – "Women are strong and sensible," the painting seems to be saying, "while men are slaves to their urges."

Another fine Baroque painter – and one of the greatest talents of the Dutch Golden Age artists – was Peter Paul Rubens. The son of a Flemish Protestant lawyer who had fled persecution in Antwerp, Rubens grew up effectively in exile, then later returned to his parents' home city after his father's death, and converted to Catholicism. Given this upbringing, religion had, unsurprisingly, a large influence over his artistic output. His mother apprenticed him to several leading painters, after which he spent a period in Italy, learning the works and styles of the masters.

When he returned to Antwerp, he quickly established himself as the leading artist in the region. He went on to undertake a number of artistic commissions as well as diplomatic missions, spending long periods working for both the French and Spanish royal families. Throughout his life, he was a strong advocate for peace, and worked hard to preserve it.

One of his most amazing achievements was a cycle of 24 allegorical paintings for the French Crown, that portrayed the rather unpopular Marie de Medici in an extremely flattering light. Although Rubens is known to have found the work unpleasant and unrewarding, the sheer intensity of producing so many large, detailed masterworks in three years makes it an unparalleled feat. The cycle works hard to depict Marie – who became regent of France after her husband's suspicious murder – as beloved of the gods, fated for greatness, and adored by the populace.

Each painting is laden with symbolic tokens of Marie's wonderful nature. A good example of the cycle is *Henri IV Receiving the Portrait of Marie de Medici*, in which Marie's future husband is shown her likeness for the first time. Armed and armoured, the king (6) is the epitome of splendour. The portrait of Marie (5) – a flattering "likeness", hiding her obesity – is presented to him by a pair of smiling, flower-garlanded angels (4), who seem to have borne it down from heaven in a cloud of glory. A cherub (8) is on the ground, playing happily with the king's helmet, while an apparent Eros (9) hides behind his shield, bow ready to strike love into the king's heart. Above it all and surrounded by splendid peacocks, Zeus (1), Hera (2) and their peacocks (3) hold hands and gaze down fondly on the king's reaction. Athena, goddess of wisdom (7), whispers words of glorious endorsement in Henri's ear as he studies the image.

The symbolism is of course lavish and unsubtle. Marie is favoured by the gods themselves, beautiful and filled with divine grace, and their union is blessed. Athena's presence indicates that the union is wise; Eros's that it is loving. The peacocks, Hera's symbolic bird, also represent immortality and eternal bliss. According to the painting, the union of Henri and Marie is a matter of divine inspiration, thrice-blessed and sanctified at every step. The rest of the cycle of paintings takes a similar tone, and Marie, naturally, was delighted with them.

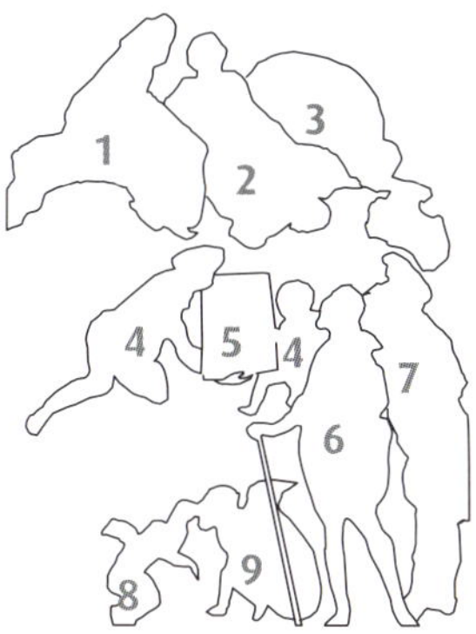

Henry IV Receiving the Portrait of Marie de Medici by Peter Paul Rubens – a classic study in workmanlike sycophancy. Marie was unpopular, and not good for the French Crown, so she sought artistic support to bolster her position. Rubens's cycle of works was as masterful and successful as it was subtly insincere.

Where Rubens was painting grand scenes of divinity, the Dutch artist Vermeer, another of the Golden Age masters, concentrated on simple indoor compositions. His typical focus was on an individual, depicted with almost photorealistic exactness, engaged in an everyday activity. These scenes generally symbolized an allegorical religious instruction or lesson. Vermeer's work is particularly famed for his stunning use of transparent colour, a technique called *pointille*.

In the representative work *Woman Holding a Balance*, Vermeer depicts an apparently pregnant young woman (1) holding a pair of scales (2) in her right hand. It appears as if she is about to weigh some gold coins (3) lying on the table's edge. The table also holds some jewels, a gold chain and some pearl necklaces (4). Beyond her, an image of the Last Judgement hangs on the wall (5), while a mirror (6) hangs on another wall, facing her.

Dressed in blue, with a serene expression and a shaft of light falling on her – emphasized by a dash of bright yellow over her belly – the woman is often thought to represent the Virgin Mary. The mirror facing her represents self-knowledge and self-awareness, reinforcing the impression of wisdom. Mirrors can also suggest vanity, which the woman is eschewing by not looking into the mirror. The light in which she is bathed is a typical representation of supernatural wisdom. Everything points to this figure being highly important. The pearls, with the gold, are a token of worldly wealth and, more importantly, worldly concern. In the painting of the Last Judgement on the wall behind her, Christ is judging souls to decide who goes to heaven or hell. The woman's head obscures the spot where St Michael would typically be weighing souls on Christ's behalf. The balance emphasizes this point strongly. Overall, the message is one of instruction: do not pay too much heed to wealth or appearances, for you too shall be judged.

Woman Holding a Balance. Vermeer's work, as understated as Ruben's Medici cycle is overstated, is no less masterful. The subtle use of colour and light is nothing short of brilliant.

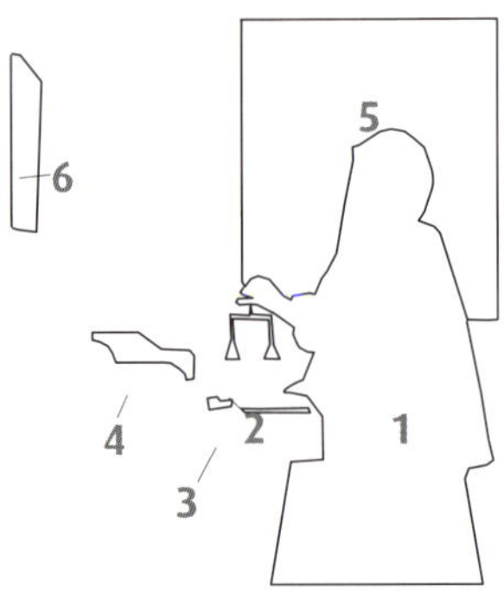

Romanticism and the Pre-Raphaelites

The Romantic artistic movement of the 18th and 19th centuries developed as a reaction to the orderly neo-classical ideals of reason and ethical sense. In place of the earlier movement's emphasis on realistic representation, the Romantic school favoured whimsical fantasy, imagination, emotional sensibility and a semi-mythical return to an idyllic vision of nature. The term derived its name from the similarly imaginative medieval tales of the 18th century known as "romances", because they were inevitably written in one of the Romance languages rather than in Latin. The movement also saw a revival of Gothic sensibilities, in a somewhat more melodramatic form. Indeed, many of the Romantic painters selected quite dark or oppressive themes for their work.

One of the early influences of the movement was Giovanni Piranesi, an Italian artist who worked primarily in engraving. Based in Rome, Piranesi was greatly inspired by the antiquity surrounding him, and often sought to depict familiar sights restored and reimagined to their early glory. However, he is most famous for his series of *Carceri d'Invenzione* (Imaginary Prisons). These depicted a series of grim, oppressive underground vaults, vast and bleak, populated with ugly staircases and huge pieces of enigmatic, hostile-seeming machinery. Tiny specks – perhaps people or prisoners? – crawl through these nightmare scenes, already broken.

For all the stark bleakness and oppression, these prisons are clearly not supposed to symbolize real jails. They display a surreal, twisted architecture that comes close to foreshadowing the modern Dutch graphic artist Escher's impossible mazes. These are prisons of the mind – of the imagination, harking back to the title – and as such are more terrible by far than any stone wall. A symbolic depiction of despair, loneliness, isolation and abject depression, they force us to remember that the mind can be a very terrible thing.

It is a warning that seems to haunt the later

Carceri #14 is typical of Piranesi's cycle of fortunately imaginary underground prison complexes. Huge, brooding vaults and caverns of stone with ant-like people and unknown devices, the *Carceri* are decidedly infernal in tone.

work of the Spanish painter and engraver Francisco Goya. Born in Fuendetodos, he lived most of his life in Madrid, and made a reputation as a chronicler of history and royal portrait artist. One of Goya's best-known cycles of work, however, was a series of prints titled *Los Caprichos* (Caprices), depicting symbolic representations of the foolishness and prejudice commonly found in everyday life. One of the better-known Caprices, *Que Viene el Coco* (Here Comes the Bogeyman) is a statement about superstition and fear. In it, a rather witless-looking woman is sitting on the edge of a bed, cowering as a cloaked figure approaches. Her two children, clearly terrified, are clinging to her desperately. Is there anything to be scared of? It's difficult to tell, but Goya makes it clear that the children, absorbing their mother's fear, will themselves grow up afraid.

In northern Europe, one of the most important Romantic painters was Germany's Caspar David Friedrich. His paintings focus on the power of nature untamed – a direct contrast to the portraitists of the Enlightenment, who tended to use soft, natural depictions to frame simple, literal images of their subjects. Friedrich was deeply scarred emotionally by a childhood tragedy

Goya's Descent into Darkness

Over the course of his career, Goya's mood steadily darkened, and his later work is strongly subversive. He went deaf in 1792, and eventually locked himself away as a recluse, decorating his house with a sequence of quite frighteningly nasty paintings depicting all manner of insanity, evil and cruelty. These "Black Paintings" (so called for their mood rather than the colour) were never intended for public view, but were rescued after his death, and had a strong impact on the Expressionist art movement.

Goya's *Caprice Number Three*, "Here Comes the Bogeyman", is a study in terror, but without giving any real suggestion that there is actually anything to be afraid of. The bogeyman figure seems neither armed nor particularly threatening.

in which he fell through thin ice over a pond. He himself was rescued unharmed, but in saving him, his beloved older brother drowned. He carried the guilt and pain of his brother's death with him for the rest of his life, and his awareness of pain and mortality coloured all his works.

In the *Stages of Life*, painted just a few years before Friedrich's death, five ships of differing sizes are sailing away from a muted beach. Five people are on the beach, corresponding to the ships. The two smallest ships are little more than skiffs, tiny things barely deserving their sails. They are closest to the shore. Likewise, the two figures closest to the sea are a pair of toddlers, playing with a Swedish flag. Moving out from the line where sea meets sand, the next corresponding pair are a larger boat with sails hanging from a clearly cruciform mast, and a girl just a few years shy of maturity. All three of these first boats are close to shore, almost within reach. The next figure, facing the viewer, is a younger man, in his twenties or thirties, elegantly dressed. He corresponds to a large, impressive ship some way out. Beyond it, the last ship is becoming indistinct, and corresponds to an old man with his back to us, watching his youthful relatives.

The link between ships and individuals is clear. Only the first three ships are close to the beach; the young man's ship is already distant, greyed by mists, fading toward the old man's ship. While all the participants seem content, Friedrich is suggesting that even at 20 or 30, the young man's life is effectively over. He stands near the children, some way from the old man, but his ship is long, long gone. Only the children, playing in the sand, have vivid, attainable ships – the hope and optimism of childhood. But all the ships are sailing away. Even at the moment of birth, the separation of shore and sea, the children have missed their boats. They too will grey. Symbolically, the ships tell the sad truth – for the old man, the past 40 years have been a slow, grey decay from the vivid colour of the first 10, as the young man is discovering, and the children will come to understand.

Friedrich's *Stages of Life* is a bleak observation on mortality, hope, and the inevitability of death and loss, a clear refrain to the painter's own emotional scarring. Life may be short, but surely that is all the more reason to enjoy it?

Drawing heavily on Romantic and neo-Gothic themes, the British artists William Holman Hunt, John Everett Millais and Dante Gabriel Rossetti founded the influential Pre-Raphaelite Brotherhood. They wanted to escape the formal realism of literal, accurate depiction which had started with Italian early Renaissance Mannerists such as Raphael – hence the name Pre-Raphaelite – in favour of the lavish colour and idealized imagery of earlier work. Although the Brotherhood was short-lived, artistic works of several kinds adhering to its aims continued to be produced for several decades after its demise.

One of the signature works of the Pre-Raphaelite movement is *Beata Beatrix*, Rossetti's painting of the death of Beatrice, Dante Alighieri's unrequited love who was to become his heavenly guide in his great poem *The Divine Comedy*. Rossetti's painting captures Beatrice at the moment of her death. Her face bears the features of Elizabeth Siddal, Rossetti's dead wife; their marriage had been short and stormy, with Rossetti frequently unfaithful, and Elizabeth, a long-term Laudanum addict, killing herself with the drug in a fit of depression some months after giving birth to a still-born baby. Although she would almost certainly have died of an overdose sooner or later, Rossetti always blamed himself for her death.

The painting is laden with symbolism of love, passion and death. Beatrice (1) is in rapture – both spiritual and sexual – fulfilment coming to her finally in her passing to heaven. A dove is at her wrist (2), representing love and physical passion. It is dropping a poppy (3) into her lap. A strong symbol of death in its own right, the poppy is also the plant from which opiate drugs – including Laudanum – are obtained. The subtext is that the drug was a physical passion. She is dressed in red and green, a combination representing youth and vitality, but a sundial (4) in front of her shows that time has caught up. Behind her, the red-clad angel of love (5) watches over her, while Dante (6), black-clad, observes from a half-hidden position in the shadows. A golden shaft of light symbolizes her ascent to heaven. With the identification of Siddal with Beatrice, Rossetti is also linking

One of the most important works of the Pre-Raphaelite Brotherhood, Dante Gabriel Rossetti's *Beata Beatrix* is a moving memorial to the artist's dead wife. By identifying himself and his wife with the Italian poet Dante Alighieri and his famous lost love Beatrice, Rossetti is making a statement of undying regret.

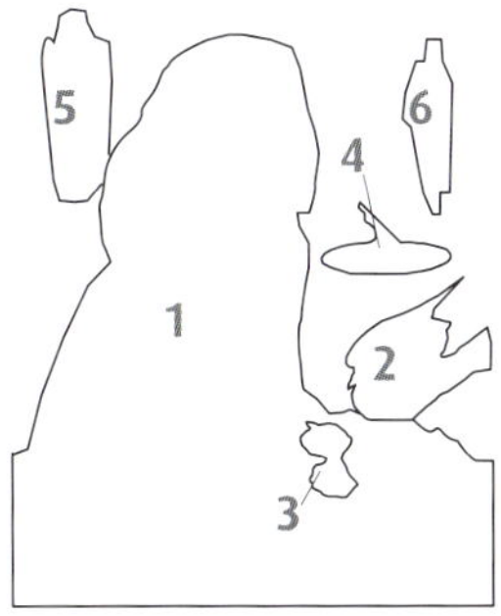

himself to Dante Alighieri, and taking on a lifelong burden of love and guilt.

Art as Propaganda

The height of art's symbolic power of course has been its use as propaganda, to convey a political message. An offshoot of the church's desire to use art as a teaching aid, artistic propaganda has become a vital tool of politics and commerce worldwide. It remains the foundation of the advertising industry, which exists solely to cajole and manipulate. In many ways, as state and commerce become increasingly cross-tied, advertising is returning to the true roots of medieval art, as a tool used by the existing power base to reinforce its key messages.

One of the most famous early political polemic artworks is Eugène Delacroix's *Liberty Leading the People*, painted at the end of July 1830 to celebrate that month's popular revolution in France, even though it did little more than bring about an exchange of kings. Delacroix was already well known for politicizing his art. A short series of highly charged paintings in support of the Greek war of independence against the occupying Turkish forces had won him a certain amount of fame.

In Delacroix's painting, Marianne (1), the personification of Liberty, is leading a group of armed citizens (5) forward over the bodies of fallen enemies. She holds a bayonet in one hand and the Tricolore (2), the flag of the revolution – now the national French flag – in the other. Beautiful, bare-chested and barefoot, Marianne is both the symbolic goddess and an attainable real figure

A powerful summary – and empowerment – of the French drive to republicanism, Marianne is the representation of Liberty in Delacroix's famous masterpiece *Liberty Leading the People*, and she has become a global symbol.

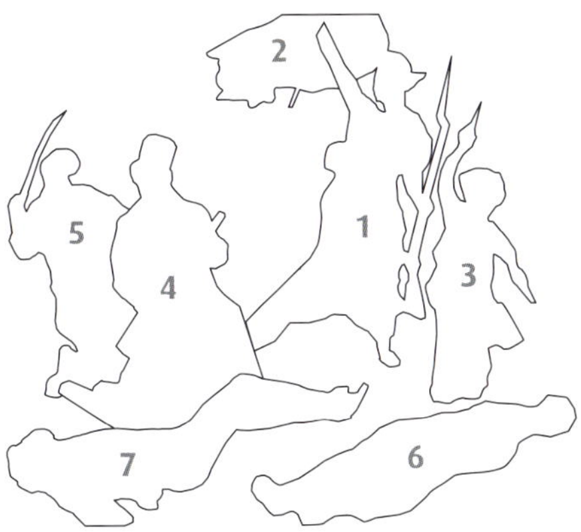

Intensely moving and powerful, Picasso's *Guernica* is a furious, scathing indictment of the insanity of armed conflict and a world that can allow it to be an accepted part of life.

striding out of the picture resolutely. The mound of corpses she is walking over serves as a pedestal. She is wearing a Phrygian cap, a type of hat originally given to slaves in ancient Greece who had earned their freedom. Her troops range from the well-off (including Delacroix himself (4), wearing a top hat) to penniless street children (3), but they are all united and dauntless. They are trampling over the corpses of the old regime, both soldiers and aristocrats, without even momentary hesitation.

Liberty Leading the People was purchased by the French government to display in the throne room and remind the king of who had put him in power. A cadre of bureaucrats, however, decided it was too powerful to risk displaying to the public, and it was first put in a museum, but then taken away even from there. Eventually, Delacroix was permitted to have the painting moved to his mother's house for safe-keeping.

Another more modern but equally intense statement on armed struggle – and still one of the most powerful images against warfare – is Pablo Picasso's *Guernica*. Picasso was born in Malaga, Spain, the son of an art professor who taught him the foundations of classical painting. His output during his lifetime was astonishing, including more than 10,000 paintings and 100,000 engravings. He is probably best remembered as the co-founder of Cubism, but he was a genuine master, able to work in all sorts of styles and mediums, and capable of creating highly lifelike works when he chose to. *Guernica* is almost certainly his most famous piece, recognized around the world.

The city of Guernica, situated in the heart of the Basque region of Spain, was horrifically carpet-bombed in June 1937 by General Franco's forces. Picasso, outraged and already in self-imposed exile in Paris, completed his furious response within days. The picture, which is executed in the Cubist style, depicts people, buildings and animals in a chaotic melange, thrown around by the sheer violence of the assault. It is painted without any colour, to highlight the dramatic intensity of the scene.

Guernica contains symbols familiar from much of Picasso's work, including bulls and minotaurs (strong symbols of Spanish male pride), broken swords indicating the futility of violence, and other, subtler references, such as a burning Punch and Judy stand representing the destruction of childhood and innocence. Everything is jumbled, agonized and threatening. It is a vastly powerful symbolic statement of the horror of war and the slaughter of innocents, and the piece itself – which is 3.5 metres tall and almost 8 metres long (about 11 by 26 feet) – has come to stand as a symbol for everything that is wrong with armed violence, as relevant today as it was in 1937.

As if the open symbolism used in the painting was not jumbled enough, Picasso also incorporated a number of hidden symbols inside the work. These are formed from the outlines and planes of other shapes, difficult to see until they are highlighted. The hidden symbols are further obscured by being rendered in the same sort of stylized manner that Picasso brought to the whole image. It has been suggested that by including these hidden images, the artist was trying to give the painting extra power to lift the viewer away from the visceral horror of the base subject – a counterpoint view that would make it easier to see how insane and unnecessary war truly is.

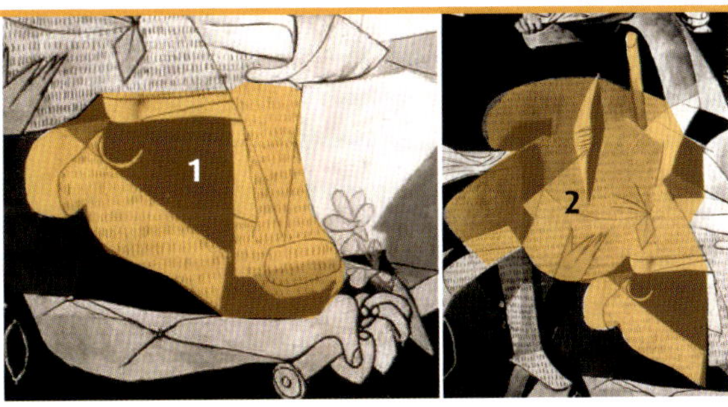

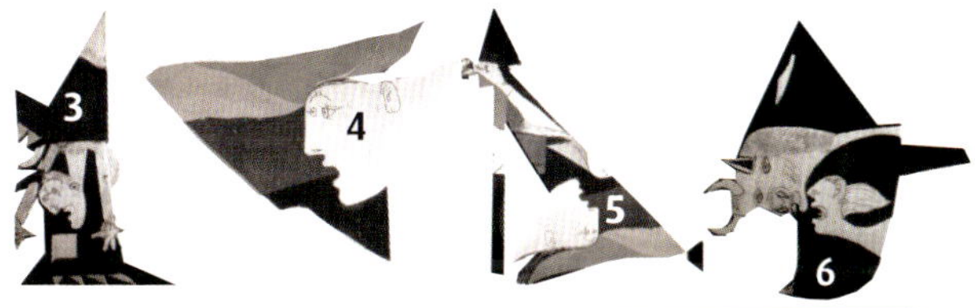

Hidden symbols in *Guernica*, from far left, include two skulls centred around the central horse's legs (1 and 2), and Harlequins in the Punch & Judy (3), as the Flying Head (4), full-bodied and leaning forward (5), and within the Bull and Woman (6).

The dominant symbol that Picasso encoded into the image was that of Harlequin, the famous trickster-clown of the Italian *commedia del' arte*, a traditional form of unscripted opera performance. Rather than having set lines and plots, each individual performance of the *commedia* would be improvised, driven by its regular cast of characters. Harlequin himself is one of the most complex of the *commedia*'s characters, a prankster and mischief-maker who nevertheless possesses deep hidden wisdom and power. He is often linked with mythological figures such as the Norse god Loki, the Voodoo Loa Legba, and the American Indian spirit of Raven, all guardians of the power over death. Picasso was particularly interested in Harlequin's mastery of mortality, seeing it as a symbolic link back to Christ and the resurrection. In Picasso's hands, Harlequin becomes a transcendent force, symbolizing the transformation of pointless death into the mercy of Christ's love and resurrection in God.

The largest, and most powerful harlequin image hidden within the work occupies the top and centre of the painting. His left eye is the easiest point to identify; toward the top-centre, it is an otherwise obscure white slash in the air between the bull on the left and the screaming horse on the right. The horse's bridle is the right eye; beneath it, a cut in the horse's body becomes a diamond-shaped tear that Harlequin is crying for all the victims of the war – the diamond shape is one of the traditional symbols associated with the character. His long, thin face stretches from top to bottom of the image, and the very wide brim of his notorious peaked hat can be seen right across the top of the image.

Other depictions of Harlequin in the painting only become apparent when the image is rotated, recognizable through his wide-brimmed triangular hat, his masked face, and his patchwork costume. A stylized head-and-shoulders Harlequin can be found upside-down in the burning Punch and Judy stand (3), confirmed by his hat and the presence of the character's traditional serrated collar. The hat is peaked by the crocodile's mouth, and following this rather Cubist start, Harlequin's mouth is square, his left eye above it a dark triangle. A clearer Harlequin is hidden in the top left, within the lines of the bull and the woman (4), rotated leftward. This Harlequin is in profile, looking right from beneath the brim of his hat, his eye formed from the woman's hair, his nose and mouth outlined in her shoulder. His expression is grim, as befits the scene.

A full-body Harlequin can also be found upside-down immediately to the left of the Punch and Judy stand (5), kneeling but leaning forward on his arms or a staff. His triangular hat frames the top of the symbol, and his lean, patchwork body coils back beneath him. The flying head in that section frames Harlequin's thighs and narrow stomach, but it is also a depiction of the character in its own right (6). Turning the image to the

One of the most mysterious characters of the *commedia del' arte*, Harlequin is a consummate trickster with the power to cheat even death itself. He walks a fine line between light and darkness.

right clearly highlights the triangular hat pointing upward, and the horrified Harlequin – unmasked, at last – staring up in horror at the descending bombs that inspired the painting.

Not all the hidden symbolism relates to Harlequin and Christ's promise of the defeat of death, however. A large skull image (3) is hidden right in the very centre of the painting, formed out of the body and legs of the horse. This is doubly apt, as the horse is a symbol of death in Spain, possibly due to the way the animal is used in traditional bullfighting. The picador's horse is blindfolded and ridden up to the enraged bull; while the bull gores the horse, the picador uses the opportunity to slice the bull's neck muscles, making it vulnerable for the matador. Today, picadors' horses wear body armour and are rarely killed, but up until the 1950s or so, very few picador horses survived a fight. As possible emphasis of this, a bull's head is hidden within the horse's legs (2), in exactly the right position to be goring the unfortunate animal. The image of the gored horse was a frequent symbol in Picasso's work, a powerful juxtaposition of death with sexual imagery.

Political artwork played a large part in the success of the Bolshevik Revolution in Russia that eventually led to the formation of the USSR. The early Bolshevik revolutionaries were fighting as much for the minds of the peasantry as against the official government, and they needed all the support they could muster. Their campaign was waged by their chief propagandists, the cartoonists Dimitri Moor and Viktor Deni. Posters were a key weapon in Lenin's vision of cultural transformation, and with the population mostly illiterate, they were the only way to speak to the masses. From 1918 to 1921, some 3,600 different posters were designed.

Moor and Deni were recruited to the new "Literary Publishing Department" once the Communists had seized control of all paper supplies and printing presses. Their brief was to coordinate propaganda efforts in a central bureau. Moor specialized in clear, simple, striking images designed to make an open appeal to the simple peasantry of the country. His recruiting poster entitled *Have You Enrolled as a Volunteer?* was churned out in one night in response to urgent manpower needs, and 50,000 copies were distributed. Simply depicting a handsome young Red Army soldier, it inspired massive recruitment. Similarly, his pro-farming labour poster, *The First of May: A Festival of Labour* showed a strong, proud, healthy soldier in front of – and symbolically supported by and borne up on – a huge crowd of ecstatic agricultural workers.

Deni was more involved with satire, pointed humour and barbed caricature. His depictions of priests and capitalists as fat, crazed monsters were a constant companion all through the civil war. Like Moor, Deni worked like a maniac to keep up a very high standard of output, despite huge pressure. After 1921, however, the end of the civil war and of the conflict with Poland meant that Communist propaganda no longer needed to be so cutting-edge, for a few years, at least.

The archetypal Viktor Deni image is *Either Death to Capitalism or Death under the Heels of Capitalism*. The poster portrays a heroic, handsome Russian worker in modest clothing and a grossly fat, monstrously distorted old man in an expensive suit, top hat and tie, with the word "Capitalist" blazoned across his stomach and a gold pocket-watch chain stretched to bursting point beneath it. On the left side, the capitalist lies peacefully dead like a wild boar, the worker's boot on his chest. The worker is holding a red flag on a pole in one hand, and a rifle in the other. On the right-hand side, the capitalist stands on the worker, one foot in his groin, the other about to stamp on his neck. He too holds a flagpole, but it is more like a spear, and the end is pointed straight at the horrified worker's face. The poster's title runs along the bottom, but even a total illiterate would understand every nuance.

Karl Marx's work, of course, was the foundation of Bolshevik political thought, and of the Communist Party movements of the 20th century. There has always been a strong current, however, of artists and activists who consider themselves Marxist, without being in support of a particular political Communist party. According to Marxist theory, the only valid function of art is as social criticism – to get people to understand, on a deep, intuitive level, what is wrong with their societies and their lives. This would then, ideally, spur them on to change their society. According to this view, art becomes a revolutionary tool, existing only as propaganda, an idea that non-Marxists tend to find depressingly prosaic and cheerless.

Saving the World

Not all social criticism has to be actively revolutionary, of course. Hans Erni is a major Swiss sculptor and painter with a strong sense of social conscience. A known activist, he has produced a number of works of social criticism, including *Atomkrieg Nein* (No to Atomic War). In it, the planet Earth is seen blending into a hideously grinning skull, complete with gaping, void eye sockets. A vast mushroom cloud is exploding out of the top of it, so big and dense that it is almost like a punk hairstyle. A big crack is running down the skull from the base of the cloud. The implication is that even one bomb might be enough to kill us all – and twice over, at that; even the skull, the symbol of death, is being destroyed.

Hooray, hooray, the first of May – Communist propaganda artist Dimitri Moor was one of the tireless artists whose flood of powerful imagery helped get the Russian people behind the Bolsheviks after Lenin's revolution.

ПРОЛЕТАРИИ
ВСЕХ СТРАН
СОЕДИНЯЙТЕСЬ
ВСЕМИРНАЯ
РЕВОЛЮЦИЯ
ДА
ЗДРАВСТВУЕТ
№ 80
Д. МООР
1ое МАЯ ПРАЗДНИК ТРУДА

4 ARCHITECTURE

The Washington, DC headquarters of the US Defense Department are known worldwide by the building's shape – The Pentagon. Very few buildings are constructed to a pentagonal plan, a fact that has fuelled much speculation over the years.

Buildings have power. Just in terms of their sheer size, they command human respect – and the more imposing, aged, skilfully constructed and ornate the building is, the more power it has over us. Expensive to site, to construct, to furnish and even to maintain, every building and structure represents an investment of resources. Buildings are thus natural bearers of symbolic meaning.

One of the most recognizable symbols of American power and authority, the White House was designed, right from its inception, to show off the imperial might and strength of America's new republic.

The most basic level of architectural symbolism is that of broadcasting the building's purpose. The White House in Washington, DC, with its covered porch, curtained windows and broad wings, is clearly a home – and just as clearly a magnificent one, built on a grand scale. Equally, Westminster Cathedral in London is obviously a place of worship. The more prestigious the building, the likelier it is to make a strong declaration on this visual level. At a deeper level, different elements of a building's specific design can also carry volumes of meaning. Even something as basic as the position and design of a window makes a statement about the building's role with respect to the outside world – large, expansive ground-level windows are an invitation in, and probably indicate a shop; little slits are a warning to keep out, and most likely belong to a prison or medieval keep.

Every piece of architecture is of course also symbolic in its own right. Buildings carry a whole wealth of significance and meaning encoded within their shape. Any structure immediately declares all sorts of information regarding its owner's or inhabitant's wealth, status, taste, history and circumstances.

Design philosophy, as well, has a significant bearing on a building's symbolic structure. Modernist architecture – the infamous, featureless concrete block – was a rallying cry of efficiency, utility, practicality and value over sentiment. When the post-Modernist backlash occurred against Modernism, it emphasized playfulness, visual impact and sheer exuberant fun – at the cost of architectural features that were utterly superfluous, useless even. But it was a strong symbolic statement: "There is more to life than soulless purpose." Perhaps inevitably, architecture since then has fallen between these two extremes, acknowledging that beauty is as important as utility, and that both cost and

The Map is the Territory

Simply by the fact of its existence and the market forces involved in owning and maintaining it, a building comes to summarize certain lifestyles and attitudes. A small, grimy, mid-terrace town house and a ramshackle old cottage may both indicate comparative poverty, but even so the two structures have very different associations.

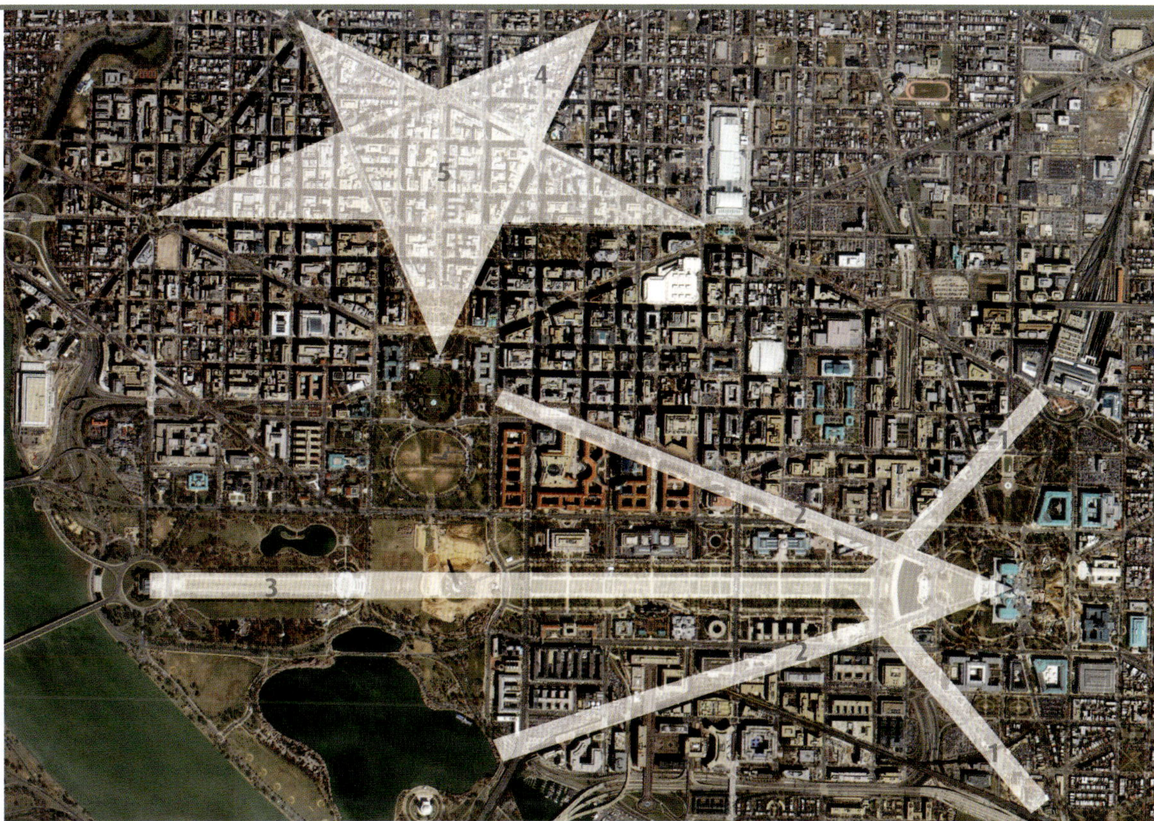

Conspiracy theorists and anti-Freemason paranoiacs have repeatedly pointed to certain patterns that can be picked out of the Washington, DC layout to bolster their claims that evil plots threaten their liberty.

aesthetics must be considered. Even so, something as superficial as last-minute exterior styling can greatly influence a building's symbolic power: consider, for example, the differences between similar buildings, with one styled after a pagoda and one decorated with mock-Tudor beams.

Which brings us back to the White House, with its high-impact white dome and pillars. Right from the start, George Washington was determined that the presidential home had to indicate the power and status of the president to other nations and rulers. It was designed to mimic imperial style, showcasing the majesty of his new republic. It had to dazzle and awe, to show that America was strong, capable of as much pomp and ceremony as any other nation. At the same time, it had to show the citizens of the nation the best that their country – and they themselves – could aspire to. Although Washington never slept in the building, his vision for it endures. It is a living symbol of American power and hegemony, the "People's House", the heart of the American Dream. With its famous reputation for excellence in all things, it strives to symbolize American culture itself.

Washington's "Masonic Zodiac"

Given the influence that Freemasonry undoubtedly played in the formation of the fledgling United States – Washington was a dedicated lifelong Mason, as were many other founding fathers – it is perhaps inevitable that modern-day conspiracy theorists and anti-Masonic detractors should seek to find evidence of gigantic cover-ups in the capital. The human mind is particularly adept at picking out patterns. It is the defining characteristic of how our brains work. So those who have sought patterns in the layout of the city have found them – and found them in abundance.

According to the conspiracy theorists, several giant symbols can be seen built into the very layout of Washington, DC. The most famous of Freemasonry's symbols is the crossed Square (1) and Compass (2). A reasonable impression of this symbol can be found starting at Capitol Hill. Taking the Capitol building itself as the head-point of the figure, the left leg of the compass is said to be formed by Pennsylvania Avenue and to extend down to stand on the White House, while the right leg of the compass is Maryland Avenue, extending down to the Jefferson Memorial. The square that crosses the design is formed by Canal Street and Louisiana Avenue.

As if this were not proof enough for the conspiracy theorists of some fuzzy evil-doing on the part of Freemasons or Satanists or, well, someone, the White House itself is said

The Jefferson Memorial, seen here at sunrise, is strongly reminiscent of a certain class of Greek and Roman temple. As a celebration of Jefferson's achievements and wisdom, it is perhaps not all that far away from serving a similar role, too.

to be the southernmost tip of an inverted pentagram (4) – a sign that has recently come to be associated by the popular media with satanic activity. The inverted pentagram spreads up north from the White House, inside the intersections of Connecticut Avenue and Vermont Avenue north to Dupont and Logan Circles, with Rhode Island Avenue and Massachusetts Avenue going to Washington Circle to the west, and Mt Vernon Square to the east. The centre of this pentagram (1), a terrifyingly evil 13 blocks north of the White House, is the Masonic House of the Temple on 16th Street. Some theorists even go so far as to include the location of a Masonic "Rule" symbol cunningly encoded into the city… in the form of a straight line (3).

Pentagons and Pentagrams

For conspiralogists looking for evidence of Satan's hand in the US government, the final nail in the coffin comes in the admittedly unusual form of the Pentagon, the headquarters of the Defense Department. Consisting as it does of five concentric, regular five-sided polygons, all the Pentagon is missing is the internal connecting threads to turn it into a "satanic" pentagram. An awful lot of paranoid conspiracy buffs take this as a certain sign that the US military machine is in league with Lucifer himself. Some even maintain that the missing links are in place in the form of underground corridors connecting the five wings, and that the spot in the very centre of the courtyard is actually a prison for vile demonic entities.

All sorts of wild claims have arisen from the Pentagon's design. Is it simply a matter of acknowledging the Army, Navy, Air Force, Marine Corps and Coast Guard, or is there some deeper symbolism at work?

The Defense Department has a predictably mundane explanation, of course. The five-sided shape of the structure was supposedly chosen to represent the five wartime branches of the US military: the Army, the Navy, the Air Force, the Marine Corps and the Coast Guard. That is as may be, although the inclusion of the Coast Guard – who are not overseen by the Defense Department during peace time – seems to be stretching the official rationale a little too far.

However, the number five has in its own right a good provenance as an appropriate symbol for the Defense Department. As well as representing vigilance (via the five senses), five was the number sacred to the Greek deity Ares (and his Roman counterpart Mars), the god of war. In the Kabbalah, the fifth Sephiroth is that of Geburah, which symbolizes the severity and willpower to do that which is necessary to protect the whole. With its five-by-five structure, the Pentagon could quite easily be an ancient Greek temple to the god of war.

The Pantheon, Rome's oldest surviving church, shows off the architectural design for which it is most famous, the Oculus, or all-seeing eye, that remains open to the heavens.

Roman Power

Architectural details can carry just as much symbolic weight as entire buildings, of course. The Pantheon in Rome is one of the city's oldest surviving structures. It was built as a temple to the Roman gods in 27BC, remodelled in AD120, and then converted to a church in 608, which is how it has survived. Its sanctity as a temple, however, is derived from a nine-metre (30-foot) hole in the top of the dome, the Oculus, or "all-seeing eye" of the heavens. All the temple's illumination is provided by the Oculus, and internal markings provide information about time, date and the equinoxes and solstices. The Oculus is the breath of the divine in the structure – light, information, access to the heavens, fresh air, a way of staying in contact with nature. It is the symbolic power of the Oculus that turns an impressive feat of architecture into a sacred space.

At the opposite end of the scale, overt power and a massive amount of work can be used to make a comparatively subtle symbolic point – even without leaving Rome. In 1929 the Vatican recognized Mussolini's Fascist Italy as a state. To celebrate, Mussolini proposed a splendid new thoroughfare, the *Via della Conciliazione* (Reconciliation Street), to lead straight up from the River Tiber to St Peter's. A slum dating back to Roman times known as the Borgo was sprawled in the way, so Mussolini had it

The Pantheon: Rome's Master Dome

Architecturally symmetrical, the temple dome is the same width as the height of the walls, a massive 44 metres (143 feet). The dome was made from concrete by Hadrian's architects – who used a technique which was then lost for well over a thousand years – and it was the world's largest dome until well into the twentieth century.

torn down, along with the buildings on either side of the existing roads and any other structures that were in the way.

In their place, the government built a wide, gleaming road lined with buildings that exemplified the best in Fascist architecture. The view of the Vatican that the new road provided from the river was – and still is – breathtaking. But the new street, wide and in perfect repair, lined with first-rate buildings, also doubled as an ideal symbolic stage for parades, marches and rallies. The Vatican at its head merely added a subtle touch of historical and religious authority to any activity. The very fact that so much havoc and relocation should be undertaken merely to provide a venue with a little extra authority is, in itself, a very strong symbolic statement of power.

SYMBOLIC SPACE

In some instances, entire landscapes can become symbolic spaces. Glastonbury is a small town in southwest England. Although it is now surrounded by farmland, until the sixth century it was almost entirely encompassed by marshland, and the Celtic people are known to have considered it a very holy place, a gateway to the next world, and possibly even the isle of the dead itself. Glastonbury is shaped and surrounded by an amazing number of Christian and pre-Christian holy sites, including two sacred

The majestic Glastonbury Tor, topped dramatically by St Michael's Church. Regarded as a highly powerful female earth energy site in its own right, it was seen by the Celts as a portal to the underworld.

Glastonbury was traditionally exempt from the law of the land and the rule of the king. That right was brutally revoked by Henry VIII, and the town's majestic Abbey was destroyed.

hills, an abbey, two holy wells and a supposed ring of earth-line figures representing zodiac signs.

The best-known feature of the town is probably Glastonbury Tor, a pendulous natural hill topped by a thirteenth-century tower, all that remains of a church dedicated to St Michael. The hill is carved with an ancient Celtic earth maze – a set of ridged paths that leads about and around the hill repeatedly in a sacred spiral dance, until it finally reaches the top. According to Celtic legend, this was the site of an entrance to the realms of Annwn, the underworld, and there is a legend about St Collen meeting Gwyn Ap Nudd, the King of the Fae himself, on top of the hill. The Tor is a very strong symbol of the power of mother earth. The hill with its tower (earlier, a stone circle or spiral may have adorned the top) is clearly reminiscent of a female breast. The spiral maze around it is a serpent-line, a physical symbol of spiritual power and energy, and the acquisition of knowledge.

The other important hill in Glastonbury is at the other side of the town. Wearyall Hill is supposed to be where Joseph of Arimathea landed following his departure from the Holy Land after Christ's crucifixion. He planted his staff in the hill, and it is said that a holy thorn tree grew from it that flowered twice a year, once around Christmas and once around Easter. At the end of the hill, Bride's Mound used to be the site of a holy well devoted to the Celtic fire goddess Brigit, along with two chapels, one to her Christian counterpart St Brigit, and one to Mary Magdalene. A stone now marks the covered well. With symbolism drawing on all four of the natural elements – Brigit, Joseph's staff, and thorns all representing fire; Mary Magdalene and the well water; and the hill itself both earth and air – this would have been widely considered to be a very powerful spot.

At the foot of the Tor, two still-active holy wells nestle in the grounds of the abbey. The Chalice Well is so called because legend says that it is the hiding-place of the Holy Grail, as deposited by Joseph of Arimathea after his arrival in Glastonbury. The well is known to have been in continual use for at least two thousand years, and possibly much longer. For a portion of the year, the waters of the Chalice Well run red, owing to its iron content. Symbolically though, it is said to represent the menstrual blood of the earth mother – and chalices themselves symbolize the divine womb from which all goodness pours forth. As such, they are the essence of life itself, the Earth's gift to sustain all living things. The Chalice Well has never failed (unlike many springs, which go dry from time to time) and thus is also symbolic of an eternal and boundless life force. For the Celtic tribes, wells and springs were gateways to the spirit world, places where, as it were, the material veil rubbed thin. With its red waters, the Chalice Well was a particularly appropriate spot for communing with the goddess.

The Glastonbury Zodiac

The most ambitiously speculative – and least known – element of the town's landscape is the Temple of the Stars, a set of 12 astrological symbols surrounding the town. Said to spread 10 miles wide, the temple was supposedly constructed on the advice of Merlin, King Arthur's wizard. It was formed from dykes, roadways, paths and earthworks, depicting the old zodiac signs in a wheel around the town. It was long lost until its supposed rediscovery in the 1920s. Real or not, a ring of signs around Glastonbury is another strong symbolic link to the feminine mystic principle – in a town already dominated by it.

The counterpart of Chalice Well at Glastonbury is the White Spring, which flows from underneath the Tor. Its waters are high in limestone, which gives them their white colour. Known as a healing well, the White Spring is another powerful gift of the earth mother, symbolizing the milk from her breast. This is doubly emphasized by the spring's origin in the Tor.

From the earliest times right up until the rule of Henry VIII in the early sixteenth century, Glastonbury town and the surrounding area had been outwith the laws of the land. The now-ruined abbey is a testament to those times, when all legal issues for the town were decided by a council of 12 priests. Even the kings had no authority over the town. Its holiness was deemed so great that it was left to govern itself. Henry revoked that right when he destroyed the abbey and slaughtered some of the monks, but the ruins of the abbey still symbolize the town's sanctity.

The Past Reflects the Present

A more enigmatic – and far more famous – use of sacred space is the world-renowned megalithic monument Stonehenge, also in southwest England. Construction at Stonehenge took place in a number of phases. The first phase, around 3000BC, involved the creation of a circular ditch and bank, the henge itself. Just inside that was a ring of 56 pits, which may have held a ring of wooden posts and crossbars; four "station stones" were arranged inside the circle in a rectangle. A break was made in the henge bank, marked by the placement of the so-called Slaughter Stone, and the Heel Stone was placed some 24 metres (80 feet) away down the avenue.

After some uncertain, possibly wooden, construction two hundred years later, the next major building phase at Stonehenge was around 2100BC, when an inner ring of five massive "trilithons" – two pillar stones joined by a horizontal lintel stone across the top – was formed. This was closely surrounded by another ring of 30 tall pillar stones, which were joined at the top by 30 horizontal lintel stones to make an unbroken circle. Over the next five hundred years, an innermost horseshoe of giant standing stones was added inside the trilithon ring, and another ring of 60 standing stones was erected between the trilithon horseshoe and the lintel circle. Finally, around 1400BC, two more rings of pits (known as the "Z and Y holes") were dug outside the lintel circle, again possibly holding wooden constructions.

Some facts pertaining to Stonehenge's symbolic meaning are certain. The giant sarsen stones, each weighing up to 45 tons, must have come from a quarry 30 kilometres (19 miles) away – a real achievement given that the builders did not have the use of wheels as a technology. The smaller bluestone rocks weigh around four tons each – a mere four tons! – but can only have come from the Preseli Mountains in Wales, almost 400 kilometres (250 miles) away. Then there is the famous matter of the monument's solar alignment. On midsummer's day, at dawn, the sun shines through the largest trilithon stones to illuminate the innermost Altar Stone, which (when cleaned) sparkles, thanks to its mica content. It is the only day of the year on which this happens. Then, a few minutes later, the shadow of the Heel Stone falls along the same path and it, too, covers the Altar Stone. The Z and Y holes consist of 30 and 29 pits respectively, which average between them 29.5 holes – the precise length in days of the lunar cycle. It must have been an important spot, because more than 400 burial mounds are to be found nearby.

There are many competing ideas regarding Stonehenge's true purpose and meaning, of course. In terms of modern symbolic thought, the concentric rings are representative of the female womb, particularly with the opening of the avenue. The sun – and shadow – piercing the symbolic womb at midsummer makes it very tempting to describe

Stonehenge, on Salisbury Plain, is the world's most famous circle of standing stones. This enigmatic monument is over 5,000 years old, and remains one of the world's most impressive feats of pre-historic architecture.

Stonehenge as a temple to the earth mother and sky father. The powerful stones penetrating the earth may possibly emphasize this aspect.

There also appears to be quite a lot of astronomical lore bound up in the rings and patterns, so much so that some theorists believe the site to be a gigantic calculator – although why, if this were the case, it would have been built in stone and not wood is never explained. The concentric rings, reinforced, have led some theorists to suggest that the site was a mystic prison, holding some mythic evil in place (now long-escaped, presumably). The presence of other, less ornate, megalithic sites have made some New Age thinkers hold that Stonehenge is a power conduit, an energy sink for a theoretical earth force. It has even been suggested, perhaps only semi-seriously, that Stonehenge is supposed to represent a giant ribcage.

In fact, there is only one thing that Stonehenge definitely symbolizes today, and that is easily its most important association – the mystery, power and elegance of prehistoric enigmas.

Imperial Space

The Louvre is one of France's most enduring

Many artists have tried to recreate Stonehenge as it might have looked at the height of its importance. Their efforts are, by necessity, somewhat speculative, as this whimsical example shows.

The transformation of art into article? IM Pei's glass pyramid entrance to the magisterial Louvre Museum clashes uncomfortably with the historic surroundings in which it finds itself.

symbols of grandeur. Now one of the pre-eminent museums in the world, it has had many illustrious functions over the course of its career. It was first built as a fortress in 1190 by King Philippe-Auguste, to protect the royal family and their valuables from thieves and attackers. In 1360 Charles V reworked the building extensively, turning it into a light and airy palace. It then remained the seat of the French kings for centuries, until the Court eventually moved to Versailles. In 1726 it started its life as a museum, but it was only in 1793 that it was opened to the public. Its magnificent collection includes European paintings from the Renaissance through to 1900, European sculpture from the Gothic period up to 1900, selected artwork from Asia and classical Greece, Rome and Egypt, and a selection of important furniture and jewellery.

For years the Louvre held a reputation for being confusing to navigate – some areas of the palace were out of bounds, pushing the museum's internal structure into a twisted L-shape – and people even had difficulty finding the way in. Its most recent reorganization aimed to simplify the internal structure, opening up a closed-off wing and restricting access to the more confusing locations. A new grand entrance was marked by an enigmatic pyramid of glass in the courtyard, designed by the architect IM Pei.

The original building is a masterpiece of palatial grandeur. Executed in classic European style, it is tastefully ornate, on a massive scale, clearly displaying power, wealth and status combined with an aesthetic sensibility. It is a building that makes one think that the inhabitants are not "richer" so much as simply "better". Like most institutional places of cultural significance, it aims to overawe and impress the visitor before they even get inside. "This is important," the architecture says symbolically – "more important than mere people. Pay attention. Learn about your superiors." While modern museums and art galleries are gradually moving away from this emphasis on architectural space, this cultural imperialism is absolutely standard in older buildings. The British Museum, like the Louvre, remains a towering, awe-inspiring edifice, a temple of knowledge to which the profane can come and worship in the hope that the merest speck of enlightenment may rub off on them.

All of which makes Pei's glass pyramid in the Louvre harder to understand. In a clear homage to ancient Egypt, it is built along the same general lines, except that it is made entirely of untinted glass. It is smaller than the surrounding building – just – so as not to detract from it, yet that merely focuses the attention more. It invites visitors in, but then dumps them in a retail zone under the museum, rather than in the museum itself. It is context free, as bland as possible, unthreatening – and so jars horribly with the shameless majesty of the Louvre. All glass and steel, the pyramid is ultra-modern, hi-tech, almost analogous to a television or computer screen: all things that the USA is, but that France is not. In the end, what it really seems to symbolize is the transformation of art into product, the great commoditization impulse of modern American culture reaching into Europe's historic roots.

Encouraging Participation

A totally different ethic was at work during the design and construction of the Canadian Museum of Civilization opposite Parliament Hill in Ottawa's Parc Laurier. Designed to suggest natural forms and geological processes, its elegant evocation of the landscape of post-glacial Canada quickly earned it significant public interest and status as an important global cultural project.

The CMC building concentrates on integration, evocation and inclusion rather than overwhelming awe. In a country of immigrants, a unified national image is a very necessary tool. Rather than trying to bully people into respecting a collection, as the Victorian-era museum movement did, the CMC seeks to get its visitors excited about learning more. In homage to the first human inhabitants of the landscape, some fifteen thousand years ago, it attempts to recall the landscape they would have encountered.

The curatorial wing (1) holds the museum's collection vaults, the massive secure storage areas where objects that are not being currently displayed are held for preservation or research. Symbolically, this is the museum's buried wealth, and the building itself seeks to reflect that. Architecturally, it is designed to call to mind the Canadian Shield, the bedrock outcrop that holds so much of the nation's mineral wealth.

By contrast, the façade of the public wing is the huge glass spread of the Great Hall (2). Designed to call to mind the front of a melting glacier, the public wing (3) is pregnant with possibility and creation. Copper vaulted roofs will eventually be covered with verdigris, symbolizing grass and vegetation reclaiming the frozen territories. At night, the Great Hall is lit from the inside, glittering across Ottawa like a jewel, tempting people to come and investigate for themselves. The hall itself is shaped rather like a canoe on the inside, highlighting its debt to native Canadian peoples.

Unlike the traditional western grid pattern, the public wing of the museum is laid out along the basis of a pair of parallel lines, intersected by a circular track. This creates the feeling of a crossroads rather than a hall – an appropriate symbol for a country that has been, culturally, a crossroads where people from all parts of the world have come and exchanged elements of themselves. In never buying the myth of the immigrant

The excellent Canadian Museum of Civilization breaks from traditional museum design by seeking actively to attract and engage potential visitors, rather than to impress and overawe them.

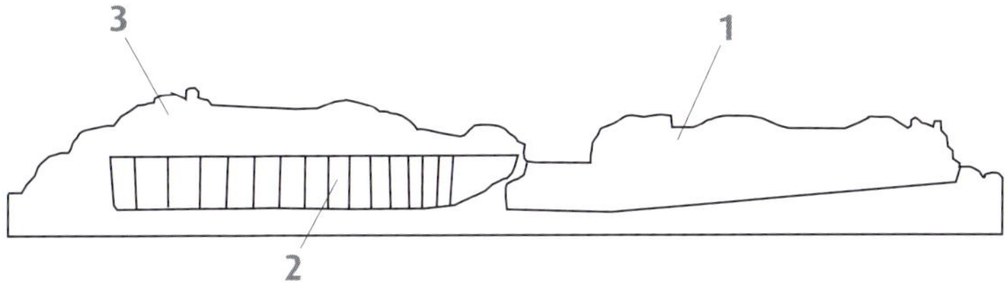

melting-pot, Canada has become something more important and honest: an exchange. The layout of the public wing symbolizes the power of that structure.

From first inception through to last stroke of execution, the CMC seeks to avoid preaching, dominating or patronizing in any way. Instead, it symbolizes the national spirit of exploration and independence – an empowering contrast to the mores of old Europe.

HOLY SPACE

There are certain symbolic elements common to the spaces that the major religions make use of, all over the world. The buildings are set apart from their surroundings, either literally by walls, hedges and distance, or figuratively by differences in architecture and style. There is an entry space, in which you noticeably move from the profane to the sacred. Inside, there is a deliberate cultivation of stillness, usually heightened by dramatic lighting and, where possible, oppressive or impressive architecture. The common idea, of course, is to emphasize those powers greater than man, and to leave the visitor in no doubt as to where he or she stands.

Traditional Power

The superlative church in Christendom – the largest, grandest, most historically rooted, most decorated with masterpieces of artwork, and so on – is St Peter's Basilica, Rome, which stands at the entrance to the Vatican, fittingly at the heart of the Catholic Church. Thoroughly traditional in its use of symbolism, St Peter's seeks to convey a strong sense of awe and historicity. To stand inside it is to be humbled in the presence of the Lord and his church. Despite the changes recommended by the Second Vatican Council to make church

The greatest of all Christian churches is St Peter's Basilica, which guards the entrance to the Vatican City. The current basilica took some 162 years to build, an incredible testament to the artistry and labour that went into its construction.

architecture and services more accessible, St Peter's remains unashamedly resplendent.

The current basilica was commissioned during the reign of Pope Nicholas V (1447-1455). The old basilica dated back over a thousand years to 325AD, and by the 15th century it was in a very poor state of repair. Nicholas asked the local master architect Bernardo Rossellino to design a replacement. Work started in 1452, but it stopped on Nicholas's death and was not resumed until the early 16th century, by which time all that had been achieved was the demolition of the old basilica. Pope Julius II commissioned another architect, Donato Bramante, to redesign the replacement. Bramante began work on a plan based on a Greek (equal-armed) cross with a large central dome.

Bramante himself died soon after taking the commission, in 1514, and the work passed to the master Raphael, assisted by Antonio da Sangallo and Giocondo da Verona. They perceived more space was needed, and changed the design to a Latin cross plan.

Construction started, but once again it outlasted the architects, with the last of them, da Sangallo, dying in 1546. After that, Michelangelo was commissioned to work on the building, and he returned to parts of Bramante's design, as well as doing some of his own design work on the dome. However, Michelangelo, as well as two further architects, Vignola and Giacomo della Porta, also failed to witness the completion of the church. The dome (1) was finally completed in 1589 by Domenico Fontana, and inaugurated in 1593. The last elements of construction – some new chapels and a façade designed by Carlo Maderno – were completed in 1614, some 160 years after work had been started.

This history alone is a strong symbolic statement of the power and authority of the building. A century and a half in the making, realized with the vision of 10 master architects and countless scores of craftsmen and artisans, this is a building that took twice as long to be constructed as most of us can hope to live. Such endeavour is a fitting symbol of the Church Eternal.

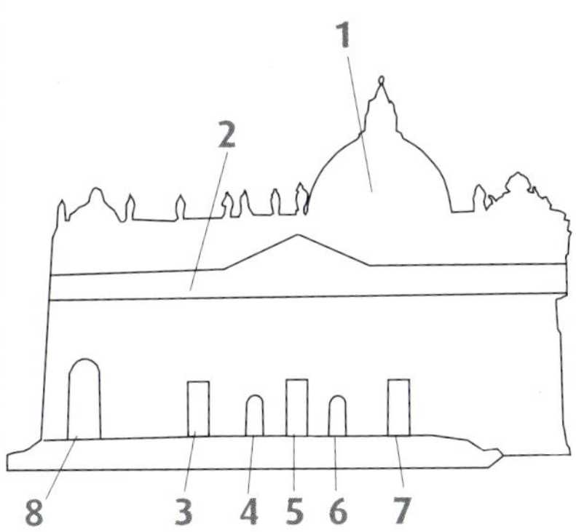

The entrance to the church itself consists of five ornately illustrated doorways, representing the breadth of human experience of religion. The leftmost door is the Door of Death (3), illustrated with scenes showing the passings of the Virgin Mary, Christ and Pope John XXIII. The next is the Door of Evil and Good (4), depicting scenes of St Augustine defeating heresy, various martyrdoms, and the Second Vatican Council. In the centre, doors from the original basilica (5) form the official standard entrance and depict scenes from the lives of Jesus and Mary, and the apostles Peter and Paul. To their right, the Door of Sacrament (6) depicts the divine grace in all acts of sacrament, and on the far right the Door of the Holies (7) is illustrated with a range of sacred scenes including Adam and Eve's fall from grace, the Annunciation by the Archangel Gabriel to the Virgin Mary, and the conversion of St Paul.

Modern Fusion

A totally different form of symbolic holy space is found in the Church of St Brendan the Navigator, in Hilliard, Ohio. St Brendan was an Irish monk in the sixth century AD who, according to legend, searched the oceans around Ireland looking for an earthly paradise known as the Blessed Isles. During his lifetime, Brendan certainly made it as far as Scotland, Wales, England and France, and it is thought that he may even have ventured as far afield as Greenland and the Canary Isles.

Building on the symbolic power of St Brendan's spiritual journey, the Ohio church dedicated to him has had its roof designed so that its front looks like the prow of a mighty ship. Symbolically, the church is Brendan's boat, and the congregation are joining him on his visionary journeys.

Sacred Boundaries

One of the features of the church's exterior is the Benediction Loggia (2), which runs above the entrances to the church. This is the balcony from which the Pope gives his Christmas and Easter blessings to the square, the city and the globe; and it is from here that the name of a newly elected pope is announced. Symbolically, the loggia – and the basilica itself – are the interface between the Catholic Church and the world at large. In keeping with this, the archway to the left side of the basilica is the Arch of Bells (8) and serves as the entrance into the Vatican State; a visa is needed to enter.

On the inside, however, the spatial emphasis is entirely different. The internal space projects upward, forming a cone over the congregants, symbolizing the tents that have been such an integral part of Old Testament lore. Tents have long been symbolic spaces where the visionary can actually contact the divine, and Christianity is far from being the only religion to consider the tent a good place for dealing with divinity. By consciously linking itself to the Tabernacle of the Hebrews, the Holy of Holies that held the Ark of the Covenant, St Brendan's makes a powerful statement about being a place outside the regular world.

The focus of this interior space is a large stone altar on a dais that thrusts into the main area of the church. Seats cluster around in semi-circles, a symbolic audience for the altar. Square-topped, but with a triangle carved out of the base, the altar is simultaneously table and tomb, container of both life and death. Its low height is invitational, but to what purpose? A tall monolith stands behind the altar, curiously reminiscent of the megalithic people – a remembrance of Brendan's Irish heritage, perhaps, but, like tent and boat and tomb, hardly a strongly Christian symbol. At what point does invitation and accessibility become dilution?

Map as Territory

Possibly the single largest religious monument ever constructed, the Hindu temple Angkor Wat was built for the Khmer king Suryavarman II during the 12th century AD. It was part of Angkor City, the capital of the Cambodian Khmer Empire from the ninth through to the 15th century, which held over a million inhabitants, a scale undreamed of by European contemporaries. In the 15th century, the Hindu temple became an important Theravada Buddhist shrine, but without losing any of its power or meaning.

Still widely regarded as an architectural masterpiece, Angkor Wat is surrounded by five kilometres (three miles) of moat (1) – symbolizing the primordial oceans from which the world was birthed – with an ornate 475-metre (520-yard) causeway (2) crossing it to its entry (3). Its proportions and sense of balance are masterful, and the detail demonstrated in the sculptures and bas-relief is equally inspirational. With its west-facing orientation and left-to-right bas reliefs – following the standard Hindu funereal patterns – Angkor Wat was almost certainly a funerary monument for Suryavarman.

Vast, complex and beautiful, Angkor Wat is a dazzling complex of towers, chambers, vaults, galleries, courtyards and porches standing up to

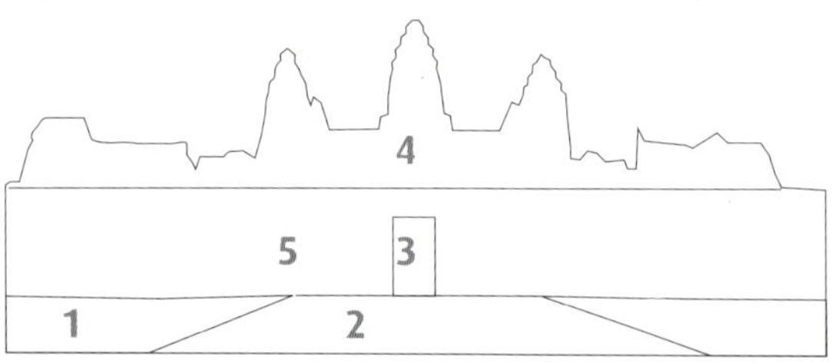

The stunning Angkor Wat, temple complex of the Khmer Kings in Cambodia. The original Hindu temple was converted to a Buddhist shrine in the fifteenth century, but fortunately the conversion was sympathetic – Hinduism and Buddhism share similar roots – and the temple's majesty was preserved.

almost 212 metres (700 feet) tall. The topmost level supports a quincunx cross of five towers (4), each with a somewhat conical shape, carved toward the top to look like tapering columns of lotus flowers. In profile, the whole temple is symbolic of the lotus, representing the true soul in the moment of its opening to perfection.

Angkor Wat is the universe in miniature, captured in stone – the cosmos symbolized on earth. Its central tower, rising from the heart of the monument, is the mythical Mount Meru at the heart of the Hindu universe. Furthermore, its five towers are Meru's five peaks. The outermost wall (5) represents the mountains at the edge of the world; beyond it, the moat is the primordial ocean. Angkor Wat isn't just sacred space, it is a symbolic map of the heavens, at once a representation and identity: it is a portal on the grandest scale, through which Suryavarman could pass into the arms of the waiting gods.

Synthesis of Space

In 1953 the Beth Shalom Jewish Community – newly relocated to Elkins Park, Philadelphia – entered into negotiations with one of America's top architects, Frank Lloyd Wright, to design a synagogue for them. Wright rose to the challenge magnificently, and the

Frank Lloyd Wright's masterpiece of Jewish-American synthesis, the Beth Shalom Synagogue in Elkins Park, Philadelphia. Although this photo does not show it, the building is actually hexagonal, to recall the Star of David.

building – which was inaugurated a few months after his death – has become one of the most celebrated modern synagogues in the Western world.

Wright spent many hours in conversation with the community's founding rabbi, Mortimer J. Cohen, and also drew on his own religious learning – as the son of a minister, he had a deep knowledge of the Bible. Determined to convey a powerful religious message, Wright created a structure that managed to embody and convey many Jewish symbols. As synagogues traditionally merge local architectural styles with Jewish symbolism, Wright wanted to create a modern American structure that still had a powerful sense of Jewish identity.

The building is hexagonally based, partly to represent the shape of the Jewish holy symbol of the Star of David, and partly to recall the look of two joined hands, because Wright felt that a place of worship should have the feel of being in God's very hands. This impression is emphasized by a pair of extensions at the front of the building that represent the thumbs of a pair of joined hands. The main entrance is shaped with a covering that resembles the Cohanim blessing gesture made by the Israelites on entering the Tabernacle, and the building's three vertical ridges are clearly decorated with Menorah (seven-branched candelabra). The roof itself is a towering edifice of gleaming planes that suggests the shining crags of Mount Sinai during God's revelation to Moses, but also, in a parallel to St Brendan's, it recalls sacred tent space, the Tabernacle of David, and even native American medicine lodges.

Symbolism without Symbols

Of all the major world religions, Islam is the least inclined to make use of symbols, considering representational images inappropriate. This has traditionally posed a few problems for mosque architects seeking to make a building as impressive or ornate as possible. There are ways to ensure symbolic power without the use of religion-specific symbols, however. Iran's best-known mosque is the Masjed-é Emam Mosque in Esfahan's Emam Khomeini Square. A stunning blue-tiled complex, the Masjed-é Emam took 26 years to build during the reign of Shah Abbas I, finally reaching completion in 1638. Its double-layered dome is over 58 metres (160 feet) tall, and its minarets – the towers from which the call to prayer is issued – are themselves over 44 metres (120 feet) tall.

The mosque is an incredible work of art. Every surface, inside and out, is covered in calligraphic and abstract designs picked out in blue tiles with gold highlighting. It is tasteful and evocative, calming and spiritual, and carries strong symbolic messages of power and sanctity without ever having to resort to depiction of any particular symbol.

The internal architecture of the mosque, which is frequently occluded, serves to heighten the sense of mysticism. The domed central chamber and the southern chamber are illuminated by gridwork windows worked into the design of the domes so as to provide a seamless light source.

The southern chamber, furthermore, is designed as a perfect echo chamber at a few spots, another technique for helping to awe and delight the faithful. Despite its absence of depicted symbols, the Masjed-é Emam remains a powerful symbol of religious strength and unity.

Despite the prohibition on symbolic meaning in artistic decoration, the Masjed-é-Emam mosque in the Iranian city of Esfahan is one of the most lavishly awe-inspiring sacred spaces in existence, a true masterwork.

Comitis Cestrie. Comitis Oxonie. Comitis Cancie. Comitis Devonie Comitis Maresealli. Comitis hutid
Comitis Lincoln. Daubeni. Willi de Mandevilla Rogi de Huntigef. Ric de Munfichet De tony
Willi de Cantelupo. Johis de bello campo. Willi de bello campo. Johis de Bassingeburne Rog de cressi. Hugonis de nou
Rob fil Walt. Hami peeche Basseth Willi de Vesci Ric de argentom Comitis Fland
Comitis daubemarle Rad fil Nichol Rob Marene Rob Munfichet Comitis Tholosie

5 POWER

One of the most common uses of symbolism throughout human history has been to convey power, might and status. In many practical ways, the deliberate application of symbolism is restricted to those who have time and money to spend on non-essentials – particularly in past eras, before the rise of the bourgeoisie. After all, if you can barely provide your family with clothes and food, using symbols, even of colour, becomes effectively impossible. So, over the years, much of the non-religious symbolism that has arisen has been created by and for the elite levels of society. The powerful often have very specific messages they want to send, and their use of symbolism can be almost an art form in its own right. Symbolism is versatile, however. While declaring your power and authority can be as simple as wearing a badge or a uniform, the same tokens can also be used to advertise your lack of personal power.

This manuscript records the coats of arms of the English nobility of the 14th century – its contents would have been used to identify individual knights and lords in battle.

The grand palace of Versailles was the brainchild of the French Sun King Louis XIV, and ate up his country's annual wealth for 30 years.

Drawing Down the Sun

One of the most famous monuments to display conspicuous wealth is the palace of Versailles near Paris. It was transformed under the directions of the French king Louis XIV, the Sun King, from a hunting lodge into a massive complex of such splendour and opulence that even today visitors' inevitable first question is: "How much did it cost?" The precise sum is unknown, but it has been estimated at about the same as the cost of a modern airport, or about $100 million. Certainly, it is often said that the construction of Versailles consumed much of France's annual wealth, and that even once it was complete, its upkeep took somewhere between 6 and 25 per cent of the country's GDP.

The construction of Versailles involved 35,000 workers and took a period of 30 years. It included not only the vast palace itself, lavishly laden with mosaics, paintings, mirror plates and grand furniture, but also some 40,000 acres of painstakingly landscaped scenery – chateaux, temples, lodges, roads, lakes, scenic paths, terrains, ornamental gardens, fountains and so on. It was an ambitious project: as the new royal court, the palace had to provide space for scores of offices and homes for thousands, including most of the country's nobility.

It's easy to see where all the money went. Largely restored during the 20th century, the palace and grounds of Versailles remain dazzling, both inside and out. Everywhere you turn, there are wonders and marvels to be seen. The name alone is symbolic of massive expenditure, unrestrained ego and kingly vanity. But the palace was not just an exercise in opulence: it was a symbol of power in more ways than one.

In 1682 Louis XIV took up official residence in the palace, some 22 years after first commissioning it. He was keen to get out of Paris, which held bad memories of poor security. The first French monarch in years to actually wield power himself rather than turn it over to others, Louis was desperate to recentralize as much power as possible, taking it away from the provincial nobility. He had already set a policy of never appointing a noble as a minister or advisor, because commoners had no power to resist him. To facilitate this, he made Versailles his court and insisted vehemently that the French nobility come and attend him for much or all of the year.

Life in Versailles was strictly ritualized and based around the figure of the king: the most influential lords

Power Houses

One of the most common ways of showing off power – because it is easy to grasp and appeals to the unsophisticated – is simply to spend an awful lot of money in a very ostentatious way. Construction is a very good way of doing that. Good land is expensive, and so is its ornamentation. There are many ways to demonstrate dominance, wealth and even ruthlessness through the use of space and the objects that fill it.

Hitler's secret attack on the Reichstag building and his subsequent manipulation of the public fear it generated was the masterstroke that catapulted him to ultimate power in Germany.

were perhaps allowed to help pass Louis a shirt as he dressed, while less favoured peers were permitted only to watch. The day was a long rote of ceremony, broken by lavish parties and entertainments. To retain any social standing, nobles had to spend a fortune on hosting such events, along with further fortunes on fashionable attire, gifts for the king, and anything else Louis could think of. Meanwhile, away from their lands and businesses, the nobility found their provincial power atrophying and drying up. Plotting was impossible, with the number of spies Louis retained. Nobles who did not attend court were made into figures of fun.

In one masterful stroke of purely symbolic manipulation, Louis transformed his aristocracy from a potentially dangerous regional nobility into useless, powerless courtiers, fluttering for attention in the most expensive gilded cage that contemporary Europe had seen. The more irrelevant and powerless they became, the stronger Louis grew, and the more desperate his courtiers became to please him.

Enabling Symbols

If the palace of Versailles proved to be a transformative symbol of power in France, then an even more dramatic use of symbolic power was Adolf Hitler's manipulation of the German Reichstag, or parliament building, during the Nazi Party's rise to power. The Reichstag building in Berlin was started in 1871 under the direction of Kaiser Wilhelm I, Emperor of Germany, following observations that the parliament buildings in use at the time were too small.

The Reichstag itself (the body of parliamentary members) and its leader, Otto von Bismark (the "Iron Chancellor") wrangled with the kaiser for several years about how and where the building should be built. Eventually, the structure was started in 1884 and finished a decade later, but it did not really come into its own until the end of the First World War in 1918, after Kaiser Wilhelm II's abdication and the transformation of Germany into a republic. It then served as intended, housing the Reichstag for 15 years.

On January 30, 1933, Hitler was appointed Chancellor of the Reichstag thanks to the popular strength of his Nazi Party after the recent elections. The platform that the Nazis stood on was very broad in its general appeal to the masses, but very narrow in its aims. Specifically, they spent much of their time warning that the country was corrupt and inefficient and that Communists were about to take it over. They claimed that the only way to prevent this happening was to pass the "Enabling Act", which would allow the Reichstag Chancellor to bypass parliament for certain vital matters of national security.

Less than a month after Hitler's appointment, the Reichstag building was set on fire. On the night of February 27, 1933, an arson attack crippled the edifice, rendering it unfit for habitation. After a mentally ill Dutch Communist named Marius van der Lubbe was found cowering behind the building, Nazi hawks

and spin-doctors portrayed the arson as a symbol of Germany's terrifying vulnerability to the Communist menace. Citing the Reichstag attack, the Nazi elite immediately demanded a special security law – the Reichstag Fire Decree – to preserve the nation's safety at the expense of some civil liberties.

With political pressure mounting after the Reichstag fire, the ageing president of Germany was swiftly persuaded to call an election, to allow the Nazis to increase their number of seats in parliament. Before the election, however, under the provisions of the Reichstag Fire Decree, the Nazis arrested the leaders of the German Communist Party, which was thrown into chaos. After the election, held before the end of March 1933, the Nazis had enough seats to pressurize most of the other parties into voting for a temporary legalization of their emergency Enabling Act.

Within a few months – with the symbol of the burnt-out Reichstag building still vivid in people's minds, and the spectre of Communist terrorism frightening the public into near-hysteria – all the other political parties had either been voluntarily absorbed into the Nazi Party, or had been banned on grounds of national security. Hitler's rise to power was complete. The Reichstag, as a symbol of terror and vulnerability at the heart of Germany's power, proved highly effective in leading the frightened public straight into a fascist nightmare.

IMAGES OF POWER

The official coronation portrait of Queen Elizabeth II of Britain is a fascinating study in the use of symbolism and visual metaphor. At first glance, the young queen seems almost incidental to the picture. She is delicate, clearly dwarfed by the massive vaulted hall that forms the backdrop. The robes of state (1) are over the arm of her throne (2), rather than wrapped around her. Even the curtains and carpets behind the throne seem to be a little too big. Elizabeth herself sits at the centre of it all, looking young, but determined.

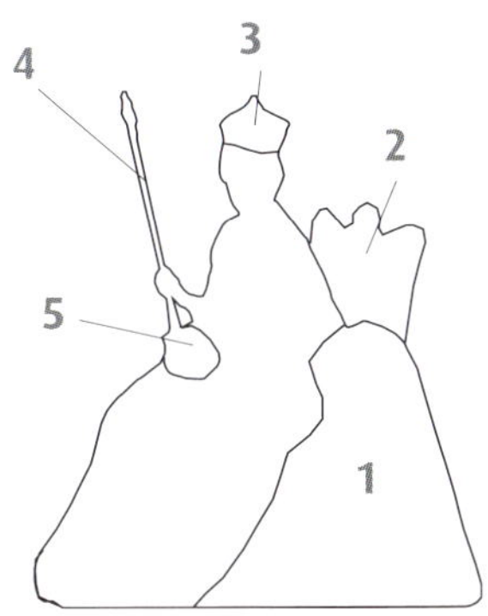

Although a young woman at the time of her coronation in 1953, Queen Elizabeth II and her advisors demonstrated subtle genius in composing her coronation portrait.

Alone, uncomfortable, surrounded by the might of the hall and its furnishings, she looks strangely vulnerable. Human. It is difficult not to feel sympathy and affection for her. Certainly, there is nothing dogmatic or bombastic about the portrait. This is a picture that is designed to avoid causing any resentment or friction. An aggressive stance, at the time of her coronation in June 1953, could easily have alienated the remaining Commonwealth nations. Instead, by presenting a seemingly vulnerable face, the coronation portrait invited the viewer to buy back into the British monarchy. It is almost conspiratorial, inviting sympathy, affection… loyalty.

The Trappings of Power

Looking again at the portrait of Queen Elizabeth II, we can go beyond our first impressions to see that there is nothing weak or compromising it. The elements that frame the queen are vast, mighty and stark. They could seem to overwhelm her and suggest that the woman is just a person in a very large role; but that doesn't change the fact that they are her support, not her enemy. The hall in particular brings to mind medieval castles, towering fortification walls, and a very real, solid reminder of the power of force. The white light shining in from over the queen's shoulder is God's grace. Symbolically, this young, vulnerable woman has the power of history, nation and even divine right to back her up.

Furthermore, of all the possible coronation items that could have been depicted, the new queen is shown with the crown (3), sceptre (4) and orb (5). It is a powerful and authoritarian combination. The three together are a direct symbolic reference to the trappings of power of the Holy Roman Empire, which also used these three symbols. The image is emphasizing the historic power of Britain, and the queen's right to wield that power. Each item has further significance, of course. The crown is the universal symbol of rulership. Specifically, it is the crown's dome of purple cloth inside the gold-jewelled crosses and fleurs-de-lys that represents that power. Called the Cap of Estate, the cloth embodies the monarch's tie to (and control of) the land.

The cross-tipped sceptre is a symbol of earthly power, representing authority and power devolving from heaven. Staves have always been a traditional symbol of force over skill, and here the queen's sceptre is a reminder of earthly might. Together, the crown and sceptre were the two tokens of biblical power used by the angelic beings known as Dominions to hold authority over the ranks of the Cherubim. In her other hand, the queen holds the sovereign's orb, or globus cruciger. This is a symbol of Christian authority dating from the Middle Ages that symbolizes God's rule over the earth being held in trust under the protection of the rightful monarch.

The items selected are all tokens of power, right and control. By selecting them for the portrait, the queen is sending the very clear message that, despite any possible

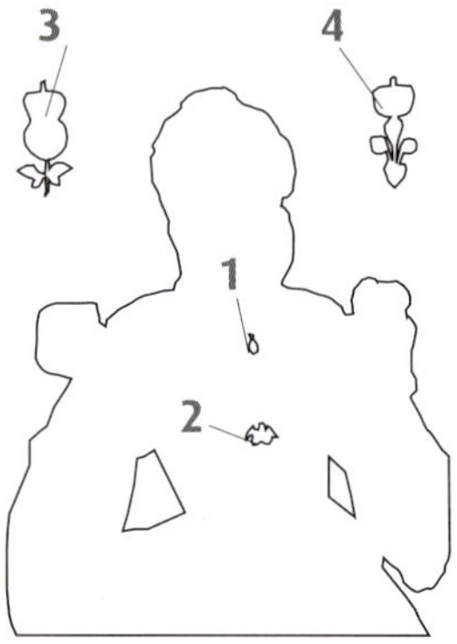

The stylised depiction of Queen Elizabeth I in the famous Pelican portrait harks back to religious iconography, emphasizing her divine right to rule.

doubts about her age or sex, she is the rightful heir, empowered by God, and backed by the very real might of her country. She could have chosen to feature the dove-tipped rod of mercy, equity and justice, or the jewelled sword of state, representing the nation itself; but instead she turned to the wider, collective Roman trappings of empire, and the dominion of God over the earth. The message is plain: support this woman, sympathize with the immensities of her role, but don't anticipate even an instant of softness or weakness – anywhere in her domain.

Virgin Queen Ascendant

One of the more famous and enigmatic portraits of Elizabeth I, Queen of England (1553-1603), is the so-called Pelican Portrait, painted in about 1575 by Nicholas Hilliard. Elizabeth was in her early forties when this painting – named after her pelican pendant – was commissioned, and she had been queen for more than two decades. Hence the purpose of the portrait was not to define her reign or to offer any support or legitimacy for her rule, but rather to make a statement of her divine nature as God's chosen for the throne.

In the portrait, there is almost no background. The painting focuses on Elizabeth as an individual, not as a composite. It is very flat too, almost cartoon-like. It is not trying to be realistic; quite the opposite. By calling to mind the style of religious iconography and early pictures of saints, the painting is trying to bring out the queen's divine nature: it is a portrait of a demi-goddess, not a person. The dominance of white in the colouring of the queen's flesh, the gems of her dress, the pearl at her neck (1) and so on, all serve to remind the viewer of her purity and famous virginity – and to emphasize her divine nature.

The pelican pendant (2) on her breast represented, according to contemporary lore, unconditional motherly love, specifically symbolizing the queen's selfless love for her country. It was said that the pelican pricked its own breast with its beak so that it could feed its own blood to its children, so symbolizing Christ's sacrifice on the cross. Also noteworthy are the two devices floating above the queen's shoulders. To the left, there is a Tudor rose surmounted by the British crown (3); to the right, a fleur-de-lys (4), also surmounted by the British crown.

The Tudor rose is a blend of the white York rose, which represented the Virgin Mary (or Rose of Heaven) in her purity and divinity, and the red rose adopted by Lancaster after the so-called Wars of the Roses. A symbol of Christ's agony on the cross, the red rose was fused with the York rose to form the compound Tudor rose, a sign of reconciliation, unity and healing that represented Britain's new royal line.

The Tudor rose device, then, is a simple statement of Elizabeth's authority to rule in Britain. The fleur-de-lys makes a similar claim, but over the throne of France, to which the British royal line has maintained a claim. The fleur-de-lys is the emblem of French royalty, signifying perfection, life and light. It is said to have been given to the Merovingian king Clovis (ancestor of the French monarchs) by an angel, its three parts representing the Holy Trinity – but many people have been quick to point out that it also looks a lot like the blade of a spear.

The repeated heavenly imagery in the Pelican Portrait is emphasizing Elizabeth's divine aspect. As a secure monarch, she had no need to shore up her place on the throne, or to play politics among her factions. The lack of background in the painting shows that the picture is about her, and her alone. Even the claim to France seems thrown in more as a matter of form than as a serious point. Instead, the painting is reminding the viewer of Elizabeth the divine, God's chosen mother for the people of England.

Spiritual Power

An interesting counterpoint to secular power looking to the divine for legitimization is provided by the papal regalia. The Pope, by definition, is the embodiment of divine selection – he has not held any official secular power since the middle of the nineteenth century, when the last of the Holy Roman states joined the kingdom of Italy. So the potential should exist for the Pope's regalia to be entirely spiritual in symbolism. In reality, of course, many of the symbols are plainly tokens of power and authority, as befits an office with as much political influence as the papacy.

The primary symbol of the papacy is the Triregnum, the Pope's three-tiered tiara. Following a general design of probably Persian or Byzantine origin, the tiara consists of three jewelled silver circlets over a white cap, a form arrived at in 1314. Various versions of the tiara were worn from that time right through to Pope Paul VI, who was crowned in 1963.

Paul VI, shown at his coronation here in 1963, was the first Pope to demonstrate his piety and humility by leaving aside the traditional tiara of worldly authority in favour of a decorated mitre signifying ecclesiastical rank.

After the reforms of the Second Vatican Council, Paul VI set his tiara on the altar of St Peter's Basilica as a gesture of humble piety and a symbolic renunciation of any hint of a claim to temporal power. Although his 1975 Apostolic Constitution required that his successor be crowned with it, the three popes since Paul VI – John Paul I, John Paul II and Benedict XVI – have all refused coronation ceremonies outright and have opted for inaugurations instead (leaving the crowning of British sovereigns as the only surviving coronation ceremony in the world). So while it is currently not part of the papal regalia, the tiara is still depicted in heraldic symbols and flags of the Vatican, the Pope and the Holy See, and it is up to each individual future pope whether or not to have a traditional coronation or an informal inauguration.

The three levels of the papal tiara are often associated with a wide range of trinities, and there is no clear answer as to whether any one of them is definitive. Even the two formal bodies that constitute the Vatican disagree. The Holy See attributes the three crowns (from top to bottom) to: the Pope's authority as universal pastor, his universal ecclesiastical jurisdiction, and his temporal power. The Vatican City, on the other hand, says that the levels symbolize the Pope as Father of Princes and Kings, Ruler of the World and Vicar of Our Saviour

Ronald Reagan's inauguration is a stark counterpoint to the lavish ceremony and ritual of some other transfers of authority – but true power does not need to advertise itself.

Jesus Christ. Other famous symbolic interpretations include a traditional claim that the crowns represent the Church Militant, the Church Sufferant and the Church Triumphant; that they reflect Christ's triple office as king, prophet and priest; that they symbolize the Pope linking the celestial, terrestrial and human worlds; and even that they represent three faces of the Pope's more important duties as teacher, lawmaker and judge. One thing that the definitions share, for the most part, is a breadth of symbolism greatly in excess of purely spiritual influence – which may be why recent popes have seen fit to continue to set the tiara aside.

Another world-renowned symbol of the Pope's office is the pair of crossed keys. One of them is silver, the other is gold, and they are tied together with a red cord. Representing the keys to the kingdom of Heaven, this image is one of the most definitive symbols of the papacy. When Jesus defined Peter's authority, he clearly demarcated the separate realms of Heaven and Earth ("Whatever you bind on Earth shall be bound in Heaven"). The two keys are the symbolic power over the two realms, the silver key to bind and unbind on Earth, the gold key to bind and unbind in Heaven. The red cord linking them is the spiritual tie between the two realms and, by extension, the authority of the Pope himself.

An even more direct symbol of papal power is the Fisherman's Ring, which takes its name from its depiction of St Peter casting his net from a coracle. The ring is remade for each pope, and has his name cast around the central design. First referred to as "the seal of the Fisherman" by Pope Clement IV in 1265, the ring is the signet that is used to seal the Pope's letters and briefs, as a stamp of authenticity. The newly-cast ring is placed on the Pope's finger when he assumes power, and then removed and smashed with a hammer when he dies. Consequently, it is the least ambiguous symbol of the Pope's temporal power, existing as it does for the duration of his reign, and being the instrument by which he verifies that he is exercising his authority.

Other famous papal symbols include the pallium, a band of lambswool worn over the shoulders, with descending strips front and back so as to appear like the letter Y in either direction. It is decorated with six black crosses and has jewelled pins at one shoulder. It is thought to symbolize Christ as the "good shepherd", carrying the lamb on his shoulders. Earlier popes also held the right to walk under a red-and-gold banded canopy (umbraccullum); to be fanned with large ostrich-feather fans (flabella); and to be carried around on an ornate chair (sedia gestatoria) for certain functions by a dozen bearers (palafrenieri). All of those tokens – many of which are still symbolic of the office of the papacy – have fallen into disuse over recent years.

Of course, the old adage that those with real power have the least need to lay claim to it is also true. Contrast the lavish symbolic richness of the Pope's regalia to the symbolic content of a US presidential inauguration: Ronald Reagan, for example, chose the west front of the Capitol building for the site of his inauguration as a symbolic thank-you to the people of the west of the country, who had constituted his power base. He also ensured that the ceremony was noisily packed with cannon fire, church bells

A lord's coat of arms, as well as serving as an identifier and badge of rank, was also a complex statement of personal qualities and history – every nuance held meaning.

and patriotic music, marking his return to Republican values after the Democrat Jimmy Carter's presidency. Personally, however, he dressed in restrained greys, eschewing any overt trappings of power. Perhaps the gradual decrease of the ritual grandeur in papal ceremonies represents a subtle attempt to demonstrate greater real influence?

SIGNS AND TOKENS

Possibly the richest vein of symbolism to develop in Europe, heraldry arose from the nobility's desire to identify itself with assorted virtues and graces, to display relative status and to provide easy identification on the battlefield. It evolved from its early beginnings as simple colour swatches to a highly precise – if arcane – art in which just about any conceivable creature or object carried a precise meaning.

The means by which coats of arms are defined and given meaning, heraldry is very much an art form. However, although the entire point of the heraldic field is to provide visual identification and symbolic associations, it is interesting to know that any given coat of arms is defined as a written description rather than as an image. This description – known as a blazon (and the act of drawing an image from a blazon is called emblazoning) – can be depicted in quite different ways but still remain the same coat of arms – provided that it tallies with the relevant blazon.

A Subtle Language

Heraldry draws on a lot of antiquated French terminology and can become incredibly precise: for example, "Argent, a Griffon Gules voided of a Trefoil Or" would be the rather strangely worded construct of a red griffon with a gold clover leaf cut out inside it, on a silver background. Particularly complex blazons can run to several hundred words and substantial training may be required to even come close to deciphering them.

Despite the precise nature of a blazon, much is left up to the individual artist when it comes to depiction. The colours do not have any pre-defined shades, for example, and the shape of the shield used to depict the coat of arms is also largely immaterial. Designs of different creatures and objects also differ within certain boundaries, although they are obviously supposed to remain identifiable as the creature or object in question.

Nuances of Meaning

As with the precision of the blazon, the meaning of the different nuances of a given creature or other symbol in heraldry could be very exact, as could the use of some rather obscure or unusual images. For example, one of the less common symbols was a morion, a 15th-century helmet worn by certain Spanish infantrymen. As a symbol on a coat of arms, it represented strength and protection attained through having sufficient wisdom to maintain a secure, safe defence, particularly when such prudence resulted in a great victory in battle.

Another originally uncommon heraldic symbol was the pineapple, which, after Columbus made a present of one to Queen Isabella of Spain, was adopted by ship's captains as a sign that they had returned from an exotic journey. Returning voyagers would place a pineapple on their gatepost, so that neighbours knew they were back. From this use, the pineapple became a rare but recognized heraldic symbol, indicating that the bearer was famed for elite hospitality among the higher social strata. In modern times it has even found use as a piece of statuary to adorn gates – a symbolic boast that the inhabitants always maintain the very highest standards of elite sociability.

By contrast, the lion, one of the most common heraldic designs, is a symbol of military might and courage, majesty, strength and justice. It also symbolizes resurrection – in mythological tradition, lion cubs were born dead and only attained life after three days, when their father breathed upon them. According to a slightly more plausible legend, the lion was the only creature to sleep with its eyes open, and thus it also represents vigilance; as the king of beasts, it represents royal power as well.

Furthermore – like all heraldic animals – the lion can be depicted in a range of different positions, each of which has its own interpretation. For instance, a Lion Rampant – that is, standing on its hind legs, in profile – indicates a magnanimous nature. However, a Lion Rampant Guardant (on its hind legs, head turned to show full face) indicates a prudent nature, and a Lion Rampant Regardant (on its hind legs, looking behind itself) indicates a circumspect nature. Even more specifically, a Lion Statant (standing with all four legs on the ground) indicates that the bearer is skilled in battle, and, if the tail is raised erect, that the bearer is not just able but ready to fight.

Pope Benedict XVI standing in the window of his papal apartment to give blessing during the Angelus prayer, his coat of arms (above) blazoned on the drape below him.

Example Shields

The symbolic meaning of a coat of arms is best assessed by looking at the various elements separately. In designing a coat of arms for his papacy, Benedict XVI has drawn on symbolism from the arms he bore as an archbishop, updated to reflect his new position. The shield itself, which typically bears tokens alluding to personal beliefs or attitudes, is shaped like a chalice, the traditional shape for church coats of arms. It is divided into territories by a notional cape shape, or chape, which symbolizes religious thought, particularly in connection with the Benedictine order. The devices inside the cape's folds (1), the Moor's Head (2) and the Brown Bear with Pack (3), are symbols associated with the areas of Munich and Freising, where the Pope was formerly archbishop and cardinal. The device in the point of honour, however, is a golden seashell (4). This symbolizes pilgrimage and the impossibility of the limited human mind to understand the infinity of God.

Around and behind the shield are the tokens that represent the bearer's authority and rank. In the case of the Pope, the main device here is the cord-linked, cross-keys (5) symbol of the papacy. Additionally, the arms are decorated at the bottom with a pallium (6), representing in this instance the Pope's sharing of his jurisdiction with the metropolitan archbishops. Finally, the coat of arms is topped with a headpiece. In the first versions of his emblazon, Benedict XVI broke with tradition and topped his arms with a simple mitre (7), representing his inauguration rather than coronation. In later versions, it seems to have reverted to the more traditional papal tiara.

By contrast, the coat of arms of Charles, Prince of Wales, is almost entirely devoid of any personal symbolism, while still being incredibly dense and complicated. His shield bears the royal arms of Britain, quartered panels bearing the three lions of England (twice), the single lion of Scotland, and the harp of Ireland. In the centre, an "escutcheon of pretence" carries the Welsh arms – four panels, each bearing a single lion – surmounted by a crown. The recurrent device of a white three-pendanted label indicates that he is the first-born son. The shield is "supported" by the English lion and Scottish unicorn, wrapped in the token of the Order of the Garter, and surmounted by a helm of rank. The whole device rests on a princely crown, flanked by the heraldic dragon of Wales and the badge of the Order of the Bath. Even his personal motto, *Ich Dien* (German for "I serve"), is the motto of the Order of the Bath.

When Prince Charles married Lady Diana Spencer, their royal coat of arms was formed from their personal arms conjoined, his on the left, hers on the right.

Of course, coats of arms are not restricted to individuals. Where the blazon is designed from the first without historic accretion, it is possible to convey a reasonable potted history of an entire community with a simple design. The coat of arms of Kingston, Ontario, is a good example. Its central design is a Martello Tower resting on blue and white wavy lines, surmounted by three gold crowns. The tower exists in reality and has been a main feature of the town's waterfront for more than 150 years; it symbolizes Kingston's military links and long history, as well as strength and resolve. The three crowns represent the three municipal districts that make up the city, while the three white waves represent the three waterways that meet in the city. The red field of the

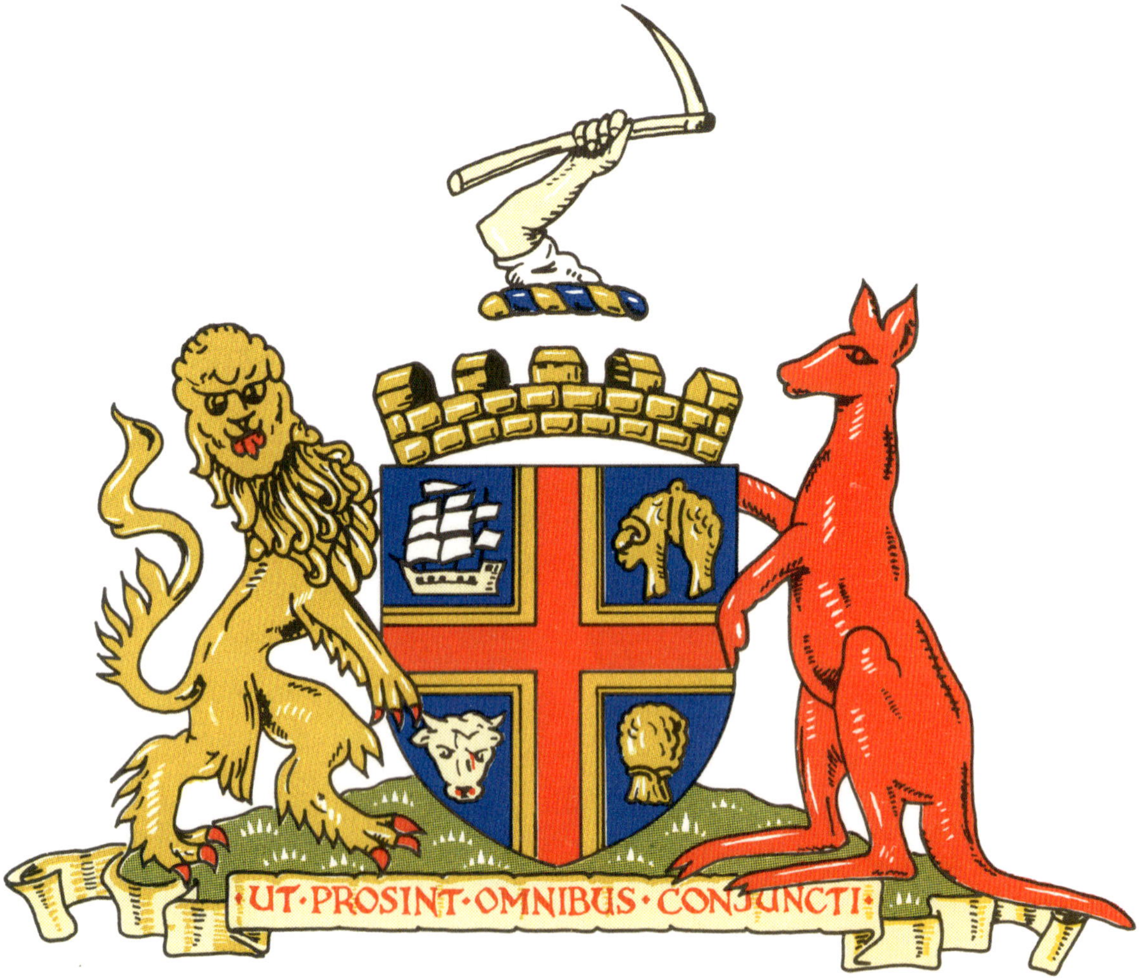

The Australian city of Adelaide's coat of arms is a celebration of the foundations that made the city great – its trade, industry and common purpose.

shield is the red of Canada. Around the shield, the crest holds a beaver, denoting the city's early origins in the fur trade; the river rocks that the animal is standing on reflect the meaning of the town's original native name of Cataraqui.

The shield's two supporters represent the joint French and British origins of the town – on the left, the griffin is associated with Count Frontenac, who founded the early settlement; the lion, on the right, is the lion of Britain. Each supporter wears a collar of maple leaves, representing their Canadian foundation. The motto, written on a gold-and-blue scroll to represent crops and water-based industry, can be translated as: "A civil and creative community with a proud past."

Similarly, the city of Adelaide in Australia bears arms that primarily celebrate its industrial strengths. The shield is dominant in the colours blue and gold, the city's traditional colours, quartered by the red cross of England. The four quarters bear a ship, representing the merchant trade, a fleece indicating sheep farming, a bull's head indicating cattle farming, and a wheat sheaf symbolizing agriculture. The crest is an arm holding a miner's pick, indicating the last of the city's traditional commercial industries. This sits above a mural crown, symbolizing the crown awarded to Roman soldiers who were the first to break into a besieged town. The shield's supporters are the lion of Britain and the kangaroo of Australia. The motto, on a plain scroll, translates as: "United for the common good."

SUBSUMING IDENTITY

It can be easy to forget that a lot of the symbolism of power is about anonymity, rather than personal aggrandizement. There is a lot of very real power to be had in losing identity. Think about the word "uniform" for a moment. As well as referring to an outfit that denotes membership of an organization or group, it also means, as an adjective, that a collection of items – or people – are the same. By wearing a uniform, you become no more than another part of the group that

LEFT: The blues of a nurse's uniform are calming, reassuring and designed to indicate a caring, professional manner, all helping to set distressed minds at ease.

RIGHT: Hotel receptionists traditionally embody the cultural and corporate mores of the establishment while retaining enough personality to make their welcome genuine.

issues it; you lose your unique individual identity.

Masks have long been known to strip inhibitions, by taking away the sense of personal identity; to a slightly lesser extent, uniforms have the same effect. They stand as symbols of power in two equally important ways: first, they give the wearers a sense of freedom from themselves and their inhibitions, a feeling of being part of something larger, therefore making it easier for them to do things that they might not normally do; second, uniforms mark the wearers out as the property of the organization or group, and particularly its leader. It may seem paradoxical that we find it liberating to hand our identity over to someone else, but in fact we are abdicating our responsibility and guilt – by escaping from our social programming.

Any uniform, even the most ludicrous or inoffensive, can be intimidating to outsiders if there are enough people wearing it, in a compact enough group. We almost instinctively recognize that a close group of people sharing an identical uniform represent a pack, in a very animal sense – much more so than if the same people were dressed in disparate clothing. Even fairly small groups can be surprisingly threatening.

For this reason, uniforms tend to be restricted to specific socially sanctioned uses: schools, football and other sports teams, certain job roles, such as hospital nurses and matrons, and so on. A political protest group that attempted to standardize itself by wearing uniforms would very quickly find itself banned for being paramilitary.

While uniforms are undoubtedly a source of symbolic power in their own right, it remains true that different types of uniform have different symbolic associations and so tend to channel their power in different directions – sometimes even against the wearer. A supermarket checkout assistant's uniform, for example, is designed to turn the individual into a seamless, featureless part of the supermarket experience; hotel desk staff, by comparison, need to have an identity that is part of the brand, but without being totally faceless, and so tend to have uniforms that are less anonymous and more a statement of corporate image. Other uniforms, however, have been designed purely to instil fear.

One of the most infamously threatening

Heinrich Himmler stands at the front of a gathering of SS officers dressed in what must be one of the most threatening uniforms yet devised.

uniforms of the past hundred years was that of Adolf Hitler's *Schutzstaffel* (protective squadron) – the notorious SS. The elite paramilitary wing of the Nazi Party, the SS were tasked with all of the most dehumanizing jobs that were to be done, including running death camps (the *Totenkopfverbände*), carrying out special black operations (the *Einsatzgruppen*), and serving as secret police (the *Gestapo*). For most of their functioning period, the uniform worn by the SS was a severely cut, black outfit with sparse silver trim and a hat bearing a silver death's-head logo. With the fleshtone beige shirt collar barely noticeable at the neck, the only significant splash of colour in the uniform was supplied by a red swastika armband.

The SS uniform served to highlight all of the colour black's most menacing attributions and, by extension, to leech humanity from the wearer, transforming him into a symbolic (and sometimes literal) agent of death. The contrasting armband's shocking red – its positivity swamped in all that darkness – mainly called up images of blood and viscera.

There is a fair amount of black in the standard British police uniform, too. However, the cut of the clothing goes a long way to offsetting the menace of the colour. The collar is much wider, for example, exposing significant amounts of white or pale blue shirt beneath and thereby automatically softening the effect. White checkerboard patterns and decorative trim further help to move the uniform from plain black to black-and-white (a combination that represents legality and justice through its overtones of precision), or even black-and-blue, representing reliable safety. Furthermore, the black jacket is often omitted entirely, or replaced with a yellow high-visibility vest. This means that even on occasions when it is being worn, the viewer will remember less formal outfits, further easing the officer's visual impact.

At the other end of the scale, the uniform of the Royal Canadian Mounted Police (RCMP) is one of the most immediately recognizable police uniforms in the world. The outfit is dominated by a bright, friendly red jacket. Blue trousers with gold trim add an element of almost regal authority, and brown boots and hat round the outfit off with a solid, reassuring grounding. The overall effect is impressive without being ostentatious, and has helped the Mounties to become the world's most popular police force, with an almost unique reputation (in police circles) for fairness, polite efficiency and honesty. Their reputation does in fact stem from their actions: their hard work providing unbiased justice on behalf of Canada's first nation tribes gave them a strong reputation for fairness, and this was compounded by their superb handling of the Klondike gold rush at the end of the nineteenth century, as well as by their generally good performance since.

Although notionally a federal police force, the RCMP also contract their services at a local and regional level

Although the British police uniform makes heavy use of black cloth, the threat levels are reduced by softer lines, other colours, prominent decorations and – in this instance – a friendly smile.

Wearing one of the world's best-known and best-regarded uniforms, the Canadian Mounties symbolize everything that is admirable in a police force.

to all of Canada's territories and the great majority of its provinces. Much of the uniform's detail derives from traditional British cavalry uniform, and the organization is in fact officially a dragoon regiment. As such it is entitled to bear battle honours, which it won for distinguished service in the First and Second World Wars, the Boer War from 1900 to 1902 (in which it was awarded the "Royal" designation by King Edward IV), and the Canadian Northwest Rebellion of 1885.

Dull Plumage

The uniforms of modern military forces have seen a standardization away from visual splendour over the past century and a half. On the battlefield, this trend makes good sense. In earlier times, easy identification of friendly and hostile troops was a significant concern. Bright, distinctive uniforms made overall strategic direction of a battle much easier, allowing a commander to retain some degree of flexibility and strategic direction as an engagement took place. Shield blazons and pennants were particularly important with respect to armoured units, because one knight in full armour looks much the same as any other. Impressive uniforms for foot soldiers helped display wealth and status too, as a further aid to intimidation.

As ranged weapons, battlefield communications and long-range observation devices all improved, however, colourful uniforms became first a disadvantage, and then a death sentence. Modern camouflage technology has patterns and outfits for every conceivable terrain to help soldiers blend into the background and become harder targets. Commanders don't need to be able to see their troops easily – there are other ways of keeping track of who is where.

The American General William Harrison – shown here in 1840 at the Battle of Tippecanoe – is a study in bright ceremonial uniform decoration.

There has also been a concomitant toning down of dress uniform as well. Dress uniforms are worn only in non-combat situations (for formal engagements and the like), when there is no requirement for visual camouflage. Interestingly, these uniforms, too, have become plain and utilitarian in most armies. With the US Army, for example, Civil War-era dress uniforms were bright and vibrant, with rich colours, plenty of gold braid and piping, ceremonial weaponry, vivid sashes and also white trousers for some ranks. By contrast, modern US dress uniform looks very nearly fit for use in a standard office – almost as if the soldiers are trying to look like business executives. Without the insignia and stripes, you would be hard-pressed to recognize the suit as military dress at all. Symbolically, this appears to be some sort of statement of serious intent, or perhaps a sober, business-like mien.

Although the precise origins are uncertain, military insignia of rank generally seem to have been passed down from earlier heraldic designs. In the US Army, the enlisted ranks are distinguished primarily by the presence of chevrons (upward-pointing angled stripes) and "rockers" (slightly curved bars). The more of each, generally speaking, the higher the rank. Symbolically, the chevron represents the roof of a house, and is awarded to a person who has demonstrated faithful service. The rocker is probably a variant of the heraldic device known as the "fesse", representing the girdle of honour, and is received only by soldiers of merit. The highest enlisted ranks are denoted with further small tokens between chevron and rocker, such as a lozenge, symbolizing honesty and reliable, constant service, or a wreath, denoting great victories in battle.

Nuances of Meaning

Badges of insignia are far from the only adornments to military uniform, of course. Bars reflect insignia styles, and there are cap or helmet adornments, trims and pipings, and all manner of other signs and signifiers that serve to identify the exact rank, specialities, experiences and competencies of a serving military member. Whole sets of books detail the minutiae of the trappings of military power, but in the end, symbolically, they come down to saying, "I am #". Like the coats of arms of old, they are a language of labels.

Signs of Rank and Achievement

US officer ranks, by contrast, start with the insignia of a bar – a heraldic symbol of high excellence, honour and conscience. Gold and silver are used to distinguish different adjacent ranks, but interestingly in all cases gold is the junior rank to silver. In heraldry, gold represents generosity and silver represents sincerity, which may have some bearing; or it might simply have been that silver showed greater contrast against cloth at some critical juncture. After a bar, the next ranking symbol is an oak leaf, symbolizing resilience, endurance, strength and high virtue. The next highest insignia is an eagle. Long associated symbolically with might in battle – each Roman legion bore an eagle standard – the eagle represents the decisions of command, discernment, readiness for action, power, courage and freedom.

Even at their most ceremonial, as the Color Guard, members of the modern US military look considerably more businesslike than in previous centuries.

Finally, the highest symbol of rank is the star. A symbol of truth and hope, it is the sign of a knight and of nobility, and a reminder of divine blessing. Every order of knighthood has borne a star as part of its insignia, so it is a fitting symbol for the highest levels of attainment of the modern military.

The most familiar military symbols, to the rest of the world, are of course medals. Awarded for specific achievements or experiences, medals are a way of earning distinction independent of rank. The various types of medals are obviously designed to reflect what they stand for, and each one has a unique colour pattern on its ribbon. As the number of medals a soldier earns gets unwieldy, the medals themselves are replaced with short strips of the medal's ribbon, sewn on to the dress uniform's chest. Even so, high-ranking officers can have

Three chevrons and a rocker denote the rank of sergeant – the solider shown here stands to attention in Little Rock, Arkansas.

very impressive swathes of ribbon colours decorating their uniforms.

Most medals are designed with a fairly basic symbolic meaning in mind. The Purple Heart is awarded by the US military to personnel who have been wounded or killed in action. It was first established by George Washington during the American Revolution, and then revived in 1932, on the 200th anniversary of his birth. The medal is bronze and heart-shaped, with a purple-coloured heart on one side bearing a profile likeness of Washington, and the inscription "for military merit" on the other side. Washington's coat of arms appears above the heart.

Symbolically, purple denotes power and status, but it is also reminiscent of bruises, veins and veinous blood, recalling the injury suffered. The heart, meanwhile, simultaneously denotes bravery and fortitude on the part of the injured, and sympathy, compassion and gratitude on the part of the armed services.

Similarly, the Medal of Honor – the US Military's top award, and the only US medal which it is illegal to trade or wear without entitlement – takes the form of a gold star surrounded by a wreath. The Army's version of the medal is then topped by an eagle, on a bar inscribed with the word "Valor". All these symbols are also badges of high rank, indicating just how exceptional the recipient is: only three Medals of Honor have been awarded for actions since the Vietnam War, all of them posthumously. The British equivalent, the Victoria Cross, is a cross patteé (symbolizing military honour) bearing a crown of royal approval, and a lion to represent both immense courage and the British nation.

Unit badges of modern military corps also tend to reflect similar veins of symbolism. In the Australian Army, for example, there is plenty of interesting heraldic symbolism still in use. All corps badges incorporate the British crown at some point, indicating their royal designation and their Commonwealth links to the British royal family. The Australian Intelligence Corps badge is a Tudor Rose – a sign of reconciliation and unity, and perhaps a symbolic statement of Intelligence's role in diplomatic efforts – on a bed of olive leaves, again symbolizing peace and concord. The badge states plainly that if the Intelligence Corps is working effectively, there will be no conflict.

The Royal Australian Electrical and Mechanical Engineers

The Purple Heart is the US military medal awarded to those killed or wounded in action – made tragically world-famous by the Vietnam War.

The Medal of Honor is the rarest and most exclusive award available to the US military. This one is the Army issue form, as indicated by an eagle standing on a bar.

The British Victoria Cross is the highest UK military decoration. Its markings symbolise both great personal courage and the might of the British nation.

are represented by a rearing horse chained to the Earth, with a lightning flash zigzagging down behind the design. The symbol is all about harnessed power – literally having the mechanical horse-power and the electrical energy to move the Earth according to the Army's needs. The Dental Corps uses the head of a dragon – a symbol of eternal vigilance – with a sword clutched in its beak. This could be a pun on the sharp, stabbing pain of dental distress, but it might also indicate fearless valour in detecting and treating oral problems. The badge of the Corps of Signals depicts wing-footed Mercury, god of communication and message-carrier of the gods, astride a depiction of the Earth, which is shown in lines of longitude and latitude – a symbolic statement that Signals can pinpoint any location on the globe with its communications. The Education Corps badge is dominated by a large flaming torch of learning, surmounted by a boomerang to represent Australia itself, and also to hint symbolically at the valuable power of applied knowledge.

CLOCKWISE FROM TOP: The Tudor Rose design of the Australian Intelligence Corps; the raw horsepower of the RAEME; the burning flame of the Education Corps; globe-spanning Mercury representing the Corps of Signals; and the enigmatic sword-biting dragon of the Dental Corps.

HELLS ANGELS
MC
CALIFORNIA

6 IDENTITY

For most people, the chief value of symbols lies in providing them with ways to lay claim to a distinct identity. As social beings, we all want to feel part of an accepted group, but we also want to retain a sense of our own individuality. For most of us, that means following society's broad outlines regarding acceptable behaviour and appearance, as policed enthusiastically by the mass media. Without those outlines, there are a dazzling array of options and choices from which you can construct your symbolic identity. Contrary to what most would-be rebels think, there are actually far fewer options outside the accepted range. The world economy is consumerist – it needs us all to spend as much as we can, and promoting uniformity is not in its interest. The farther you step from the acceptable, the less support – and the fewer options – you enjoy.

Group identity is conveyed through uniformity of dress, and it can be an immense source of power and personal liberation – or a dehumanizing anonymization.

PLUMAGE

Our physical appearance is the single greatest symbolic statement that we can make to the world on a day-to-day basis. Whenever we step outside our houses, we are going to be seen by many more people than we will get a chance to talk to. Equally, each onlooker will make an instant, fleeting assessment of us based on the perceived symbolism of our appearance as a whole. The assessment may not even register consciously, and without some excellent reason to keep it in mind, it will almost immediately sink into long-term memory storage. It stays in place though, called up every time the person in question is remembered or encountered.

The impressions we convey take shape in a gestalt moment of perception – a unifying summary of all the symbolism and associations related to our appearance – blended with the observer's personal opinions and attitudes. We can no more stop it happening than we can dictate what the other person thinks. What we can do, however, is attempt to stage-manage the impression we make, according to what sort of person we wish to seem: in other words, we can manipulate the symbols we display in order to convey our sense of our own identity. While that may sound manipulative, it is something that every person does, consciously or unconsciously.

The choices you make about your clothing and appearance will be interpreted, rightly or wrongly, by everyone who sees you. Everything, from the age and manufacturer of each item of clothing you are wearing through to how carefully you brushed your hair in the morning (if at all), goes toward painting a picture of your life by which other people will judge you. The assumptions they make may be right or wrong, but they will be real, and will be applied to you whether you like it or not. Careful stage-management – identity construction – gives you a great deal of latitude, provided you are willing and able to invest the time and money required. You can lie with a coat as effectively as with a word or a kiss.

Social Groups

Sociologists and urban anthropologists bat exact group definitions to and fro, and will do so until the world ends. But we all have some understanding of social groupings, usually defined by who we ourselves are; and every area will have certain groups that are dominant, and others that are less common. Groups such as "Soccer Moms", "the Beautiful People", "Jocks", "Apartment Dwellers" and so on are common right across the modern world, the result of unavoidable similarities in certain types of lifestyle. Other groups have a deliberately constructed image that all its members consciously adopt. Symbolically, the latter groupings tend to be more interesting.

Group Identity

The most common overt use of stylized appearance management is in the construction of an identity as part of a group. It is something that all of us see on a daily basis, and understand at a very basic level. The human mind categorizes and analyses patterns by default. We look at a person, and the patterns that they fit rise up and take over our perceptions. It's entirely automatic and entirely natural, although not entirely desirable (and not always accurate): suit and tie equals businessperson, for example; tired woman with child equals housewife.

One of the most visually striking recent groups is the Punks. Less prevalent now than in its heyday in the 1970s, the Punk movement was a powerful statement of youthful anger at the perceived restrictions of society. Nowadays, its imagery has been mostly absorbed and softened into other, less extreme youth cultures, but there is a remaining core. Punk, above all else, was angry, and its image strongly reflected that. Extreme hair styling and coloration was adopted as a shock factor, along with aggressive use of extreme black-and-white clothing combinations. Leather and denim – both seen as protective fabrics, thus symbolizing readiness for combat – were prevalent.

Punks were furious with society, with the population at large, and even with themselves – and they made sure everyone knew how angry they were.

A true post-modern aesthetic, tattooing is the ultimate way of playing with your own body and how it is perceived – the most efficient images are often the most meaningless.

This was sometimes offset with splashes of bright, high-intensity colour in clothing or make-up as a counterpoint. Chains, studs and other pieces of metal added to the symbolic stress on readiness for violence. Emphasizing extremity and danger, the movement sought to demonstrate, symbolically, that it was more than ready to express its rage physically.

Every deliberately cultured group seeks to emphasize its puissance, of course. At the opposite end of the spectrum, Haute Couture has long sought to achieve exactly the same results as Punk, but with a very different approach. Both styles seek to intimidate onlookers, but where Punk is physically threatening, Haute Couture desires to establish a sense of visual and cultural dominance – to control with beauty and an implication of superior taste and understanding. The language of fashion has always been aggressively elitist, using jargon and faux artistic sensibility to exclude outsiders. Media commentators translate creators' visions into pithy soundbites for the masses.

The clothing itself is often highly stylized, going beyond recognizable symbolic meaning into incoherency: the whole circus itself has become a symbol that claims elitism, glamour, taste and wealth. There are almost no real-world venues where high-profile catwalk creations could actually be worn – the occasional parody disco or nudist beach, perhaps – but then the point is not to demonstrate clothing, but to dominate through an implied sophistication that goes beyond the understanding of the viewer.

The desired dominance is further emphasized by keeping models firmly within a very narrow band of supposed physical beauty. An almost impossible bodily form and facial aesthetic is cultivated – partly by forced selection of a tiny proportion of the population, partly by unnatural nutritional and exercise regimes – and then sold ubiquitously as a standard of beauty and elegance. Its unattainability for the vast percentage of the population ensures that its power to dominate remains strong. Unlike Punk, however, which alienated by symbolizing a tangible threat, Haute Couture remains aspirational by a careful symbolic suggestion of perfection, desirability, glamour and privilege.

Body modification is a different sort of symbolic affiliation – more radical, yet also considerably less formal. It is more a statement about attitudes and sensibilities than it is about any particular political or commercial message. There is nothing new about using tattoos to indicate group membership, of course. But there is a difference between tattoos as a form of branding, to indicate ownership, loyalty, affiliation or similar notions, and the more post-modern aesthetic of the tattoo as simple decoration.

By using abstract or fashionably decontextualized designs – swirls, spirals, Celtic knotwork images, and so on – the tattoo's meaning is moved from the symbolic content of the image itself to the fact of its existence. In other words, simply possessing the tattoo is more relevant than what it looks like. For the body modification group, this represents freedom, a playful spirit, having fun, and not taking anything too seriously. This applies to the

Playful, sensual and erotic, a pierced tongue usually indicates someone who is more interested in the joys of life than its restrictions.

more common piercings as well – of eyebrow, tongue and belly button.

GANG AFFILIATION

A more serious use of symbolism is its application as an identifier for street gang membership. Over the years, the role and nature of street gangs have changed as larger-scale criminal gang activity worldwide has matured. In fact, it is difficult to consider street gang activity in the modern world meaningfully without looking to the larger criminal organizations. Over the course of the twentieth century, the world economy globalized. As transportation, communication and finance became truly worldwide phenomena, corporations and other large-scale businesses swiftly followed suit.

It may seem odd to consider them as such, but large crime organizations are basically businesses, albeit ones that habitually engage in criminal activities. Unburdened by following financial regulations or trade agreements, the major crime groups very swiftly globalized and federalized. In law enforcement circles, they are now referred to as "Transnational Criminal Organizations", or TCOs. The Sicilian Mafia, the Japanese Yakuza, the Colombian and Mexican Cartels, the Albanian Fares and all the rest are now just as likely to work together, using each others' strengths, as they are to be in conflict.

So, for example, in a typical human trafficking route from the former USSR to the sex industry in the USA, the Russian Red Mafiya will trick (or abduct) young women from trouble-racked areas away from home. These unfortunates are then passed to the Albanian Fares – who are particularly adept at smuggling people – for transport to a soft area in South America. They are then taken by Mexican Cartels and smuggled into the US, where the American Mafia take charge of them and assign them to various areas depending on requirements. The motorcycle gangs – Hell's Angels, Pagans and others – are then contracted to distribute them to their final destinations along the east and west coasts. The motorcycle gangs' infamous clubhouses have themselves become symbolic of lawless licentiousness, and many of the trafficked women are abused in these "bars" before reaching their final destinations. Most of the brothels and street districts they end up in are run by the street gangs. More than two million women are trafficked annually worldwide, mostly from China and from the former USSR.

Street gangs, whether in the USA or other parts

The Hell's Angels trade on their reputation and criminal attitude. Without the trappings of group membership to invoke the necessary power, a Hell's Angel would be just another big, psychotic biker.

By inverting the five-jewelled crown and writing the word "King" backwards and upside down, this logo is declaring itself the enemy of the People Nation, and therefore a badge of affiliation to the Folk Nation.

of the world, have become part of the TCO network. In the same way that almost all the different brands of washing powder are actually owned by one of two major pharmaceutical corporations, so almost all street gangs are now effectively local distribution units for one or more of the TCOs. For the street gangs, symbolic identity creation is an important part of membership. Tattoos, clothing logos, graffiti and so on play a large part in establishing an identity. This is particularly important in the USA at present, when gangs all across the country are affiliating with each other.

There are two broad unions of street gangs operating in the USA. Known as the People Nation and the Folk Nation, the two groups are officially hostile to each other, although the requirements of the modern criminal business environment have damped down the violence between them. The two unions originated in Chicago, but have now spread to polarize every street gang in the USA, and they are even dispersing abroad.

The People Nation gangs include the Latin Kings, the Kents, Black P-Stone and, generally, the infamous Bloods of LA. Their symbols often reflect the use of the number five, and include: a hand with two fingers and thumb pointing up and two folded down (representing a devil's horns and tail); a five-pointed crown with three points in front and two behind as a disguised version of the hand; a five-pointed star; a walking stick and top hat; a die showing five spots or the number five; a Spanish cross (which, like the shepherd's crook and crescent moon, is a religious symbol used in a sardonic way); and a champagne glass and a Playboy-style bunny head, both representing the spoils of crime. In addition to these signs, the People Nation gangs also use a number of variant symbols pointing or indicating left, or representing left-handedness. These can be as subtle as leaving a left shoe untied, or placing a left hand in a pocket.

Gangs associated with the People Nation tend to incorporate one or more associated symbols into their own range of identifiers, often merging a People Nation sign with an original symbol of their own as a mark of their affiliation. For example, Latin King imagery includes a skull wearing a five-pointed crown, a five-pointed star in a crescent, the letters LK separated by a five-pointed star, and crossed walking sticks with a top hat in the right-hand quarter and a champagne glass in the left-hand quarter. Blood signs and graffiti tend to focus on a crossed-out letter C and other "anti-Crip" identifiers, since the Bloods originally formed as a defence against the Crips gang.

Folk Nation gangs are generally allied with the LA Crips, and include the Black Gangster Disciples, the Cobras, the Latin Disciples and the Two Sixers. Their primary numeric indicator is the number six, from a stylization that involves carrying the loop of the six on and down to make it into a curled tail, terminating in a triangular spike, as in cartoon depictions of a devil's tail. This imagery is carried on as a number six, a six-pointed Star of David, and a die showing six spots or the number six. The devilish theme is further developed with symbols such as a pitchfork, a pair of devil's horns and, somewhat mistakenly, an inverted swastika. Another group of symbols appears to have developed in reaction to the People Nation: these include a crown turned upside down, a bunny head with a bent ear, and the use of right-hand symbols, including rolling up the right trouser leg a little. Uncategorized imagery includes a winged heart, a sword and the letters BOS, an acronym for Brotherhood Of the Struggle.

As with the People Nation, Folk Nation gangs tend to incorporate broader affiliated symbolism into their imagery. While the People Nation gangs often have a range of different symbols, however, Folk Nation gangs tend to focus on just one or two. The Black Gangster Disciples, for example, use a six-pointed star with the

The ups and downs of gang life: the cartoon Crip in the background goes from predator to prey in a heartbeat. Likewise, real gang members are sanguine about their dreadful life expectancy.

letters BGD written across it and a pair of pitchfork heads pointing up out of the top of the star like horns. The Cobras use a logo of a raised cobra with pitchforks behind it, while the symbol of the Latin Disciples is a heart with horns and a devil's tail, bracketed by raised pitchfork heads. Crip signs and graffiti tend to focus on the six-pointed star and images of their C hand sign.

Hiding in Plain Sight

Moving away from the criminal world and the use of symbolic identifiers as an overt blazon of affiliation, there have been plenty of groups historically that have sought to declare membership openly, but only to those who know what to look for. Private clubs and organizations often opt for this approach. In this sort of instance, members of the group who want to declare their affiliation will typically wear a signet ring, brooch, tie or hat pin or some other understated piece of personal ornamentation. The item in question will then bear a logo or device that is known to the rest of the organization's membership.

Identifiers of this sort are subtle rather than secret; they are used when group members wish to avoid ostentation, or don't want to make a big song and dance about their membership. This sort of behaviour does not indicate that the group is in any way secret, or even secretive, merely that it is restrained. Secret societies, to the extent that any really survive in the modern world, tend to avoid any visible symbols that would be clearly recognizable; it is simply too dangerous to risk such obvious exposure.

Something of a crossover case is the loose federation of societies known as Freemasonry, which is not only the most famous group of this sort but the oldest and most widespread. Originally founded in the early eighteenth

A gang of young LA Crips in their colours flash a range of identifying hand signs. For anyone else to be caught using them would mean almost certain execution.

century out of the remnants of the ancient stonemasons' guilds, Freemasonry is an international collection of closely related fraternal societies dedicated to guiding its members down the path of moral and spiritual self-improvement. It has a rich and vibrant mythic core, reaching back to the early biblical times of King David and King Solomon, and it takes much of its internal symbolism from the art and science of architecture, and from the semi-historic construction of Solomon's Temple in Jerusalem.

The Square and Compass of Freemasonry is one of the most emblematic of the secretive society's designs. It embodies deep layers of subtle meaning about rectitude, probity, responsibility and faith.

Freemasonry has millions of members spread all over the world – tens of millions, in its heyday – and has never attempted to be a secret society, despite what some detractors claim. Some of its recognition criteria are still kept officially secret, despite being easily available on the internet, but its visual logos and symbols are openly displayed on lodge halls all around the world. As the lodges themselves tend to list their addresses in local telephone directories, the symbols are – and always have been – comparatively easy to discover.

The most famous Masonic symbol is a crossed pair of set square and compass to form a rough diamond shape, often with the letter G in the middle. The symbolism behind the image is quite intricate, and delves deeply into Masonic lore. In short, however, the set square is a method for measuring a right angle, the most stable angle under aligned pressure and therefore the strongest way of constructing simple buildings. It therefore represents strength of character, moral rectitude, an upstanding attitude, square dealing and, in general, the necessary foundation to build a strong, responsible social attitude on.

The compass, by contrast, is the tool used to draw a circle, and is therefore representative of the circle's completion, perfection and synthesis. As such, it symbolizes the entirety of heaven and earth, the perfection of God and the spiritual realms, and the all-encompassing nature of divine love and provenance; it is the counterpart to the set square, the spiritual dimension. Joined together, the square and compass represent the ideal person, honest and true, in the light of God's love. The G is said to stand simultaneously for God and geometry as the representatives of the spiritual and physical aspects of construction.

The square and compass symbol has many intricate layers of meaning, but it is not unique in that respect – all of Freemasonry is highly loaded with symbolic power of this sort. In fact, in some senses, the symbol is simpler than many others connected with the Masonic craft, which may be why it has become the particular iconic emblem of Freemasonry as a group of organizations. A Mason wishing to advertise his or her membership would typically display the square and compass on a signet ring, tie, tie pin or monogrammed handkerchief.

The success of Freemasonry, particularly in its role as a source of charitable work for the

Another of the world-famous benevolent societies, Rotary International's cogged wheel represents each Rotarian's belief that he is a cog in a giant machine that can work wonders – vital, but just one part, with a role to play.

community, has led over the years to the creation of a number of similar high-profile organizations. Two of the best known of these charitable fraternal bodies are Rotary International and the Lions Club. Rotary was founded in Chicago in 1905 by an attorney named Paul Harris, who wanted to recapture the spirit of mutual assistance he remembered from his small-town youth. It has grown to encompass millions of members worldwide, united by the common goal of "service above self". Their emblem is a cogged blue-and-gold wheel with six spokes.

The Lions Club was also founded in Chicago – in 1917, by a businessman named Melvin Jones – with the idea of expanding the remit of business beyond commerce into helping to support the community. The Lions also have in excess of a million members, and their motto is, "We serve". The symbol of the Lions Club is a gold letter L in a scrollwork circle, on a blue background. As with Masonry, Rotary and Lions emblems may be spotted on signets, ties and lapels all around the world.

A rather different organization to the three above is Mensa, founded in 1946 by the British scientist Lawrence Ware and the Australian barrister Roland Berrill. Mensa is dedicated to fostering and promoting human intelligence for the benefit of mankind as a whole. Membership is open to anyone who scores more than 98 per cent in an approved, standardized IQ test. Members – there are more than 100,000 worldwide – meet informally or in topic-driven discussion groups to explore ideas, engage in cultural and social activities, and enjoy like-minded company. Their logo is a stylized letter M topped with a globe, shaped overall to be reminiscent of a human head, shoulders and torso. The symbol is typically rendered in tones of gold.

The Lions Club seeks to expand business beyond just profit-chasing into being a vital and vibrant part of the local society itself. It is a great shame that its ethos is not more widely spread.

Mensa is the world's most important High IQ society, a forum for the most intelligent members of the population to exchange ideas, enjoy like-minded company, and help advance the world.

Not all group affiliation tokens are as weighty, high-powered or serious, of course. To take just one example, a square ringed by a circle with a tangential triangle pointing up toward the top right is an uncommon symbol that nevertheless does crop up globally: it is the logo for Clan Tremere, a sorcery sect that exists only as a group of characters within a game produced by an Atlanta publisher called White Wolf. The logo symbolizes the occult power for which the sect is known – within the game world. Players of the game with a particular fondness for the sect can purchase and wear striking lapel badges displaying the sect sign.

An even less formally organized grouping is represented by the presence of a pentagram – a five-pointed star drawn with five straight lines – worn around the neck. The word means "five-lined", and in fact a

The symbol of the secretive sorcerer-vampires of Clan Tremere, who play an important role in the delicate power structure of the vampiric conspiracy in White Wolf's "World of Darkness" game *Vampire: The Masquerade*.

proper pentagram must be composed of exactly five lines. As such, it inevitably contains an interior perfect pentagon – it cannot be any old hollow five-pointed star. It can also be constructed by drawing the capital letter A five times together, and in this form it is also known as a pentalpha. Some users maintain that the symbol should be called a pentacle if it is surrounded by a circumscribing circle, others that the term pentagram applies in either instance. Because, when it is drawn properly, the pen returns to its starting point, the symbol is also sometimes referred to as the Endless Knot.

The pentagram has been a symbol of the planet Venus – and thus also of the goddess of the same name – since ancient times, when it was observed that the planet appeared to trace a five-pointed star shape around the sun once every eight years, returning to its precise location after five such eight-year cycles. A popular symbol in ancient Babylonia and later in Greece, it represented Ishtar/Aphrodite/Venus, the goddess of love and beauty, and in early Christianity it was emblematic of Christ's five wounds. Since then, it has acquired extensive occult and magical associations.

The pentagram is an ancient symbol of eternity and goddess-power, particularly the love and lust associated with Aphrodite. It was tailor-made for adoption by the witchcraft revival of modern times.

The Rallying Cry: Identity and Belief

A large part of our self-identity is bound up with our religious and political convictions. Most of us identify ourselves, even inside our own heads, as members of the groups that fit closest to our personal beliefs. Buddhist, Christian, Jew or Muslim, Conservative, Democrat or Socialist – the labels we choose for ourselves carry a lot of implications with their symbolic meanings. Right-wing political views, for instance, tend to be most commonly espoused by those from a comfortable or privileged background, or by those who expect or strongly desire to attain comfort and privilege. Left-wing political views, by contrast, tend to be found among those who have the least wealth, and also among the intelligentsia, who tend to have a less hands-on view of reality. In a world where popular support is literally equal to power and wealth, the competition for allegiance – both political and religious – is fierce.

The pentagram is commonly worn to indicate interest in pagan faiths and/or magical and spiritual matters in general. It is a common emblem of the modern witchcraft-revival nature religion known as Wicca, and it saw frequent use through the Middle Ages and afterward in association with conjuring and other feats of magic. It is also said to symbolize the perfect unity of the four elements with the motivating force of spirit; a human being with arms, legs and head outstretched; and the entirety of the scope of creation in heaven and earth – as above, so below. As such, it is a benevolent and protective symbol. Thanks to frequent media misunderstandings and associated lazy reporting, the pentagram has also come to be associated with black magic, Satanism and evil in general.

Raising the Standards

The dominant political parties, in particular, put a lot of effort into symbolic branding that is designed to appeal to as wide a spectrum of voters as possible, while still conveying a message that their core support base approves of. Every nuance of image and statement is carefully tuned by experts to be, simultaneously, as confident, triumphalist, inoffensive and encouraging as possible. The politics of individuality are long gone, replaced by a political ethic of bland charm that makes career politicians of all parties sound increasingly identical. Symbolic differentiation in other areas therefore becomes doubly important.

The dominant political party in Britain at the time of writing is the Labour Party, founded at the turn of the twentieth century. Originally a staunchly socialist group, the Labour Party was set up to represent the interests of the industrialized working masses. Working men were poorly enfranchised at the time – and women not at all – and the political landscape was dominated by the pro-establishment, right-wing Conservative Party and the more radical, non-conformist Liberal Party.

Labour quickly gained enough popularity to exploit a serious split in the Liberal Party during the First World War, and when full male suffrage was established at the war's end Labour pushed the Liberal Party firmly into third place, where it has remained ever since. Labour had some victories, but remained consistently weaker than the Conservatives until 1994, when new leader Tony Blair and a cabal of supporters moved the party ideology from left-wing to mild right-wing. The resulting pressures split the Conservatives badly, weakening them enough to permit Blair's Labour three continuous easy victories, and the prospect of at least one more.

Ideologically, the Labour Party has had to revise itself to appeal to the moderate right wing that makes up most of the voting electorate in Britain, while still ensuring that its traditional power-base of left-wing support is not abandoned. Its symbol – a stylized drawing of a red rose with a green stem and leaves – reflects this clearly. The two primary symbolic skeins within the image are the colour red, and the concept of the rose. The international colour of Communist and Socialist politics, red has long been the identifying colour of the Labour Party. Radical and exciting, it once represented the left wing's desire for sweeping social change. To abandon the colour would be to fully and permanently alienate the left.

By containing it within a red rose, however, the symbolism is transformed and made safe. The rose is the emblem of England, a symbol that the dominant moderate right-wing middle class recognize immediately with pride and affection. It allows the target audience of voters to identify with the party, conveying the historic associations of authority and establishment that help them feel secure. The plain green base to the rose further calms and suggests compassion, and helps imply both an understanding of environmental concerns and an affinity with Britain's famously green countryside. If the logo has any weakness, it is that it is somewhat exclusionary toward the other countries that make up Britain – Scotland and Wales – but the main Labour party does not contest those territories, instead working through localized junior branches. In terms of its goals – appeasing the British left, while appealing to the English centre-right – the symbol is undoubtedly a masterpiece of design.

Tony Blair, the architect of the British Labour Party's reinvention and subsequent rise to power, is seen here above the Rose he and his advisors so carefully designed.

In the USA, the modern Republican Party was founded in Wisconsin in 1854 in opposition to the expansion of slavery. Its current ideological base really dates to the realignment undertaken by William McKinley for the election of 1896. At that point, the Republicans aligned themselves firmly with business and industry, gaining the funds required to ensure sweeping victory. Socially conservative, financially isolationist (but disinclined to regulate business interests) and militarily expansive, the Republicans are generally considered to be pro-establishment, and have often had particularly good relations with the British Conservative Party. Also known as the Grand Old Party (or GOP), the Republican Party has dominated US politics for much of the last century: it has won the presidency for almost two-thirds of the past 38 years and has had a clear majority in Congress for all but two of the past twelve years.

The symbol of the Republican Party is the elephant, styled in its current incarnation to be reminiscent of the American flag. The use of the animal as such is chiefly the work of *Harper's Weekly* cartoonist Thomas Nast. He first depicted the Republicans as an elephant blundering headlong into a pit in a landmark cartoon for the 1874 election (which they did indeed lose).

Nast's image held enough resonant power and versatility to ensure that he then regularly depicted the party as an elephant in a variety of attitudes, depending on its fortunes – from triumphantly stomping a Democrat Party lion into the ground during the presidential campaign of 1876 to lying badly wounded in the grave of Democracy during the electoral college controversy of the following year. By 1884, the cartoonist's depiction had become a near-universal association. The symbolic attributions of the elephant certainly wouldn't have hurt the Republican image – as well as their famous mythical long memory and patience, elephants also symbolize massive strength, cunning intelligence and wit, and powerful ambition. As a common mount of royalty in lands where they are indigenous, elephants are also associated with wealth, power, dignity and temperance: all attributes the Republican Party remains keen to identify itself with.

In Canada, the Liberal Party has lost only nine elections since 1896, earning it the nickname of Canada's Natural Government – all its leaders since the beginning of the twentieth century have managed to win at least one election to serve as prime minister. The party first ran for government in 1867, as a fairly radical collection of reformers who sought responsible government from the British. It remained a mostly opposition party from its inception through until it was reorganized by Sir Wilfred Laurier for the 1896 elections. He restructured party interests, capitalized on his opponents' alienation of several groups, and moved the party into the dominant position it still enjoys.

Like most successful modern parties, the Liberal Party of Canada follows moderate right-wing policies while campaigning on a portfolio that includes many moderate left-wing ideas, thereby occupying centrist ground and still pleasing business backers. Its logo is a stylized snow-capped mountain with a red Canadian maple leaf emerging from behind it

The stylized elephant of the Republican Party is now very carefully designed to be reminiscent of the American flag, a potent symbol indeed in US politics.

The Canadian Liberal Party has dominated the nation's political landscape for as long as there has been a Canadian political landscape, earning it the nickname of Canada's Natural Government.

like a dawning sun – a symbolic new Canadian era of solar wealth and glory emerging from the strength of the united land.

The Liberal Party of Australia, like that of Canada, is a chiefly conservative party occupying the centre-right that has dominated the country's political scene in recent years. In fact, the Australian Liberals have only been out of power for 15 years since the party was founded in 1945. The brainchild of Robert Menzies, it was assembled from a collection of smaller conservative parties and groups opposed to the then-current leadership of the Australian Labor Party, including Menzies's own United Australia Party, the Young Nationalists and the Australian Women's National League.

Menzies himself led the new party, taking power in 1945 and retaining it for a record-breaking 23 years, until he finally retired in 1966. Current leader Paul Howard, who leans toward the neo-Thatcherite "new right" in most areas, has himself been prime minister since 1996. In the most recent elections in 2004, Howard won a clear majority in the Lower House and an absolute majority in the Senate. The logo of the Liberal Party is a stylized letter L made up of three flags, coloured Australian blue. The corner flag of the three is marked like the flag of Australia. Symbolically, this is primarily a nationalist statement – but then the party has been so dominant since its inception that it has hardly needed a cleverly manipulative logo.

Tokens of Faith

Like political parties, religious groups have long made use of iconic images to rally believers and provide them with a symbol of group allegiance. While all developed

Australia's Liberal Party makes use of a simple logo, an Australian flag with blank flags above and to the right – a simple statement of identity and power as befits a massively dominant party.

religions necessarily acquire a large body of intricate symbolism – at least, those religions that do not specifically forbid the use of symbols – they vary in the amount of emphasis they place on one specific iconic sign, and this has been the case throughout history. Even in ancient times, some of the major polytheistic religions had core symbols, while others did not.

The ancient Egyptian religion, for example, made such strong iconic use of the Ankh symbol (a cross with a loop in place of the top bar) that it is still commonly seen. By contrast, the Greco-Roman religion entirely lacked a central symbol, and while many of the symbols of the individual gods' cults still retain some meaning today – for example, Zeus's lightning bolt and Mercury's winged staff of healing (or Caduceus) – there is no image that specifically invokes the faith as a whole.

During the first years of the spread of Christianity – before the Edict of Milan in 313 – it was a suppressed religion, and its members often had to meet in secret to escape persecution and arrest. The secret symbol that they used to mark their

This section of Egyptian cartouche is from the funerary temple of Queen Hatshepsut in Luxor. Even after thousands of years, the eternal Ankh is still clearly visible, the second character in the row.

Originally used as a covert signal of direction to a place of worship, the Ichthys is still a common symbol of faith in Christianity.

meeting places, or as a visual challenge/response, was the Ichthys (the Greek for "fish"), which consists simply of two intersecting arcs, one up and one down, that are reminiscent of the profile of a fish.

Because the Christians' meeting places were typically changed every week to avoid discovery, the symbol was used to mark routes to new locations as well as to indicate the end site. It had to be simple enough to scratch easily into stone and rock, and able to face different directions to indicate routes, yet still be unobtrusive enough not to attract attention from the authorities. It has been claimed that it was also used as a person-to-person identifier. When two Christians met, one would casually trace a simple arc on the ground with the end of his staff, and his companion would complete the shape with the other arc, to signify their joint belief.

The symbol itself may have been derived from several possible sources. For example, as previously mentioned, there were certain practical requirements to be met, and the fish symbol certainly fitted those well. A cross would have been similarly practical, but that was already a known Christian token and therefore an indiscreet choice. Other associations of the fish were Jesus's role as "fisher of men"; the story of the miraculous feeding of the five thousand; and the earlier existence of a similar symbol, Pythagoras's *vesica pisces*, which the philosopher believed encoded certain mathematical and mystical principles.

The Ichthys is still in regular use among Christians wishing to announce their religious affiliation. It is particularly common as a simple metal badge on the back of a car, but it is also frequently seen as a design element in business logos, as a lapel badge, as an exterior house decoration, and as a drawn logo on backpacks, shoulder bags and similar items. Its position as the iconic Christian rallying signal gave way to the Latin cross once the need for secrecy was removed.

The Latin cross is the symbol of the central mystery of the Christian faith: the death and resurrection of Jesus Christ and his identity as part of God in the form of his Son. It is the sacred focus of every church, the mark of identification on bibles and holy books of scripture worldwide and the preferred symbol of personal ornamentation for hundreds of millions of Christians around the world. From its original use as a primitive instrument of execution and torture, it has come to represent the salvation offered by Christ's sacrifice, the promise of life eternal, and God's love for all.

Another iconic religious symbol which has come to stand as a visual representation of an entire faith is the Taijitu of Taoism, known colloquially across the West as the Yin-Yang (see page 18). It takes the form of a circle divided into

The clear, classic lines of the Latin cross form a stark but beautiful counterpoint against the blue of the sky. Despite its gruesome origins, the cross's modern meaning is salvation.

two equal, teardrop-shaped portions by a reversed S. One half is coloured black, with a white dot at the centre of its thickest point; the other is white, with a complementary black dot. It represents the dual forces of Yin and Yang in counterpoise and harmony, giving way to each other, eternally balanced in perfect opposition.

Unlike Western dualist philosophies, in which good is all that is desirable, and evil is everything baneful, Yin and Yang are both neutral, both vital. Too much Yang will burn; too little will stagnate. Too much Yin will freeze; too little will decay. In Taoist thought, Yang represents the active principle – light, energetic, rising, upward, right, day, the sun and so on. Yin is its opposite, the passive principle – dark, relaxed, sinking, downward, left, night, the moon and so on. Each contains the seed of the other, and so can be subdivided – in temperature, for example, Yang is hot and Yin is cold, but hot itself can further contain scorching (Yang) and warm (Yin), just as cold can be freezing (Yin) or cool (Yang). Together, in the Taijitu, the two represent balance – the eternal perfection that is the goal of all Taoism – and, by association, the Taoist way itself.

In Hinduism, the central symbol of the religion's doctrine is the syllable Aum. Sometimes referred to as the Udgitha, or primal mantra, it is prefixed and suffixed to all Hindu incantations and mantras. According to Hindu lore, Aum is the first manifest form of Brahman, the Divine Whole whose manifestation resulted in the universe. In other words, it is the vibration that gave birth to all matter; in effect, the name of God.

One of the implications of the symbolism surrounding Aum is that worldly existence is not the full truth of reality. We can only come to perceive the truth by moving intuitively beyond infinity and the nature of duality into a divine sense of entirety that contains all being and all non-being simultaneously. Aum is the instant of enlightenment, when the barriers between knower and known are undone, and the self becomes pure understanding. On a less metaphysical level, this is said to be represented by the notion of the three in one – a recurrent symbolic theme in Hinduism – where the three are: being, unbeing and the infinite. Note also that Buddhism and Hinduism share certain roots, and the syllable is also holy in certain Buddhist doctrines (as "Om").

Buddhism itself acknowledges a rich range of symbols, but does not have one in particular that serves as an iconic symbol. In the West, perhaps the best known is the Sacred Lotus (species *Nelumbo nucifera*). In Buddhism, the lotus (see Chapter Eight) represents the purity of mind, body and soul needed to rise above the gross carnality of physical attachment, desire and lust – in other words, the discipline that leads to balance and enlightenment. This symbolic meaning probably derives from the way the flower grows up from its lily-like base in the usually muddy water of lakes and streams. The Buddha himself is frequently shown sitting on an open lotus flower. Buddhist use of the lotus as an image almost certainly stems from earlier Hindu practice.

Judaism and Islam both specifically forbid the representation of God by any idol or graven image. Islam goes a little further, generally proscribing the use of any symbolic image in case Muslims should be confused or tempted into idolatry. The only symbol that can be applied to Islam at all, in fact, is the colour

The first manifestation of the primal cause – the chord from which the universe sprang – the Aum is in effect the sound of the instant of the Big Bang itself.

This nineteenth-century image of a Turkish Sultan in battle clearly shows the Turkish forces rallying under the green banner of Islam.

green, because it is said to have been the Prophet Muhammad's favourite colour. He is reported to have worn a green cloak and turban.

Judaism is less restrictive, and there is a range of symbols which are important to most Jews. They are all very specifically not representative of God or the religion as a whole, however. There are two symbols generally thought of as being preeminent. The blue, six-pointed Star of David is an emblem of Judaism and particularly of Jewish nationality, and is now incorporated in the flag of Israel. The earliest known references to it in Jewish lore are at the start of the 14th century AD. Despite its relatively recent provenance, it is probably the best-known Jewish emblem worldwide, although it has a longer history as a mystic image.

The other common symbol of Judaism is the seven-branched Menorah. An ancient design of candle holder, a Menorah is said to have been kept perpetually alight within the inner sanctum of King Solomon's Temple in Jerusalem, so that God's House on Earth would never fall into darkness. Most modern synagogues also contain a lit Menorah

ABOVE: The flag of Israel has the Star of David as a prominent device. Reminiscent of God's clasped hands cradling mankind, it is the emblem of the Jewish faith.

RIGHT: Another common Jewish symbol is the Menorah, a seven-branched candlestick representing the ever-burning light in Solomon's Temple.

or, as a substitute, a lantern or oil lamp. Small Menorah symbols also see some use as a lucky charm or amulet.

Sporting Colours

Although many politicians would be loathe to admit it, many people in the modern world consider their sporting affiliations at least as important as their political ones – they certainly devote a lot more time, emotional energy and attention to the former than they do to the latter. A few die-hard sports supporters would even place sporting affiliation above religion in determining their identity.

In general, the sports world keeps its symbolic content fairly minimal. This is not really an area of life in which subtle implication is rewarded or appreciated. If a team is known as the "Bulls" – and several are, worldwide – the chances are that their symbol will be a bull (the symbolic meaning might include strength, tenacity and/or the idea of a fierce charge). In the case of other teams whose nicknames are more abstract, the meaning may derive from some historical circumstance. For example, Charlton Athletic Football Club is said to take its nickname "the Addicks" from the time in the early twentieth century when players had to use a fish-and-chip shop as a changing room ("Addicks" being a play on the word "haddock").

One of the most popular sporting teams across all fields worldwide is the British soccer club Manchester United. Its team logo features a red devil on a gold shield, a reference to its nickname, the "red devils", which it acquired after changing the team colours to red and gold in 1902. Manchester United is still famously associated with bright red, the colour of its shirts, and it is interesting to note that recent studies have shown that sports teams dressed in bright red have a measurable advantage over competitors dressed in any other colour. This is thought to be due to red's associations with aggression, strength and other warlike qualities – unconsciously, opponents are intimidated by the colour.

In the US National Football League (NFL), the Tennessee Titans took their nickname in 1999, having

Manchester United is one of the world's most successful soccer clubs. Could its reputation be due in part to its canny choice of shirt colour?

The Tennessee Titans American Football Club takes its nickname from the ferocious giants of Greek legend. Symbols of strength and prowess in battle, the Titans were feared throughout the ancient world.

been the Houston Oilers when they were first founded. Mythical giants in Greek mythology, titans symbolize strength and brute power, appropriate enough for an American football team. The nickname has the advantages of starting with the letter T to alliterate with Tennessee, and may also obliquely refer to their stadium, the Coliseum, named after the mighty theatre in Rome. The team's logo is a central T ringed by three stars and surrounded with a flaming circle. The circle and stars are reminiscent of the flag of Tennessee; the flames represent speed, energy and prowess; and the central T is designed to look a little like a sword-blade, possibly an oblique reference to the sword-wielding fire giants of Norse mythology.

In Australia, the Tasmanian Cricket Association logo makes noteworthy use of Aboriginal symbolism in its logo. The focal point of the logo is a stylized image of a thylacine, an indigenous, hyena-like canine known colloquially as the Tasmanian Tiger. The animal is possibly extinct: the last captive specimen died in 1936, and despite repeated rumoured sightings, no clearly verified live animal has been found since. It remains an important signifier of Tasmanian identity, however, and is a perennially popular image with the residents.

In the logo, three of the tiger's stripes are drawn up from its back and across the surface of a gold circle in such a way as to suggest strongly both the three stumps of a cricket wicket and the stitched seam on a cricket ball. At the same time, however, the lines also manage to suggest vegetation in front of a blazing sun – a particularly clever use of artistic design that combines direct sporting reference with strong natural imagery and also pays homage to native sensibilities.

A similarly clever interworking of sporting symbolism, local relevance and respect for the native

A particularly clever interweaving of different elements – traditional, sporting and cultural – the logo of the Tasmanian Cricket Association blends disparate elements into a powerful united whole: a good symbol for the island itself.

populace can be found in the logo of the National Hockey League's (NHL) Vancouver Canucks ice hockey team. The logo is in the broad form of a stylized C, the first letter of the team's name, coloured in ocean tones of deep and light blue. The top half of the letter takes the form of an orca (the dominant dolphin species, more commonly misnamed "killer whale") surging out of the water. The creature is drawn in a style strongly reminiscent of, and respectful to, the art of the indigenous natives of the pacific northwest. At the same time, the orca in the logo bears an expression of ferocious determination, and the whole image is vibrant with energy and power, as befits an ice hockey team. Orca in general are seen as lethally powerful creatures, often associated worldwide with hell, demons and killing. Note however that there is no known instance, modern or historical, of a wild orca displaying any aggression toward human beings – only to other marine life.

Another sympathetic blending of traditional local art with Western sporting tribalism, the orca of the Vancouver Canucks is a study in furious energy.

Stars, Bars and Stripes

As a final note, it is vital to acknowledge that one of the most important cornerstones of personal identity is one's nationality. The places and cultures we grow up immersed in automatically and indelibly leave strong marks on both our personalities and our perceptions of ourselves. This is a combined result of education, media exposure, national history and acquired characteristics from the previous generation; different nations unavoidably provide different environments. The defining symbol of

CLOCKWISE FROM TOP: The flag of Tibet has become a powerful symbol for the fight against expansionist aggression worldwide in the aftermath of China's annexation of the tiny Himalayan country; the Australian national flag is derived from the British flag, representing the modern state's early origins; while, by contrast, the Australian Aboriginal flag depicts the natural world in balance, earth below and sky above, with the baking sun in between.

national identity is the flag. As a symbol in its own right, a flag is a strong summary of its nation's history, culture and perceived idiosyncrasies. Some become powerful worldwide – the Tibetan national flag has become symbolic of that tiny country's ongoing struggles for freedom. In fact a national flag is one of the key symbols that contribute to most people's sense of identity.

All nations have explanations regarding the meaning of their chosen flags, of course, but there is little commonality in that symbolism. The same colour, symbol or graphic can mean different things in different places. Even on different flags of the same country, the same colour can have two very different meanings – on the Australian national flag, the red comes from the British Union Jack, and harks back partly to St George killing the dragon, and partly to St Patrick's Cross of Ireland. By contrast, on the Australian Aboriginal flag, the red field represents the colour of the earth.

HAZA

7 INSTRUCTION

Instructional symbols occupy a special place in the world of symbolism. Unlike any other area of symbolic content, instructional signs are required to be as plain as possible so that people from a wide range of social and cultural backgrounds can understand them clearly. As life gets increasingly globalised, it becomes less and less possible to rely on the public – or, indeed, people in business or politics – being fluent in the local language, or even having any real knowledge of local idioms or customs.

Given the internationalization of everyday life, crucial warning signs and instructions have to be as clear as possible to people from all over the world. Roads, transportation hubs and other major public thoroughfares are particularly important areas where instructional indicators are needed, especially when the viewers concerned will not be in a position to seek advice in case of confusion.

When it comes to important matters of safety, clear, unequivocal visual instruction is necessary. The risk of assuming everyone will read written warnings is too high. Symbols plays a crucial role in passing on vital instruction.

ISOTYPE: THE THEORY OF INTERNATIONAL SYMBOLISM

The work underpinning just about all modern international warning and instructional symbols in use today was pioneered by an eccentric Austrian social scientist named Otto Neurath. He was highly interested in Marxism, which he saw not as a political or philosophical concept, but as a scientific method for improving the lot of humanity. His early work focused on ways of organizing economic structures without money – an "economy in kind" – which led him to being drafted into government planning during the First World War. After the war, he was retained to help socialize the economies of Saxony and Bavaria, and his work prepared the ground for two political coups that brought two different Soviet-style republics into existence in the region.

Neurath was arrested for high treason when the German government restored order, but he was eventually cleared when it became blatantly obvious that he was barely aware of anything outside his own work, and had hardly even noticed either coup. Afterward, he returned to Vienna and organized a project called the Social and Economic Museum, which attempted to teach complex societal issues to the uneducated, near-illiterate public through the use of instructional symbolism.

Otto Neurath was certainly unconventional, and had the sort of total absorption in his own interests that often accompanies mild autism, but his insight was crystal clear, and his intentions always the very highest.

Neurath's Social and Economic Museum work led him to the Vienna Method – the development of a concrete methodology for reducing important information to graphic elements. Neurath hoped it would become the basis of a new wave of education. He strongly believed that unified scientific doctrine, moral freedom, benevolent Socialism and symbol-based education all interlinked – and that if people could be taught the realities of life in a way they understood, social improvement would follow. Social Realist philosophers have often accused Marxist thinkers of being too optimistic about human nature.

When Hitler spearheaded the "reunification" of Austria in 1934, the country became politically dangerous for all left-wing theorists. Neurath moved to Holland, leaving the museum to close. He was now devoted to the idea of an international language of visual tokens that would be able to provide instantly recognizable symbols to illuminate or explain any aspect of daily life. He restructured the Vienna Method slightly into what was known as ISOTYPE, an acronym for International System Of TYpographic Picture Education. Developments in pushing ISOTYPE as an international language ceased in 1940 when the Nazi expansion caught up with Neurath again, now aged 60. He fled to Britain and set up the Isotype Institute, while supporting himself by working for a public housing authority, but he died a few years later.

While ISOTYPE never fulfilled Neurath's dream of an international standard language of education, it did find important use in the preparation of genuinely international warning and instruction symbols. The commonality of such symbols worldwide – which, while desirable, was never guaranteed – is a testament to the strong foundations provided by his work.

The official logo of the ISOTYPE Institute was an image of a man holding up a viewing screen, as if to highlight the potential of learning. Ironically, optical illusion (field inversion) effects can make the logo very hard to decipher at first!

Warning Symbols

There is naturally some variation in international symbolism, particularly for less commonly-encountered hazards, but by and large the images encountered today remain surprisingly similar. Part of this is undoubtedly due to the cross-pollination of ideas and exposure to earlier symbolic development in other countries, but widespread acceptance of ISOTYPE theories and practices has also played a part. Most symbols include a simple written component in the local language, but the goal of ISOTYPE was to render such extra support basically irrelevant, and by and large it succeeds in doing that.

The International Warning Symbol (IWS) for sonic and audio hazard areas is a stylized human head in profile with a large muffler or protector covering the entire ear area. Following on faithfully from ISOTYPE principles, the image is mostly black, with white used for outlining. The head is very basic – just a rounded square with eyehole and slanting nose indicators. Along with the coloration, this helps to make it utterly international in scope. Without features, there can be no racial identification to muddy the message. The image is instantly recognizable to anyone who has seen headphones or ear protectors before, and even if someone has not, it clearly depicts a person with a device covering their ears.

More familiar to many people, the Corrosive Materials IWS is particularly vivid. In this image, a bar of some solid substance – the implication is that it is metal – and a hand are side by side.

The Audio Hazard sign uses mufflers or ear protectors to convey the message that there is a possibility of damage to your hearing in a given area unless such protective devices are used.

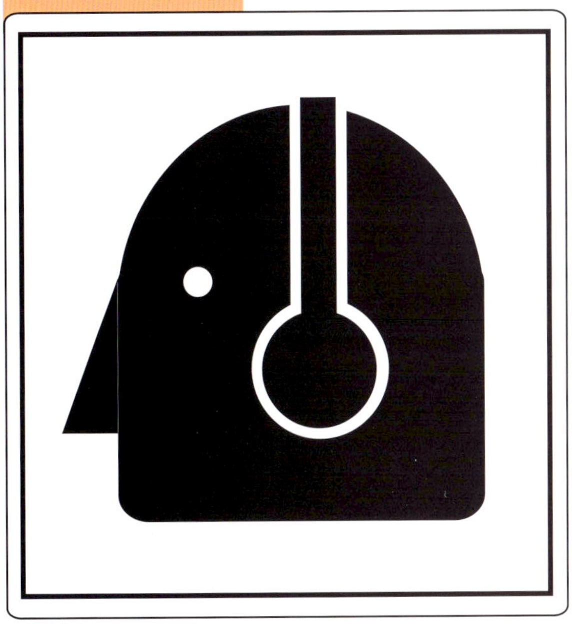

Almost guaranteed to make you wince, the large hole being burnt into the hand on the Corrosive Materials warning sign looks extremely painful – which is rather the point, of course.

Above each icon, a test tube is tipped so as to spill a drop of liquid. That drop is impacting on both bar and hand, and rather than spreading out, it is clearly burning a wide hole straight through each object. The core message – that there is a liquid in the proximity which will eat through flesh – is reinforced by the solid bar next to it, because the acid is burning both substances away with equal vigour.

The Carcinogen/Cancer Hazard IWS is a rather specialized symbol. Cancer is not an easy concept to convey in a simple visual icon. The symbol is based around a stylized letter C, which obviously will convey little information to anyone who does not know the relevance. However, in an attempt to make it more meaningful, the C is linked top and bottom to similar units in a chain that somewhat resembles DNA. Seen like this, the break in the C can be seen as damage – and damaged DNA strands often give rise to cancerous cells. While the end result is still far from clear, it is a valiant effort with a particularly abstract topic.

An alternative approach to dealing with abstract topics is to create a memorable symbol that has no prior context. Charles Baldwin was working for Dow Chemicals in 1966, developing containment systems. Symbols were very poorly standardized at the time, and Baldwin realized that a general hazardous biological agent sign was needed. He turned to Dow's marketing team, and asked its graphic designers to come up with a range of striking images that were free of any prior meaning or context and would be easy to draw with a stencil. Additionally, having the logo symmetrically

The IWS symbol for Carinogens/Cancer Hazard is a valiant attempt to illustrate an abstract idea.

three-sided meant that it would keep its meaning regardless of orientation.

Once the designers had come up with a selection of different images, Baldwin asked the marketing department to run focus groups up and down the country. In these tests, members of the public across the USA were shown 24 different symbols, including the new designs, big brand logos, political icons, and so on, and asked to guess what each one was. Then, a week later, the same people were called back again and shown the same symbols, mixed up with 36 other preexisting logos and icons, and asked to pick out the one that was most memorable from the previous session. One particular icon got the least guesses as to its meaning but the most selections regarding its memorability: this was the biohazard logo.

The new logo – with its proposed meaning along with the methodology behind its design and selection – was written up for the journal *Science* and then taken to the major operational groups of the time. It met with immediate approval and was duly accepted. Since that time, it has been increasingly used and recognized globally. Its strikingly threatening design and stylish execution have even led to its adoption by certain areas of rebellious youth culture.

Where the hazards in question are less abstract in nature and more practical, it is possible to be considerably more direct in illustrative style, eliminating almost all ambiguity. The Overhead Hazard IWS typically shows a featureless outline of a head – marking just ears and hair – being struck on the crown by a

Threats do not get much more tangible than the danger of knocking the top of your head on some large piece of hanging machinery, as the Overhead Hazard IWS clearly demonstrates.

The Biohazard logo, with its sharp spikes and strange interlocking curves, looks inherently dangerous on some subconscious level. No wonder it has been adopted by rebellious music bands around the world.

The Fragile Roof IWS has a hard job conveying complicated ideas in a simple, culture-free manner. Even the task of depicting a piece of roof in ISOTYPE-style imagery is surprisingly tricky.

large, complex solid black shape that is suggestive of a piece of machinery of some sort. To indicate the impact, small lines (that could be symbolic of either motion or of gouts of blood) radiate out from the point of impact. The head is shown in outline and, in this instance, full face, partly to indicate how much harder the hazardous object is than a human skull, and partly to highlight the head's hair – the presence of hair means that the person is not wearing any sort of safety helmet.

The Fragile Roof symbol has a little more work to do than something as easy to understand as Overhead Hazard. Roofs come in all shapes and sizes, and it is not always easy to depict a section of roof in a way that makes it clear it is not the ground. The concept of fragility itself is also somewhat abstract. The IWS tackles these issues by using a strip of surface to indicate the roof. Where a path, pavement or road would be horizontal, or perhaps vertical in a few cases, the strip is angled diagonally downward. To highlight its nature further, the surface is shown as corrugated, partly to symbolize the sorts of sheeting that tend to be used as roofing in industrial settings, and partly to suggest rounded tiles – a more residential roofing material. A human silhouette is walking along the strip, and there is a jagged hole under its leading foot. The person is clearly in the process of tumbling into the hole: the foot has already sunk into the hole and the whole body is tipping toward it. The symbolic implication is that the hole has just appeared as the person has stepped on it.

Information

Informational signs tend, for the most part, to be somewhat less dramatic than warning signs. Fire exit indicators are generally in safe colours – green, most commonly, but occasionally in blue. They tend to have large background fields, to emphasize the reassuring colour. The fire exits themselves are depicted as white rectangles to symbolize a doorway to the outside world, with a white figure running through the doorway to escape. A large white arrow next to this core image typically shows which way to go to get to the exit.

Large and green so as to immediately calm rather than cause concern, fire exit signs typically show a person running toward the white light of the outside world. The fire remains an assumed peril rather than a clearly depicted one.

LEFT: The Emergency Telephone IWS clearly depicts a telephone, but relies on the non-Anglophone viewer's intuition to figure out that normal telephones are not signposted in this manner, so the emergency phone must be there for some special purpose.

RIGHT: The deep blue of the Disabled Access sign is an uncommon colour in the world of safety signage. The combination of deep blue with white is associated with medical care and institutions, which may be the colour's source.

In instances where the sign is intended to be a warning rather than an instruction, the dominant colour becomes red. This generally is the case when there are concerns about possible blockage, and people are being instructed to make allowance for the fact that there is a fire door present. Signs of this sort typically also indicate the doorway as a white rectangle. Some have become a little more creative and may indicate the doorway as a white outline, the inside of the building through the door as a red field, and then the fire itself as white flames licking across the building and out of the door. Typically with signs that are this complex, one or more figures are fleeing away from the flaming doorway. The risk with increasing the complexity of any sign, of course, is that it becomes increasingly open to misinterpretation, and ends up causing extra confusion.

The standard sign for an Emergency Telephone is at the other extreme, relying almost totally on context. The symbol itself is just a profile silhouette of a standard telephone receiver. The image is immediately recognizable to anyone who has had any exposure to traditional telephones. There is nothing in the image to suggest crisis or assistance, however. It is left entirely up to the trappings of the warning sign itself to convey, by association, that the telephone it refers to is for emergency situations.

The Disabled Access sign is one of those that is most commonly coloured blue, rather than the more usual yellow, green or red. This may be because disability is seen as a medical condition and the combination of blue and white has very strong medical associations. It may also be because blue is quite frequently used in traffic signs, and disabled access is related, however tenuously, to travel and movement. It may also simply be an encouragement to the disabled that it is safe to proceed. The sign itself is a stylized wheelchair with a person sitting in it. The mechanism of the wheelchair on the diagram is implicit rather than specifically picked out.

One of the best-known (and probably most divisive) symbols worldwide is the No Smoking sign, which is plain, simple and unequivocal. The central image is a lit cigarette, the tip already turned to ash, with a small plume of smoke curling up toward the ceiling. A thick red bar strikes through the cigarette – a clear sign of prohibition, as is the thick red border around the circular sign.

With both a big red circle surrounding it and a thick red bar across the middle, the indication that lit cigarettes are forbidden could hardly be clearer.

Minimum Safe Distance assumes perfect driving conditions, in daylight, travelling no faster than the speed limit. As conditions worsen and speeds increase, MSD rockets through the roof, and yet some near-suicidal drivers still tailgate at 160kph (100mph).

International Road Signs

A thick red border around a white circle is, of course, a common indicator of prohibition in traffic signs. On its own, an empty red-bordered white circle means that a road is closed to vehicles. A symbol of a specific type of vehicle inside the circle indicates that the depicted vehicles may not enter. Common restrictions of this sort include trucks, motorbikes and bicycles. Sometimes, specific "No Entry to X" signs may have a red diagonal bar across the circle, further emphasizing the ban. Just as often, however, they do not.

The more general No Entry sign is a solid red circle, maximizing the impact of the colour, with a small white horizontal bar at its centre. The bar is a symbolic barrier, representing a gate or a wall, while the red field emphasizes the danger and restriction. Some prohibitions are more notional than the simple No Entry one. The Minimum Safe Distance sign follows the basic pattern of a red circle around a white field, and shows the front of one car and the rear of the one behind it, with the safe distance between the two clearly marked. The distance shown will always be the minimum safe gap between cars travelling at the speed limit for the road; it increases almost exponentially as vehicular speed increases.

In contrast to prohibitive signs, orders to take a specific action are usually displayed as white icons on blue circles. In both instances, a circle indicates that the message is compulsory; but while red says "you must not", the blue says "you must". This use of blue as a command colour is linked to its associations of safety; the expanded injunction is really: "you must do this in order to remain safe from danger"; just as the red signs are saying, "you must not do this because it is dangerous". Therefore, a Mandatory Left Turn sign is a blue circle with a white outline of a left-bending arrow.

Because some prohibitions and other instructional road signs have bars through them and others do not, and because the various designs are so diverse, standardizing a sign to indicate end of restrictions provided certain challenges. It was not possible to come up with just one sign to indicate that the previous conditions had been lifted, because there are frequent instances where motorists are under multiple restrictions, and some end before the rest do. The final decision was to reproduce the original restriction sign in black and white, fading to grey, with

About as densely red as you can get, the No Entry sign puts up a small white central bar as a symbolic barrier, but mainly relies on the alarm caused by its visual impact.

a broad three-striped bar cutting diagonally across the sign in the opposite direction to usual. The grey image symbolizes the original instruction fading away, while the diagonal slash emphasizes that this is a cancellation.

By leeching all the colour out of a prohibitive sign and then emphatically crossing it out from another direction, the End of Restriction sign seeks to illustrate that a previous command no longer applies. The sign is rectangular because it is informative, rather than restrictive.

The Alphabet of Mathematics

The symbols associated with the various mathematical operations date mostly to the fifteenth, sixteenth and seventeenth centuries, as far as anyone can tell. In terms of their design, they are like the letters of an alphabet, coming from a wide range of different sources and symbolic reasonings. Some of them are obscure in their provenance, while others are fairly definite; in a few cases, the first known user has specifically explained their logic in producing the sign, while in others the symbol just appears with a terse note indicating what it represents, and we can only speculate on its origins.

The symbolism of the plus sign (+) is fairly sure. It first appears in the manuscript *Algorismus Proportionum* written by Nicole d'Oresme in about 1360. In this text, the symbol is an abbreviation for the Latin word et, meaning "and". The fashion at the time was to write et very quickly, almost as a diphthong. Written swiftly and closely, it is easy for the word to become a slanted +.

The minus symbol (-) first appears as a complement to + in a printed book titled *Mercantile Arithmetic* by Johannes Widmann, published in 1489. In this work, Widmann uses the two signs to indicate surplus and deficit in examples related to trade and business. It has been suggested that Widmann, who was a professor at the University of Leipzig, may have taken the symbols from earlier manuscripts found in the university library, which may make the symbol quite a lot older. Some historians have even claimed that the history of the minus sign goes back to Classical Greece.

In road traffic usage, a blue circle denotes a positive order – you must – rather than red's negative order – you must not – or green's permission – you may. If the sign is rectangular, then it is not an order, but rather a recommendation. A red rectangle, which would imply approximately "it is better not to", is rarely encountered.

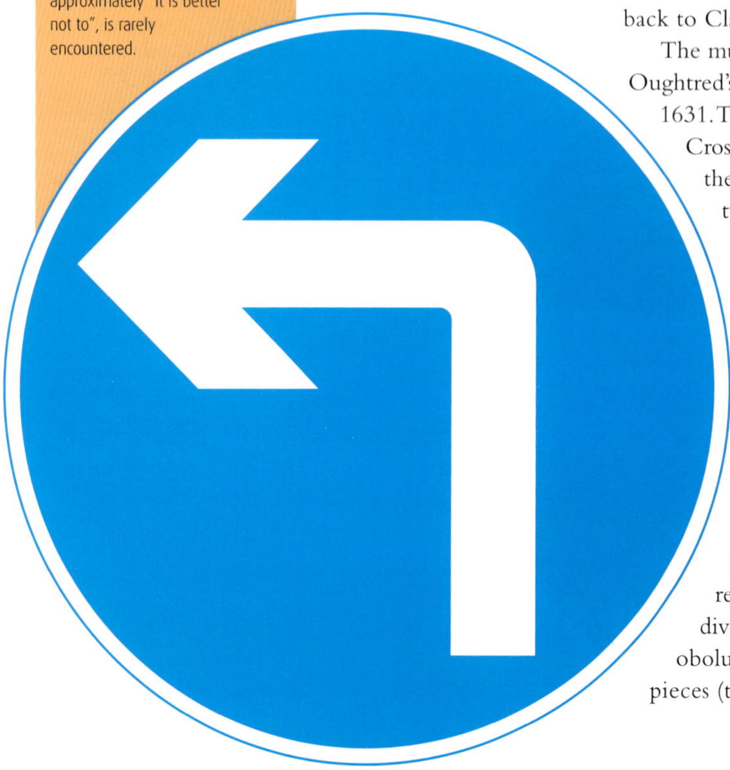

The multiplication sign (x) dates from William Oughtred's *Key to Mathematics*, published in London in 1631. The x sign has been likened to a St Andrew's Cross, and it may be that the use of it derives from the plus sign. Where addition involves summing two numbers, multiplication can be seen as summing one number to itself as many times as the second number indicates. Notionally, therefore, the second number represents a column of instances of the first number. Tipping the + sign over could serve as an indication of this progression.

The division sign (÷) is properly called the "obolus". It was first used to indicate division by Johann Rahn in his 1659 work *Teutsche Algebra*. The book was translated into English with the division symbol retained, and it spread from there. Since division, conceptually, is splitting something, the obolus may be symbolic of an item split into two pieces (the dots above and below), demarcated by

Calculators and computers have made the basic operand symbols of modern arithmetic familiar to us all. Even more fundamentally, scientists have suggested mathematics can form a universal language understandable to all sentient beings, even alien ones.

a clear separator to indicate the split. The use of the diagonal slash (/)to indicate divisions and fractions in computer-friendly scripts may therefore draw upon the same symbolism, indicating the symbolic concept of splitting.

The equals sign (=) is one of those where we know for certain what the creator was thinking. The English mathematician Robert Recorde proposed the symbol in 1557, the year before his death, in a manuscript entitled *The Whetstone of Witte*. His explanation was concise and elegant: "I will indicate equality as I often do in my workings, with a pair of parallel lines of one length, thus: = , because no two things can be more equal than these."

It is known that the infinity symbol (∞) first saw use in John Wallis's 1655 work *On Conic Sections*. Some scholars have suggested that the symbolism is biblical, and that the sign is derived from a covered lower-case omega (Ω). Omega had long been symbolic of the ultimate end of all things. However, another possibility is that the symbol derived from an out-of-use Roman symbol for 1000. Although the Romans came to use M for 1000, it was originally represented by putting C and D together into a CD symbol. M may have come to stand for 1000 by gradual corruption of the CD sign; there are some remaining Roman antiquities where the CD resembles the infinity sign quite closely, and also bears a likeness to M.

Finally, the variable symbol (x) is an interesting case for a number of reasons. The French philosopher René Descartes (in *Géométrie*, published in 1637) was the first person to introduce the letters z, y and x as symbols for unknown quantities, to match the a, b and c symbols used for known quantities. By rights, z should have become the dominant unknown variable, to balance the dominant known letter – a. However, when the printer was typesetting the book, he found that he was running out of the letters at the end of the alphabet – y and z are common in written French – so he had many more x stamps available than the other two.

After studying the text for a while, the printer asked Descartes if it actually mattered which of the unknown quantity letters was used in any given equation. Descartes replied that it made no difference whatsoever, so long as a substitution remained consistent in any given equation. The printer therefore routinely swapped x for y and z throughout the book. The habit caught on, and x became the standard unknown variable.

Over the centuries, the mathematical use of x as the unknown factor has spread right across our cultural experience. It is now a well-recognized symbol of the unknown, unexpected and mysterious in its own right. X-rays were so named, for example, when the German scientist Wilhelm Röntgen, who had been researching them, referred to them as being "radiation of type X" in a paper presented to a medical journal in 1895, indicating that it was unknown and mysterious. Associations such as the "X-Files", the "X Factor", even "X marking the spot", all derive from the mathematical variable.

Universal Language

The symbols of mathematics are particularly interesting because almost all of them can be explained by working up slowly from first principles, using just a single stroke or dot to represent each unit. This means that our entire mathematical lexicon could be made self-explanatory to any being with the wit to unravel it, in a way that no proper language could. This has prompted scientists interested in such matters to state that in the event of us eventually encountering alien life, mathematics would be the first mode through which we could communicate.

8 ESOTERIC SYMBOLS

The richest veins of symbolic content are to be found within religion, mythology and other belief systems that deal with the spiritual element of life. In considering the unknowns, absolutes and infinites of humanity and divinity, one has to move outside of the area where simple words and explanations can cope. There are no words in any human language to discuss adequately the deeply cosmic and the deeply spiritual. Mystical experience is too far outside the realm of daily life to be broken down into easily conceivable bricks. That means metaphor and allusion have to take the place of plain description, and when metaphor becomes codified, the result is symbolism.

All across human history – and possibly even before – people have been trying to find ways to understand and predict the ineffable. These magic systems, mythologies and religions represent some of the deepest, wisest thinking of which our species is capable. The symbols that surround these esoteric systems are attempts to convey, clarify or summarize things that can barely be put into words. To unlock their meaning is to open centuries of profound thinking.

Esoteric knowledge is designed to be obscured, hidden from the masses. Every religion and mythic cycle makes use of hidden knowledge and symbolism to convey ideas and notions which are simply not suited to words.

The global religions have provenances stretching back millennia, and most of them have developed very rich symbolic treasuries. Many of the greatest minds of the past two thousand years have devoted themselves to the mysteries, images and implications of these religions. The result is a set of incredibly potent traditions. There isn't room in a work of this scope to do more than scratch the surface and look at some of the more notable religious symbols, but even so, the results can offer some important insights into the thinking that has gone into these ancient systems.

Buddhism

Buddhism was founded by Siddhartha Gautama, the Buddha (or Enlightened One), who lived in India from 566 to 486BC. From its Indian heartland, Buddhism spread throughout central Asia to the East and Southeast Asian countries, including China, Tibet, Japan, Vietnam, Thailand, Sri Lanka, Korea and Mongolia. Some 400 million people worldwide follow its teachings. today

Buddhism aims to help its practitioners free themselves from repeated reincarnations into the suffering of the physical world by awakening them to a full understanding of true reality – in other words to achieve enlightenment. With enlightenment, or Buddhahood, comes a state of permanent bliss known as nirvana and freedom from the cycle of reincarnation.In order to reach enlightenment, it is necessary to follow the laws of karma – to avoid negative acts that cause harm, to deliberately cultivate positive acts that spread good, and to learn to purify the mind and body. In moral terms, this amounts to harming nothing and no-one and acting in moderation. Buddhism acknowledges that there are supernatural beings in the world, and while it feels that they have the potential to have a direct impact on the world, it does not believe they can bring enlightenment, pass judgement, or adopt some other important role.

Some of the most important symbols of Buddhist lore are collected together in a group known as the Eight Auspicious Symbols (Ashtamangala in Sanskrit). They are a recurrent feature in both public and private decoration, and they are ubiquitous in key ceremonies such as marriage. The symbols are: the Right-Coiled Conch, the Silk Parasol, the Banner Proclaiming Victory, the Golden Fish, the Wheel of Dharma, the Pink Lotus, the Precious Knot, and the Vase of Treasure.

The Right-Coiled Conch symbolizes the fearless spread of the Buddha's true teachings – known as the dharma – in all directions, and the call to wake up to enlightenment out of the sleep of ignorance. Conch shells have been used as trumpets and

By mimicking the movement of the heavens, the Right-Coiled Conch shows it is in tune with the harmonious order of things, making it a particularly sacred and powerful symbol of the spread of Buddhist teaching.

By imitating that which is desired – in this case, by carrying copies of the Banner Proclaiming Victory – early Buddhists sought to make their defeat of ignorance and death into reality, giving it the status of inevitability.

horns for millennia, and in the ancient Indian epic tale known as the *Bhagavad-Gita* the mythic heroes carry gigantic white conches, many of which actually have their own name. They were used as battle horns to rally the faithful and sow terror among the enemy and the conch still retains symbolic associations of authority, power, rulership and the force to drive away evil. In the natural world, conch shells can coil either to the right or the left, but right-coiling ones are rarer and are seen as being particularly sacred, because it is believed that the heavenly bodies also follow a right-spiralling motion.

The Silk Parasol is a symbol of protection and safety, not just from the elements, but also from illness, curses, troubles and those who wish harm. A parasol specifically is an umbrella used for protection from the sun (the word "umbrella" originally meant "small shadow"). Symbolically, umbrellas represent both protection and privilege, since at one time they were the preserve of royalty. The protection offered comes symbolically from wisdom – represented by the dome – and compassion, represented by the hanging drapes. This protection is extended symbolically from the heat of the noonday sun to the spiritual fires of pain, burning desire and other harmful spiritual forces.

Wisdom and compassion give the spiritually advanced powerful protection, as symbolized by the Silk Parasol, from the evils of pain, desire, wrath and other extreme and undesirable emotions.

The Banner Proclaiming Victory is symbolic of Buddhism's inevitable triumph over ignorance, death and all the other evils of the world. The Buddha is said to have used the image early on in his teaching mission, placing it on the top of the mountain at the heart of the world to symbolize the victory of knowledge over stupidity. He also made use of the banner to indicate his triumph over the four Maras, demons of spiritual adversity, on his path to attaining nirvana. Representing desire, emotional impurity, fear of death and pride, they are the obstacles on the path to immortality, and it is their defeat that the banner symbolizes.

The Pink Lotus, as mentioned in Chapter Six, symbolizes purity of the self – body, mind and spirit – within the world, as well as the liberation of performing good deeds in an impure society. One of the best-known symbols of Buddhism, the lotus appears in every important deity's picture, either as a cradling seat, or as something to be held. Although there are many plants that bloom on the water's surface, the lotus is the only one that has a stem strong enough to regularly hold the flower as much as a foot clear of the water. The flower's growth is symbolic of the soul's growth through the mud of childhood ignorance and physicality into the water of adult experience and up into the bright sun of enlightenment; therefore the full-grown flower represents the attained state. White lotuses symbolize a pure mind, red lotuses a pure heart and soul, and blue lotuses a pure body (specifically, purity of the senses). They are combined in the motif of the pink lotus, which represents total purity and the Buddha himself.

The Golden Fish are free, happy, fertile and united, and dressed in golden scales. This makes them a perfect metaphor for personal happiness and the state of enlightenment.

The Golden Fish symbolize freedom from suffering and, by extension, spiritual freedom from the wheel of life. Because they have the perfect freedom to swim in every direction, even straight up and straight down, fish are considered to be a symbol of personal happiness in Buddhist thought. They can breed quickly, and so represent both personal fertility and also general abundance. As a pair of fish, they further represent marital bliss, and their golden colour emphasizes their fortunate and bountiful nature.

Rising out of the muddy waters of a churning river to unfold into shining beauty as much as 30cm (1ft) above the water's surface, the Lotus is the ultimate symbol of purity and purification.

The Wheel of Dharma is the process of learning and understanding the Buddha's teachings. It is said that his first disciples, who learned directly from him, became enlightened during the course of three

The Wheel of Dharma is the cycle of learning. First, one must understand that one is ignorant. Then comes the desire to correct this ignorance. The student finds instruction, learns, and digests. Finally, understanding corrects past ignorance, but raises new questions, and the cycle begins again.

"turnings of the wheel" – that is cycles of listening to his words and absorbing their import. The auspicious symbol represents this process of turning the wheel, both in terms of studying and understanding, so as to bring the joy of nirvana.

The Precious Knot is an abstract geometric design that turns back in on itself in an endless complex pattern. Through its intertwining right-angled loops and balanced, symmetrical harmony, it represents the unity of opposites, the interlinking of all phenomena, and the closed nature of the cycle of cause and effect. Its intricate, far-reaching design indicates that all things are interlinked – in a way that quantum mechanics is just starting to catch up with. This makes it popular as a decoration on presents, emphasizing, as it does, a sense of connectedness. It is also a reminder of karma, however, linking this life's actions to the next

Linking each thing to all other things in a continuous dance, the Precious Knot is symmetrical and harmonious, symbolic of connections, the eternal strength of karma and the infinity of Buddha's wisdom.

As a direct metaphor for the wisdom and power of Buddhist teaching, and the prosperity that following such teachings will bring, the Vase of Treasure can never be emptied. All who take from it find that they have left the original contents undiminished.

one's experiences. The knot is also infinite, and so represents Buddha's infinite compassion and wisdom.

Finally, the Vase of Treasure represents – unsurprisingly – wealth, material prosperity and a long life, all through the spiritual benevolence of Buddhism. There are, of course, many mythological stories and associations in which the motif of the vase or pot that never runs out occurs. The Vase of Treasure of Buddhist lore refers not just to a literal vase filled with treasure – such as are offered at shrines to bring greater wealth and harmony in return – but also to the eternal spiritual treasure of the Buddha's wisdom, which cannot diminish, however much it is partaken of or given away.

Christianity

Christianity is based upon the teachings of Jesus of Nazareth, as recorded by his first followers, who eventually wrote them down in the four gospels of the New Testament. It also shares a lot of early mythological content about the nature of God and the creation of the world with Judaism and Islam through the so-called Abrahamic tradition, as described in the Torah (Judaism), the Old Testament (Christianity), and the Qur'an (Islam). Followers of the three religions are sometimes referred to collectively as the People of the Book. For Christians, the Old and New Testaments together comprise the Holy Bible, the sacred book of scriptural doctrine and teaching.

Christianity's primary doctrine is that faith in Jesus Christ and God, repentance of misdeeds, and obedience to the dictates of the Bible will allow a person to be cleansed of their "sins" – bad deeds, flaws, faults and failure to obey the teachings of the scriptures. After death, those who have been duly purified are rewarded with eternal paradise in Heaven; those who have not must suffer in Purgatory or Hell. Christian belief states that Jesus was sacrificed by God, his father, to open the way for humankind to partake of salvation. God is perfectly loving and forgiving, and, traditionally, all of the world's ills are the work of God's arch-enemy, Satan, the fallen angel Lucifer, who rules Hell just as God rules Heaven.

The main symbol of Christian belief, the cross, has already been discussed in Chapter Six, but the religion is rich in other symbols. One of the best known and most widely spread is that of the Lamb,

Three in One

Christianity is currently the largest religion on earth, with some 2.1 billion followers – a third of the earth's population. It has three main divisions: Roman Catholicism, Eastern Christianity and the Protestant Churches. The single largest sect is the Roman Catholic Church, with over one billion members, twice as many as the second-largest division (the Protestants).

As a symbol of purity and innocence, lambs were sacrificed in pre-Christian days to redeem oneself of the sins one had committed. Jesus was sacrificed to redeem all the sins of mankind, thus replacing the sacrificial lambs from that moment on.

which refers directly to Jesus Christ: he is the Lamb of God, as depicted in the Gospel of John. The Lamb is also a prominent figure in the Book of Revelation, the final Book of the bible, as an apocalyptic figure of blood and fire, ruling victorious over Armageddon at the end of all days.

However, the symbolism of the lamb in early Judaeo-Christian culture has also to be taken into account to understand the symbolic impact of the Lamb of God. The annual sacrifice of the Easter ("Paschal") Lamb – and, specifically, its blood – protected the Israelites from danger and evil. Paul makes the specific link that Christ is the Easter lamb of the Christian faith.

More important, perhaps, the practices of the Old Testament make allowance for "sin offerings", the practice of redeeming sin through sacrifice to God. Lambs were a popular sin offering; the sacrificial killing and exsanguination of an unblemished lamb, conducted by a properly authorized priest, would bring a person forgiveness. In the same way, Christ's sacrifice and blood-letting as the Lamb free Christians from the burden of sin. There is also an element of symbolic acceptance and meekness bound up in the symbolism of the sacrificial lamb – the proverbial "lamb led to the slaughter". All of these threads are united in the idea of the Lamb of God as Jesus Christ the Redeemer, protecting, saving and cleansing through his own self-sacrifice.

Another widespread Christian symbol – if mainly through the focus of modern media – is the Holy Grail. This is said to be the cup or chalice that Jesus used at the Last Supper, the night before his crucifixion. Joseph of Arimathea then used the cup to catch Jesus's blood during his crucifixion and after he had been stabbed in the side by a spear. The blood conveyed miraculous powers, and the cup, known now as the Holy Grail, gained incredible powers of healing, blessing and inspiration. According to legend, after Jesus's death, Joseph took the Grail to England and hid it, founding a lineage of guardians to watch over it.

The Grail appears in early medieval legends – along with the Spear

The ultimate metaphor for God's power to heal, bless and forgive, the Holy Grail has been seriously sought after ever since rumours surfaced that Joseph of Arimathea had taken it to England after Christ's death.

Marked and scarred by the horrible torments he had suffered, wrapped in thorns and set aflame by the power of the cross, Christ's Sacred Heart is a powerful and enigmatic symbol, and a strong reminder of his suffering.

of Destiny, the spear that pierced Jesus's side, and an enigmatic broken sword – as a relic in the possession of the Fisher King, a mystic ruler whose injury is blighting the land, with which he is connected. The Fisher King asks a hero to understand the meaning of the Grail, and in doing so heal him and the land, but the hero cannot, and the king is doomed. This tale later became conflated with the Arthurian legends, and the Holy Grail became the object of a near-impossible quest, often interpreted as a metaphor for the search for personal perfection.

Depictions of the Grail vary wildly, according to how concerned the various authors are about historical plausibility. Some depict it as a mighty chalice of gold, studded with jewels, emeralds and rubies; others as a simple cup of fired clay. Regardless of appearance, the Grail has become a common symbol for near-impossible goals and wild dreams, and represents purity, perfection, healing and immortality.

The Sacred Heart is a symbol peculiar to Catholic Christianity. It is so popular, indeed, that some Orthodox and Protestant thinkers have voiced concerns that it borders on becoming an object of idolatry. The Heart is supposed to be Jesus's, marked by his experiences – there is a cross embedded in the top, wreathed in flames at the point where it makes contact, and a crown of thorns wrapped around the middle.

Symbolically, the Sacred Heart is said to represent perfect, divine love. It also refers to Jesus's moral and emotional existence, as well as his great love of humankind, and it emphasizes the importance of loving Jesus in return. The thorns and the wounds they leave are a depiction of Jesus's pain at those who reject his teachings, and the thorns and cross also recall the nature of Jesus's death and the sacrifice he made. In the Middle Ages, it was common among alchemists and mystics to group the Sacred Heart with the Rose Cross as symbols that possessed a hidden meaning.

Although less frequently used in modern times, the peacock was a common Christian symbol of immortality, resurrection and the soul through most of the past 1000 years. Its association with immortality comes from a number of different symbolic and mythic threads. The simplest is that every year the peacock sheds its splendid tail-feathers and then regrows them (the peacock is by no means unique in renewing its plumage, but few birds have such an obvious change). The bird is thus associated with perpetual renewal, and therefore immortality.

Undoubtedly magnificent, the peacock is a potent Christian symbol for the soul, specifically in the sense of its immortality and its resurrection at the Last Judgement.

There is also a Roman association between the peacock and Juno, the immortal Lady of the Heavens; the Romans felt that the peacock's tail was starry, and because of this and the bird's ostentatious beauty, they placed it in Juno's heavenly realm. Medieval lore also held that the flesh of the peacock would not decay – that the bird was incorruptible, just as certain saints are said to have been. This miraculous supposed preservation was another sign of its immortality. A final linkage is the striking resemblance of the bird's erect tail to any number of long-standing solar symbols. The spread feathers very closely represent a circle of sun rays, and the sun is one of the oldest symbols of immortality and resurrection, dying every night only to be reborn, whole, the next morning. With so many different symbolic attributions of immortality, the peacock is a powerful signifier of the immortal soul and the resurrection of the body at the end of time.

One of the more enigmatic Christian symbols is that of the All-Seeing Eye – also known as the Eye of Providence. It takes the form of an eye housed inside a triangle. It is typically either surrounded by light (or a halo of glory) or is depicted with near-horizontal rays beaming out of the centre. Probably originating in the seventeenth century, the symbol is famous for appearing on the back of American one-dollar bills. The symbol represents God's omniscient watchfulness over mankind, but it also indicates his favour, as well as blessings such as success, health, fortune and happiness.

Hinduism

Hinduism is probably the world's oldest extant religion, possibly dating as far back as 3100BC. Founded upon the Veda scriptures, Hinduism both acknowledges and encompasses a wide spectrum of religious paths, beliefs and sects as alternative valid routes to the same end: the search for the divine, or Brahman, and the hidden truth that will set the practitioner free. There are approximately 1.2 billion Hindus, making it the world's third-largest religion.

Common threads running through Hinduism include: the belief in the natural laws of dharma; the spiritual laws of karma, the principle of cyclic reincarnation; and the end goal of moksha – liberation from reincarnation through social, mental, physical and spiritual practices or yogas. As the residue of free-willed actions, karma dictates the soul's journeys through multiple lifetimes. Virtuous behaviour is rewarded with incarnations better equipped (both mentally and socially) to advance spiritually; unenlightened actions in one life draw the next one back closer to the carnality of the flesh.

The most fundamental Hindu symbol, the syllable Aum, has already been discussed in Chapter Six. However, it is far from being the only important and interesting Hindu symbol. For example, one of the most ancient and propitious of all Hindu symbols has recently become one of the most feared and loathed signs in the Western world – namely the

This unusually complex sun-wheel, with its arms which are themselves turned into spiral paths in and out of each point, represents the entire scope of creation. The symbol is more usually found in its simpler form, the swastika.

Swastikam, or swastika. Before its unfortunate (and unfair) adoption by the Nazi Party, the swastika was a complex, multi-level signifier of luck and fortune.

Originally said to have been given to humanity by the elephant god Ganesha, the swastika is said to carry the luck and good fortune that he represents. It is also clearly solar in inspiration, representing the passage of the sun and the cycle of life, death and rebirth. It is said to protect against evil spirits and bad luck, and is commonly found patterned into the borders of rugs and cloths. The crooked arms of the design represent the way that life's path – and the journey to Brahman, or divinity – is full of unexpected twists and turns, responsive to intuition rather than direct logic.

Together, the whole swastika symbol represents the entirety of creation, in all four directions, wheeling forever around the fixed heart of God, which exists in all things. Separated out, its four arms are symbolic of the four Noble Aims of humanity: adherence to the natural law (dharma, or righteousness), love, wealth, and liberation from the cycle of reincarnation (moksha). As a symbol of good fortune on all levels and a sign of prosperity and benefit, the swastika may be the emblem most commonly found throughout the world, occurring especially in South, Central and North America, Europe and the Near East, as well as, of course, the Indian subcontinent, where it first appeared.

In general, the right-handed swastika is seen as being specifically solar, representing the sun's east-to-west path. It is also said to be a sign of outward dispersion, a spiralling out of power that results in the formation of the world and the scattering of the stars. In many situations, the left-handed swastika is interchangeable with the right-handed version. However, in this alternative version it is also said to represent the universe unwinding back into pure divine energy. It is also associated with the mystic left-hand path of awakening through sensual overload; the orgasmic rites of Shakti, the black mother Kali; and with the close of the year.

Other prominent Hindu symbols include a set of "auspicious symbols", broadly similar in nature and relevance to those of the Buddhists, and a set of depictions of the various gods and goddesses, all of whom are seen as different faces of the one true divinity (although the different sects disagree as to precisely which that is). Thus it is common to find statues, paintings and even body jewellery depicting favourable deities such as Ganesha, the elephant-

With his elephant-head, Ganesha has all the legendary powers of intelligence, gentle wisdom and memory of the mighty animal. As the god of education, he is a guardian of knowledge, the gatekeeper who guards the doors to power.

headed Lord of the Hosts. Symbolically, his elephantine head represents the legendary intelligence, memory, wisdom and gentleness of that animal.

Ganesha rides on a mouse, Mooshka, which symbolizes intellectual rigour, with the precision to discover any truth or secret, no matter how small or well hidden. The mouse is also a sign of Ganesha's humility and probably the source of the Western folk idea that elephants are afraid of mice. Ganesha is the god of intelligence, education and writing, good luck, wisdom and common sense. He is also the guardian of gateways and doorways of all sorts and, as such, resembles Hermes/ Mercury, Legba and other gatekeeper gods who guard the doors to power, divine influence and knowledge.

The great god Shiva, who is the embodiment of both creation and destruction, is shown here in the Natraj stance in his role of Lord of the dance of life and death.

Another very popular Hindu image is Natraj – the god Shiva in his role as the Dancer. This is not a Hindu version of the classical muse of dance, Terpsichore, however: Shiva's dance represents the twisting spiral of life and death, creation and destruction. The god's four arms symbolize different aspects and powers. In his Natraj stance, his upper arms hold the opposed forces of creation (a damaru drum in his right hand) and destruction (a flame in his left hand). Meanwhile, his lower right hand is making a gesture called *abhaya*, which removes fear and brings protection and safety, while at the same time his left hand is making a gesture called *gahajasta*, or the elephant trunk, symbolic of Shiva's wisdom. With one foot raised and one lowered, he also represents embodiment on earth and release from it. He is surrounded by a ring of fire, a symbol of his mighty power.

At the other end of the cosmic scale, in the tradition of Hatha yoga, there is a series of energy centres known as chakras within the spiritual energy field of every human being. Different emotions, energies and elements of physical life are powered and represented by different chakras. All have to be balanced and healthy if the body and mind are going to be healthy, and each one has a symbol that is representative of its nature and spheres of influence.

The base chakra that supports all the rest, for example, is called Muladhara, and is seated at the base of the spine. It is the home of the body's connection to the primal animal energy force, or kundalini, and is linked to the Earth, personal psychological foundations such as nationality and culture, physical energy, fear, anger and desire, and the colour red. Its symbol is a square contained by four red lotus petals. Inside it, a downward-pointing triangle contains a lingam (a phallic image representing Shiva) around which a snake is wrapped three-and-a-half times. The square symbolizes the world, backed up by the four lotus petals, representing the four quarters. The downward triangle represents female sexuality by recalling the pubic triangle; similarly, the lingam is the symbol of male sexuality (note that it is inside the female triangle, representing intercourse). The snake represents the kundalini force, which can be awakened – among other methods – by sexual (Tantric) yogas.

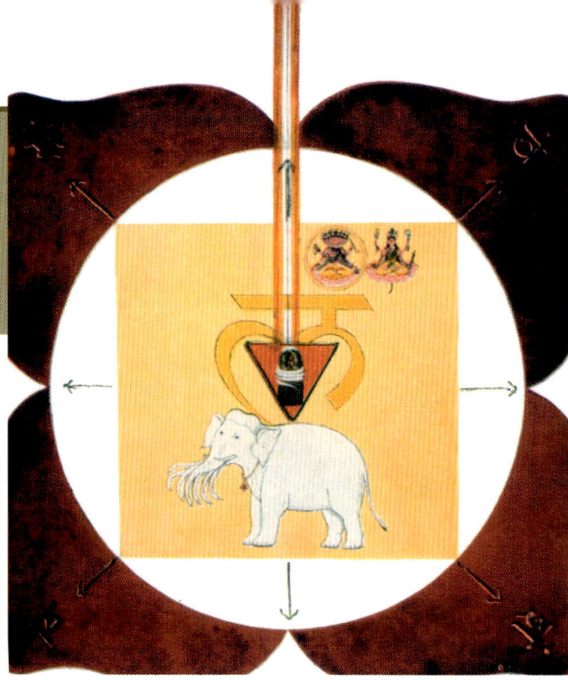

The symbol of the Muladhara chakra, which is the repository of the body's store of kundalini, the primal energy. Awakening the kundalini can energise the entire body, opening it into a very powerful state of total awareness.

Islam

Literally meaning "submission to God", Islam is the world's second-largest religion, with approximately 1.5 billion followers (known as Muslims) worldwide. One of the Abrahamic religions, Islam was founded by the Prophet Muhammad, who was born around AD570. Islam holds that all of the great prophets sent by God – Adam, Noah, Abraham, Moses, Jesus and Muhammad – have basically carried the same message. It therefore teaches that Christianity and Judaism are essentially the same faith, but that certain elements have been distorted, forgotten or censored out of both religions. Accordingly, the holy book of Islam, the Qur'an, which is believed to be the final, perfect and flawless word of God, is considered to be corrective of the Bible and the Torah. There are three main branches of Islam – Sunni, Shi'ite and Kharijite – which came about because of historical arguments over whom authority passed to after the Prophet Muhammad died.

The use of symbolism and symbolic imagery is specifically prohibited within Islam to ensure that the religion does not descend into idolatry. As a result, there is no actual symbolism to discuss meaningfully in relation to the religion; it is included here because that fact alone is itself highly noteworthy.

Judaism

Dating back to about 2000BC, the religion of the Jewish people is one of the oldest faiths still extant. With 14 million followers worldwide, Judaism is far from being one of the largest religions in terms of numbers, but its beliefs and teachings have been of great importance in the religious development of Christianity and Islam, which have their roots and founding tenets in Judaism. From the Judaic point of view, however, the other two Abrahamic religions are heresies rather than entirely different (i.e. pagan) faiths.

The main core of Judaism is the strict and exclusive worship of the one true God and obedience

The one image associated with Islam is that of the crescent moon with a star between its points. It appears on the flags of several Islamic countries, including Tunisia's, seen here. While it does indicate Islam, the image does not have symbolic meaning..

to his Law, the Torah, a perfect sacred scripture dictated by God himself. God is perfect, complete and unimaginable, and it is forbidden to attempt to depict him, for the human mind cannot apprehend his magnificence. Much of the Torah is shared with the Christian Old Testament (and with the Qur'an), and the Jewish faith is concerned with following its dictates and laws – the 613 Mitzvot – and living a clean, decent life.

Judaism is not as strict as Islam about forbidding symbolic content, but it does specifically prohibit depictions of God and Heaven, and it also bans the use of any image or symbol that people may bow down in front of and serve. As such, its symbolic development has been a little stunted, but there are a number of important images that it does recognize. The two main symbols referring to the faith as a whole, the Menorah and the Star of David, are discussed in Chapter Six. Other common Jewish symbols used as signs of luck and good faith include the Mosaic Decalogue, the Yartzeit, the Scroll of

The Decalogue, a Greek term meaning literally "ten pronouncements", is the name given to the stones bearing the Ten Commandments of God, as revealed to Moses on Mount Sinai.

With its distinctive pattern of seven upward-pointing branches with flames rising from them, the ancient candelabra symbol of the Menorah is one of the most famous Jewish images.

the Pentateuch and the Tree of Life.

The Mosaic Decalogue is the name given to the stone tablets that bear the Ten Commandments, as revealed to Moses by God on Mount Sinai. The tablets are usually portrayed together, looking like a book, with the first three commandments on one side (referring to man's relationship to God), and the other seven on the other (referring to man's relationship to society). They represent not only the divine commandments themselves, the word of God, but also obedience and virtue, and, by extension, good living, the laws of the Mitzvot, and the need to have order in society.

The Yartzeit is an oil lamp of ancient design consisting of a stone basin filled with oil and lit via a wick threaded through a floating pad. It is traditionally used to commemorate the dead and is commonly found on Jewish memorial stones. It symbolizes the soul and its onward journey, with the basin of oil being the physical matter that goes to make up the body, and the flame dancing above it representing the spark of God, the immortal soul that brings the body to life.

The symbolic Scroll of the Pentateuch (i.e. the Torah or the first five books of the Old Testament) depicts a thick parchment scroll. Its meaning is similar to that of the Decalogue – it calls to mind the laws of God, obedience to them, and the virtues associated with maintaining a safe, stable society. In its specific meaning as representing the Torah, it also symbolizes the rabbinic teaching tradition and rabbinism in general. The scroll can also be depicted as a group of five, rather than one single item.

One of the most esoteric Jewish symbols is the Tree of Life. Lying at the heart of the mystical teachings of the Kabbalah, the Tree of Life is a symbol and blueprint of near-infinite versatility. On the one hand, it represents the actual act of creation – the route taken by God's energy as it substantiated and diversified into the whole of the created universe. Thus the tree is a map of the descent from the godhead down to the smallest detail of the physical world. At the same time, however, it is a guide for the human spirit to gain some insight into God, even to catch a glimpse of that which is ineffable. Rising up through the tree is to tread the path to enlightenment and purification. Furthermore, because it is a symbolic map of the creative process, the Tree of Life can also symbolize and illuminate any system, such as the interactions between the mind, body and soul, the structure of nature, and even the workings of a car.

LEFT: This illustrated manuscript page shows the famous King David on his throne poring over a scroll of the Pentateuch. The Pentateuch itself is often used to symbolize orderly society in Jewish lore.

RIGHT: The Tree of Life has been at the heart of the Jewish mystical tradition of Kabbalah for thousands of years. It is thought to depict the blueprint of creation, although this colourful version seeks to explore its possible literal depiction as a tree.

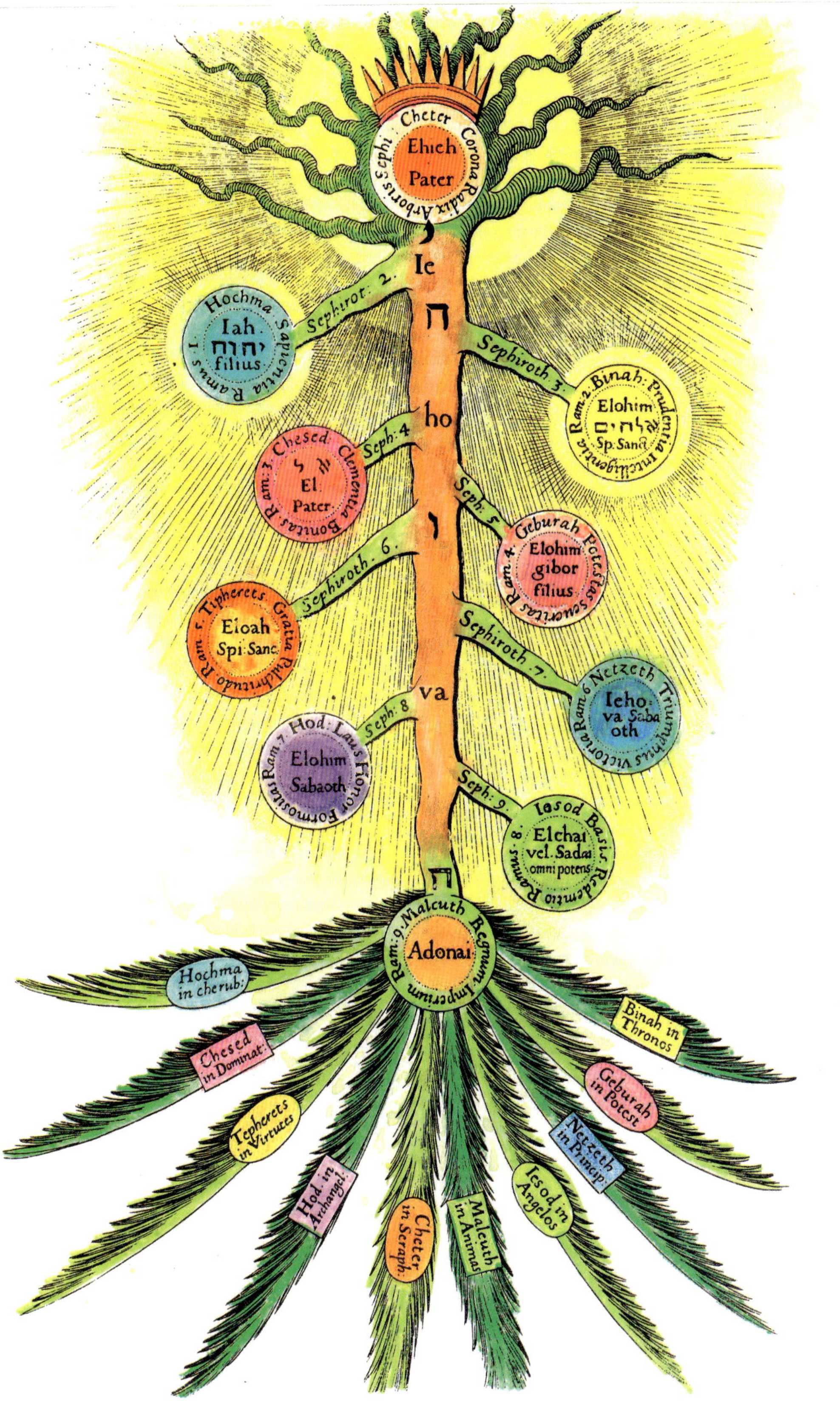
Ehieh
Pater
Ie
Iah
filius
Sephirot: 2.
Sephiroth 3.
Elohim
Sp: Sanct
ho
Seph: 4
El
Pater
Seph: 5
Elohim
gibor
filius
Sephiroth. 6.
Eloah
Spi: Sanc.
Sephiroth. 7.
Ieho
va Saba
oth
va
Seph: 8
Elohim
Sabaoth
Seph: 9
Elchai
vel. Sadai
omni potens
Adonai
Hochma in cherub:
Binah in Thronos
Chesed in Dominat:
Geburah in Potest
Tepherets in Virtutes
Netzeth in Princip:
Hod in Archangel:
Iesod in Angelos
Cheter in Seraph:
Malcuth in Animas

Myth and Magic

When religions and related belief systems of the past have died, they have left behind them a corpus of legends, mythic cycles, parables and techniques of worship that have retained their fascinating richness and power all over the world. In recent years, ancient Greek religion and history have seen a particular cultural renaissance, inspiring TV series such as "Hercules" and "Xena: Warrior Princess", major films such as *Troy* and *Alexander*, and many other types of entertainment. The old mythologies retain the power to interest us because in the last resort, like all religion, they are based on trying to make sense of life – and the experience of being human hasn't changed all that much over the millennia. The gadgets are better, but love is still love – pitfalls, pain and all.

Ancient and Traditional Symbols

One of the most prominent symbols to survive from the Greek myths is the Caduceus, Hermes's staff. Tall and thick, the staff is intertwined with a pair of snakes spiralling up it in a double helix, and it is topped with a pair of wings. It represented commerce originally, but through its wide use in alchemy it has come to be popularly linked to medicine and healing. This is also partly due to confusion with the staff of Aesculapius, the Greco-Roman symbol for a healer, which consists of a wingless staff with one snake spiralling up it. Other common Greek symbols include Athene's owl, which, with its penetrating, wide-eyed gaze and soundless flight, remains a strong emblem of wisdom and intelligence; and Zeus's thunderbolt, which still symbolizes destruction, death and vengeance.

The mythology of ancient Egypt is almost as popular today as are the ancient Greek tales. The most powerful Egyptian symbol is the Ankh, described in Chapter Six, but many other signs have also survived. The Eye of Horus is a stylized drawing of

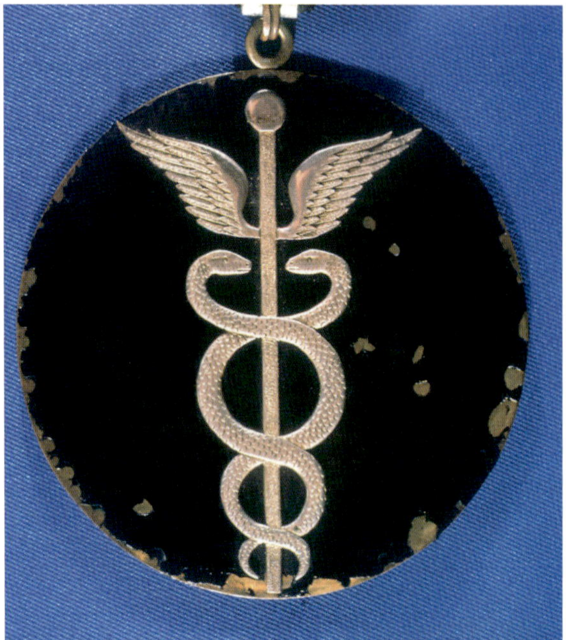

ABOVE: The Caduceus, Hermes's winged staff, represents commerce because Hermes was the God of messengers and merchants. It is still sometimes used as the sign of a pawn shop.

LEFT: Athene's wide-eyed owl was the eidolon of wisdom and intelligence, frequently a messenger for its mistress, and the bringer of her favour and assistance.

This detail from a depiction of a solar barge clearly shows an Eye of Horus, the sun, on its journey through the day in the top half. Below the dividing line, the God Horus himself looks down, examining another depiction of his eye.

LEFT: A stone tablet bears a clear scarab beetle design.

BELOW LEFT: an image from the tomb of Horemheb shows the beautiful goddess Hathor wearing her headpiece, a pair of cow's horns framing a golden disc.

BELOW: A North European symbol, the Celtic cross indicates the union of the encircling heavens with the four compass directions of the manifest world. The ever-looping knotwork decorating the cross's surface is a reminder of the eternal infinity of the divine.

an eye with a cursive design beneath it. Originally a symbol of royal power and indestructibility, it has come to signify protection and rebirth. The eye itself was thought to be the sun, and thus the symbol carried all the protection that light gave against darkness. Another protective sign was the scarab, a stylized depiction of the dung-beetle. The Egyptians compared the scarab beetle's habit of rolling large balls of matter around to the god Ra moving the sun through the sky, therefore bringing good fortune. The sign of Hathor, by contrast, was a stylized image of a pair of cow's horns framing a disc that could either be the Sun/Ra (in her role as the Milky Way, circling the sky) or a mirror (in her role as the eidolon or ideal of beauty).

The Celtic cross is a symbol from Northern Europe. A cross with a circle behind it, the symbol originally indicated the union of Heaven and Earth. The ornate tracery and knotwork often associated with crosses of this type emphasized the infinity of the divine, and the triquetra, or three-leafed Celtic knot, being never ending, is a strong symbol of eternity and infinity in its own right. In its earlier form, with equal-length arms, the Celtic cross was originally the sign of Odin, chief god of the Norse people. This attribution has led to an unfortunate association in recent years, with white neo-Fascist political parties across Northern Europe adopting a simplified version of the symbol as their common logo, because of the Aryan connection.

With his wings spread wide and his haughty gaze stretching to the horizon, Thunderbird is ready to channel the energies of the storm for the good of the Haida people, at the top of this memorial pole carved by Willie Seaweed.

In Mesoamerica, invading European forces did a very thorough job of destroying the rich, enigmatic mythic history of the Maya people. Culturally advanced in many important ways, the Maya had a very detailed cosmology complete with one of the most accurate calendar systems ever devised. Their highest god was Hunab Ku, who rebuilds the world after the Great Cycle destroys it (which has so far happened three times, with the next cycle due to end in 2012). His symbol, the Galactic Butterfly, was a complex symmetrical pattern of light- and dark-stepped spirals, radiant arcs and other devices. It was said to symbolize all of creation and be the gateway to other galaxies beyond the sun, and gazing upon it could supposedly transport a viewer's perception beyond the barriers of time and space. Other Maya gods tended to have more representative signs: Uinal was reminiscent of a toad or salamander, while Katun had a hawk-like head. The general sign of divinity was a circle swirled into segments of increasing size.

Elements of the Maya's artistic styles survived in the art of some of the Native American peoples, especially in the Pacific Northwest. For example, the Haida symbol for the trickster-god Raven clearly shows such an influence. One of the more commonly encountered symbols from the tales of the Native Americans is that of Thunderbird. This powerful spirit is depicted variously, but most usually with

RIGHT AND FAR RIGHT: The Mayan people of Mesoamerica had a very distinctive artistic style, with specific peculiarities in the way they depicted solid objects on two-dimensional surfaces. Their gods got the same treatment as everything else, as these images of the gods Katun (right) and Uinal (far right) indicate. The Mayans also believed that the world would come to an end when their incredibly complex and accurate calendar wound down to the finish of its cycle – due in 2012.

his wings spread wide. Symbolically, this is to catch the power of the storm and channel it. Another popular symbol is the Dreamcatcher, which takes the form of a hoop with feathers attached to it at various points and containing a pattern of weblike strings, some decorated with beads. The Dreamcatcher is a symbolic gateway, a labyrinth through which good dreams can pass, but which will stop nightmares dead in their tracks.

The Dreamtime symbolism of the Native Australian peoples is different from any other symbolic system on the planet, both in imagery and scope. Dreamtime paintings make use of the whole palette of native symbolism to tell a story, using progression and canvas placement to unfold their narratives. Paintings of this sort may symbolize and signify an entire Dreamtime experience, and can be immensely complex. For example, a common Dreamtime symbol is a set of concentric circles radiating from a point. Depending on the context and placement, the symbol can indicate a camp site (from the traditional circular design around a fire pit), the fire pit itself, a stone well, a hole in rock, a female breast, and even a piece of fruit. Sometimes, different meanings are indicated simultaneously – breasts, wells and fruit can all symbolically be sources of thirst-quenching

ABOVE: Australian Aboriginal Dreamtime paintings are more than just symbolic artworks, they are evocations of actual patterns through the landscape, unfolding tales and even lessons to those who can decipher their meanings. This concentric circle design, surrounded as it is by four banks at the four compass directions, probably indicates a well or a fire pit.

BELOW: The similar symbol below however, being part of a track itself, is more likely to represent sites of rising earth energy along a Dreaming Track.

The astrological wheel of the signs of the Western zodiac. The glyphs for each sign are meant to be reminiscent of the astronomical constellations they are drawn from, as well as bringing to mind certain qualities of the sign itself.

liquid. Some symbols are inherently composite; the sign of a Dreamtime track with points of rising earth energy conflates several different concepts into one powerful symbolic indicator whose nearest Western equivalent may be that of a ley line.

In traditional Chinese belief, the most common symbol is arguably the Yin-Yang circle, as we have seen in Chapter Six. Another important Chinese symbol is the trigrams – groups of three lines, either whole or broken, that are said to embody certain qualities and fundamental principles. These trigrams are grouped into mutually opposing pairs, such as Heaven and Earth, and fire and water. Together, one on top of the other, they form the 64 base hexagrams of the *I-Ching*, or Book of Changes. The book was, and is, used for general guidance on the future or for a particular course of action. In this respect, it bears a resemblance to Western astrology.

The Western zodiac, unlike the Chinese one, draws its symbolic content from the constellations of stars and the meanings assigned to them over the ages. Zodiac symbols are all founded on core astrological imagery dating back to classical times. Therefore the symbol for Taurus (Latin for a "bull") is a stylized horned bull's head; the symbol for Gemini (Latin for "twins") is a pair of upright lines

The eight trigrams of the I-Ching, arranged around a circle in opposing pairs and topped, in this instance, with designs supposed to represent the blessings of the stars, are used to ward off evil spirits – particularly when they are marked around a mirror, as here, so that the demon will be reflected.

side by side; and the sign for Leo (Latin for a "lion") represents a lion's head and mane.

If occult symbols are often about protection, projection and conjuration, alchemical symbols by contrast were chiefly concerned with elements and elemental processes. The four cardinal elements were represented by paired opposing triangles, with fire and air, as male, pointing up and earth and water, female, pointing down (representing phallus and pubic triangle respectively). Fire and earth, as forceful elements, are represented as normal triangles, while water and air, as receptive ones, are indicated by a line across the centre. Each of the substances worked with had its own alchemical symbol, as well – gold, as the supposed perfect state of matter, was represented with a solar-style symbol of a circle with a dot in the centre, for instance.

These simple signs and signifiers are only the very tip of the alchemical use of symbolism, however. Because of the esoteric nature of alchemical research, all through their long history alchemists have had to obscure their lore, techniques, conclusions and theories by heavy use of symbolism, codes and other such techniques. Religious bodies throughout history have viewed alchemy with great suspicion, often placing it just one small step above necromancy and witchcraft. In order to avoid persecution, investigation and even execution, alchemists made sure that their writings and diagrams were highly allegorical in nature.

These allegorical symbols served multiple purposes. As well as providing the alchemist with a degree of security, well-thought-out symbolic associations and allegorical diagrams were used to extend theories, ideas and qualities, and shed light on its implications, subtle secondary qualities and other aspects. One of the more common veins of alchemic symbolism was related to the animal kingdoms. Figures such as the Black Toad, the Green Lion, the Two-Headed

Signs of the Occult

Occult attempts to manipulate the world indirectly have drawn on all sorts of mythic and world imagery over the years. The archetypal magician's circle is a triangle inside a circumscribing circle. It is supposed to be a protective design preventing bad things from crossing it – the lines of the triangle represent the Holy Trinity of Father, Son and Holy Spirit, offering divine protection, while the circle is the seamless boundary, the perfect symbol of unbreakable eternity. The Seal of Solomon adds a second triangle to the design, in opposite orientation to the first, to make a design like a Star of David. This second triangle unites the power of the magician's will with the holy purpose of the divine, making it many times stronger. A different sort of seal is indicated by the occult symbol known as the Chaosphere. This is a circle with eight arrow-headed shafts projecting out of it. Rather than protecting or suppressing, the Chaosphere is a symbol that projects infinite options, powering them out into the world with all the force it can muster.

The four alchemical symbols for the cardinal elements of air, fire, water and earth. The maidens are standing on the designs in the order of water, earth, air and fire. The creatures in the jars on top of each maiden give further clues as to each element's identity and characteristics.

Eagle and the Worm Orobouros all had very subtle levels of meaning.

The Worm Orobouros, for example, is depicted as a gigantic serpent swallowing its own tail. As such, it represents the cosmic cycle of disintegration and resurrection. Because of the eternal balance of the cycle, the Orobouros also becomes a token of cyclic infinity, suggesting cycles of time and space surprisingly close to some of the cutting-edge theories of modern physics. By extension, the symbol is related to personal immortality, and the search for the fountain of all self-renewal, the Philosopher's Stone. Similarly, the Black Toad represented the first alchemical process of decaying away the base matter of the substance to be transformed, while the Green Lion symbolized the power of nature, and the transformative energy of sulphuric acid.

Other major alchemical symbols often related to certain archetypal human characters – the White Queen, the dying Old King, the Knight Errant, and so on. Like the animal associations, these figures could represent concepts, processes, materials, spiritual essences or even all four. Complex tableaux illustrations would be built up featuring the symbolic characters, animals and other designs required to convey detailed information about the way substances should be treated and the interactions between them required to bring about certain specific results.

However, it is important to understand that the symbolic language of alchemy was not narrowly defined, labelled and restricted. While many symbols had a specific core meaning and interpretation, context and surroundings remained powerful modifiers – and not all alchemists used all symbols in the same way, even among the better-defined symbolic elements. While that does make it harder to study alchemy as a general field, familiarity with the work of a particular thinker does go a long way toward making their particular symbolic language more readily penetrable.

Some of the specific symbols related to the deeper mysteries of alchemy could get incredibly complex. It is no exaggeration to say that some of the very deepest and most speculative symbolic meanings lie within the field of medieval alchemy. We started our journey looking at some of the most primal and basic symbolic attachments, so it is only fitting to bring it to a close with a look at one of the most complicated, esoteric and allegorical symbols ever devised – and even so, we will barely be able to touch its surface.

The Monas Hieroglyphica of John Dee was a compound design that looked somewhat like a crowned Ankh. Within its form, the symbols of the seven primary alchemical metals can all be traced, along with many planetary symbols, the *vesica pisces*, and all sorts of other elements. The sign is the subject of Dee's best-known manuscript, which bears the same name. In his preface to the manuscript, which consists of 24 theorems derived from study of the Monas, Dee makes it clear that he believes his work capable of revolutionizing not only astrology, magic and alchemical research, but also mathematics, music, linguistics and even engineering – quite a claim. Unfortunately for Dee, the manuscript which follows is universally acknowledged to be so allegorical and obscure as to be almost impenetrable, and if the work does indeed hold such immense potential, it is yet to be tapped.

Looking at the design of the symbol itself, Dee maintains that the straight line and the circle are the two most fundamental forms within creation. United within the glyph, they supposedly represent the most primal energies of the universe – the beginnings of a key for unlocking the power of creation itself. In addition to being the alchemical symbol for gold, a circle with a dot in the centre is the ancient Egyptian hieroglyph for the sun. In the Monas, Dee maintains this association, identifying the circle itself as the sun, and the dot in the middle as the planet earth. The crescent that then intercepts the circle becomes representative of the moon. Conjoined as they are, they become the cycle of daily life, the eternal round of terrestrial reality, even a link back to the first day of creation.

Beneath the unity of the point, the cross attached to the bottom of the circle is used to invoke both two and four. The vital necessity of duality for awareness has been covered elsewhere; suffice it say that if there is just one point of reference, observation is impossible. You need a second reference point – a mirror, a counterpart, a duplicate, whatever – before the first point is able to perceive anything, and before it is able to become aware of itself. Duality is associated with opposition of course, as the two points become the diametrically opposed end termini marking the boundaries of the spectrum of their differences.

Further, by treating the cross as four arms rather than two, the four classical elements that make up the universe are evoked: air, earth, fire and water. This also encompasses the entire physical universe through the four cardinal directions, and the path of creation itself in the four worlds of the Kabbalistic Tree of Life. Another reference to the Tree of Life – with its ten spheres – is implicit in the cross, because numbering and summing the four arms gives 1 + 2 + 3 + 4 = 10. The curve at the bottom of the design – the "leggs" – is a compression of the zodiac symbol of Aries, and is primarily associated with the creative fire required to power the symbol and its mysteries. It also provides an implicit three, providing the trinity with their way into the sign's mysteries.

Dee and others have taken the mystic symbolism of the Monas Hieroglyphica considerably further than this surface level, of course. It goes on to link with several astrological signs and aspects, Latin and Greek letters, numerology, divine names and words, the Book of Genesis, angelic Enochian scripts, and much, much more. And that, of course, is the beauty of symbolism as a subject – it is a fascinating gateway to ever-deeper mysteries.

The Monas Hieroglyphica of John Dee is one of the most complex and esoteric composite symbols ever created. Dee had great hopes for the Monas, but our ingenuity has yet to find the keys to its meaning that were lost on Dee's death.

A

all-seeing eye – Christian symbol of God's omniscience, benevolence and favour, and, by extension, of success, health, fortune and happiness.
anima – the symbolic representation of the female side of a man's personality.
animus – the symbolic representation of the male side of a woman's personality.
ankh – ancient Egyptian symbol of eternity, rebirth, eternal life, the power of the sun, cleansing light.
archetype – a class of Jungian symbol that is supposedly understood by all humans through their access to a theoretical telepathically-shared human intelligence, the Mass Mind.
armour – artistic symbol representing warfare, battle, martial prowess, military service, and, less commonly, protection and security.
arrow – artistic and Freudian symbol for an erect penis.

B

bald eagle – the national symbol of American identity.
bane, the – an evil spiritual being apparently composed of energy, linked to negative thought forms and associations.
banner proclaiming victory – Buddhist symbol of victory over ignorance, the elimination of death and the banishment of evil.
bar – heraldic symbol of conscience, honour and excellence; also military token of rank.
black – the colour of fear, the unknown, night, evil-doers, tragedy, sin, Satanism, rebellion, independence, sophistication and occult power.
blue – the colour of relaxation, calm, peace, protection, sleep, safety, authority, stability, depression, loneliness, obsession, injury and madness.
bogeyman – common symbol of irrational fear of unknown or imagined threats.
bridge – general symbol for linkage and connection, particularly between the world of the material and the divine, of passing between realms, and of being initiated from a lower level to a higher one.
bronze – symbol of splendour, craft, technological progress, the quality of precisely directed force, and the glory of victory.
brown – the colour of human life, decay, practicality, reliability, comfort, warmth, honesty, stability, restraint and dullness.
bull – symbolic of male power, masculinity and virility, especially in the Spanish culture.

C

caduceus – Greek symbol of a winged, snake-wrapped staff, representing commerce, specifically that the wielder is ready to trade.
cap of estate – the dome of cloth inside a crown that represents the monarch's direct link to the land he or she rules, so that it shall prosper or sicken as he or she prospers or sickens.
cat – symbolic of beauty and grace and, by association, of enchantment and bewitchment.
cave – Freudian symbol for a vagina.
cave – landscape representing a step outside reality, moving outside time, liminal existence, divinity, the dead, the underworld, hidden power, initiation and rebirth.
celtic cross – European symbol representing the union of heaven and earth, and therefore infinity and the protection of the divine.
champagne flute – modern symbol of wealth, luxury, privilege and the millionaire lifestyle.
chaosphere – occult symbol representing infinite options and the diversity of the routes to power, along with the myriad ways in which the magician's will can be realised.
chevron – token of rank, symbolising faithful service.
child – Jungian archetype symbolising innocence.
chimney stack – Freudian symbol for an erect penis.
cigar – Freudian symbol for an erect penis.
circle – Symbolic representation of the wheel of time, particularly in the sense of eternity and infinite duration.
city – artificial landscape representing worldly power, resources, opportunity, knowledge, communication, vice, danger and intrigue.
compass – Masonic symbol for perfection, God's love, spirituality, the union of heaven and earth, and the provenance of the divine.
crossed keys – symbolically, the keys to the kingdom of heaven, a token of the power held by the Christian pope.
crossroads – common cultural symbol of choice, transition, solitude, motivation and reflection; a dangerous place where barriers break down, and gods and demons may be found.
crown – artistic symbol of monarchy, nobility, government, and other forms of worldly authority.

D

dark stranger – Jungian archetype symbolising mystery and hidden past.
desert – landscape representing spiritual and physical trial and challenge, deep wisdom and enlightenment, and perfect, impartial honesty.

dove – symbol of love, passion, partnership, devotion, beauty, peace, spiritual advancement and generosity.
dragon – symbol of eternal vigilance.
eagle – symbolises might in battle, discernment, power, freedom, courage, readiness for action and the discernment of command; also military token of rank.

E

earth – symbolically nature and the natural world, therefore both the warm, comforting source of all we have, and also the cold grave populated by monsters and poisonous plants.
east – the direction of birth, childhood, happiness, energy, home, mystery, wonder, immortality and heaven.
eight – the number of regeneration, rebirth, transformation and physical perfection.
elephant – strength, cunning, patience, memory, strong ambition, dignity, power and royalty.
eleven – the number of impending trouble, isolation and uncertainty.
eye of horus – Egyptian symbol of indestructibility, endurance, royal power, protection against dark forces, and rebirth.

F

fire – symbolises energy, cosmic power, achievement, development, the quality of irresistible power, movement, light and warmth.
five – the number of life, human experience, protection, spirituality and individuality.
fleur-de-lys – a stylised iris (or perhaps sword) used as a symbolic emblem of French royalty.
fleur-de-lys – enigmatic French symbol representing perfection, life, the forces of light, and the monarchy of France.
forest – landscape representing uncertainty, trickery, the unconscious mind, fairy tales, magic and the unknown.
forty-two – symbolic of the ultimate answer to all of life's mysteries.
foundation symbol – one of the primal symbols derived from human experience and used as building blocks within larger, more complex symbols.
four – the number of stability, manifestation and the physical world.

G

galactic butterfly – Mayan sign of the chief god, Hunab Ku, which symbolised all of creation and purportedly could act as a gateway to other galaxies and the barriers of time and space.
Ganesha – Hindu deity considered symbolic of learning, wisdom, intelligence, education, writing, good fortune, common sense and gateways and doorways.
gold – the colour of success, top quality, victory, the sun, wealth and opulence.
golden fish – Buddhist symbol of enlightenment, spiritual freedom, perfect happiness, fertility, abundance, marital bliss and general good luck.
green – the colour of nature, wealth, currency, health, ecology, safety, permission, harmony, jealousy, inexperience, greed and death.

H

helmet – artistic symbol of military skill and power, personal protection, nobility, and the occult power of invisibility.
helmet of Athene – symbol of the greek goddess's wisdom and skill in battle.
holy grail – Christian symbol of the quest for self-realisation and other near-impossible goals and dreams; also purity, healing, perfection and immortality in general.
horse – symbol of energy, libido, travel and freedom, along with intelligence, daring, charm and impetuosity; also the traditional heraldic sign of the German peoples.
horse – symbol of harnessed power, the force required to actually do work.
house – artificial landscape representing personal privacy and space, empowerment, control and protection.

I

ichthys – christian symbol used to denote hidden faith in times of oppression, said to represent a fish.
indigo – the colour of dreams, mysteries, psychic powers, the third eye and the fore-runners.
iron – symbolic of hard solidity, the quality of indomitable spirit and resistance, the material world untouched by the spiritual, animalistic instincts and brutality.

J

jewellery – symbolises worldly wealth and privilege, money, avarice, even open greed.
jungle – landscape representing unchecked fecundity, chaos, confusion, lethal danger, mystery, hidden secrets and enigmas.

K

kangaroo – the national symbol of Australian identity.

L

lamb – Christian symbol of selfless sacrifice and Christ's role in redemption, the cleansing of sin, protection, redemption and purification.

latin cross – Christian symbol of Christ's sacrifice and rebirth, the power of redemption and the promise of eternal life in heaven.
lion – heraldic symbol of courage, might, strength, military prowess, justice, majesty, resurrection and vigilance; also the national symbol of English identity.
lotus – the urge to rise above the physical; also therefore purity of mind, body and spirit, discipline, balance and enlightenment.
lozenge – token of rank, symbolising honesty and reliability.

M

machinery – artistic symbol of dehumanisation, oppression, the power of the mechanical world, mass production and the irrelevance and disempowerment of the individual.
magician's circle – occult symbol representing the protection of the trinity of father, son and holy ghost extended to eternity; by extension, a powerful seal of protection that no malign spirit could pass.
maple leaf – national symbol of Canadian identity, from their extensive population of maple trees.
Marianne – the name given to the French revolutionary character symbolising Liberty.
maze – symbol of insanity, mental illness, anguish, confusion, beguilement and imprisonment; or, as a path, a symbol of the twisted route required to gain power, generally in a spiritual sense.
menorah – Jewish symbol of divine light, understanding, wisdom and protection.
minotaur – Greek mythological creature with the body of a man and the head of a bull, symbolic of man's worst bestial side.
mirror – wisdom, self-awareness, vanity, the act of learning.
monas heiroglyphica – alchemical symbol representing the union of the planets and their embodiment within the classical elements.
morion – heraldic symbol of the protection and security that results from a strong, safe defence.
mosaic decalogue – Jewish symbol of the ten commandments, representing obedience, virtue, clean living, the order of society and the word of god itsef.
mountain – landscape representing dominance, permanence, unyielding resilience, the centre of the world, magnificence, purity, sanctity and majesty.

N

Natraj – Hindu symbol of the deity Shiva in a specific dance pose representing the spiral of creation and destruction.
nine – the number of magical power, energy directed and creativity fulfilled.
north – the direction of modernism, materialism, science, industrialisation, aggression, coldness and dynamism.

O

oak leaf – heraldic symbol of resilience, strength, endurance and virtue; also military token of rank.
ocean – landscape representing cruelty, timelessness, infinity, lack of identity, hidden depths, barriers.
old man – Jungian archetype symbolising wisdom.
olive leaf – Christian symbol of peace, cessation of danger, new accords and fresh hope.
one – the number of unity, fellowship, individuality, loneliness, sterility, the spark of life and infinity.
orange – the colour of warmth, stimulation, appetite, sociability, wholesomeness, confidence, charm, adventure, seduction, political rebellion and the Dutch.
owl – according to tradition, can symbolise wisdom and protection, or witchcraft and death.

P

pallium – a band of lambswool, symbolising the lamb that the good shepherd carried on his shoulders, and therefore selflessness, kindness and dedication.
peacock – complex symbol for immortality, transformation, joy, creation, worldly value, sincerity, courage, beauty, vanity, power, isolation and narcissism.
pearls – semen, rebirth, reproduction, long life, energy, marriage, protection from poison, clear sight.
pelican – Christian symbol of unconditional motherly love, from the myth that it would feed its own children with its heart's blood if necessary.
pen – Freudian symbol for an erect penis.
pentagram – a five-pointed star in a circle, associated erroneously in the press with black magic and Satanism.
pentagram – symbol of feminine mysteries and the power ofVenus in ancient times, now more usually associated with spiritual protection, witchcraft, paganism and the unity of the four elements with spiritual energy to create a living being.
Pentateuch – Jewish symbol of the laws of god, the virtues of stability in society, the teaching tradition.
Phrygian Cap – a type of hat symbolising freedom from slavery, as used to be worn by slaves who had earned that reward in ancient Greece.
pineapple – symbolic statement that the bearer always keeps to the very highest standards of sociability amongst the elite.
pink – the colour of sweetness, childhood, girlishness and male homosexuality.

pink lotus – Buddhist symbol of purity in mind, body and spirit, and of the joy of performing good deeds.

plate – Freudian symbol for a vagina.

poppy – symbolic of oblivion, death and unconsciousness, but also of the underworld, rebirth and ecstasy.

precious knot – Buddhist symbol representing the unity of opposites and the interconnectedness of all things.

purple – the colour of imperial wisdom, power, luxury, ceremony, arrogance, cruelty, excess and homosexuality.

R

red – the colour of blood, life, mortality, fire, power, sexuality, rage, destruction, excitement and war.

right-coiled conch – Buddhist symbol of enlightenment, waking out of ignorance, driving off evil, the spread of dharma, and of authority and power.

river – landscape representing time, eternity, passage, escape, adventure, resistance, fertility and independence.

rocker – token of rank, symbolising exceptional merit and bravery.

S

sacred heart – Christian symbol of divine love, Christ's emotional life and his love for mankind in particular, and the importance of returning that love.

sailing ship – artistic symbol representing an individual's life, especially with regards to the course of events and passage through time.

scarab – Egyptian symbol of the sun, and therefore protection, bounty and good luck.

sceptre – earthly power, the force controlled by authority, armed might and the application of military resources.

sea – Freudian symbol for sexuality and sex drive.

seal of Solomon – occult symbol of two triangles interlocked inside a circle, each representing the holy trinity of father, son and holy ghost; by uniting the two, one for the will of magician and one for the purpose of heaven, the resultant seal was thought to be irresistibly powerful.

seashell – Christian symbol of pilgrimage, extended travel, and the difficulties of understanding the limitless infinity of God.

set square – Masonic symbol for strength of character, fair dealing, social responsibility, moral conduct and upstanding behaviour.

seven – the number of divinity manifest, the path to God, integration, schemes of existence and synthesis.

shadow – Jungian archetype symbol for a person's self-destructive urges.

shaft of light – a common artistic symbol for wisdom, divine inspiration, protection, the influence of heaven and the light of God's love in general.

shield – Freudian symbol for a vagina.

shield – solar symbol for the disk of the sun itself, along with a more general meaning as a source of protection and security.

shore – landscape representing peace, beauty, romance, evocation, safety, calm, contemplation and retreat.

silk parasol – Buddhist symbol of safety and protection, privilege, wisdom, compassion and calm.

silver – the colour of moonlight, witchcraft, enigmas, women's mysteries and second place.

six – the number of equilibrium, balance, harmony, the state of grace, good luck, health and mankind.

skull – common symbol of death and, by extension, disease, old age, lethal threats, violence, decay and putrefaction.

south – the direction of innocence, intuition, holism, feeling, playfulness, peace, warmth and spiritual wellbeing.

sovereign's orb – Christian symbol of God's delegation of authority and rulership over a land to its sovereign; that is, of the divine right to rule.

spear of Athene – symbolic representation of the power of lightning.

sphinx – symbolises enigmas and mystery, along with vigilance, power and strength.

spiral – as a natural shape found in nature, considered symbolic of life and growth, breath, expansion, progress, evolution and regeneration, and the building and channelling of power.

staff – the weapon of the element of fire in classical thought, representing energy, power and applied force.

staff of Asculapius – Greek symbol of a staff with a snake coiled around it, representing the healing arts and power over death.

star – symbol of truth, hope, nobility, divine blessing and knighthood; also military token of rank.

star of David – the symbol of Jewish nationality and identity.

stone – said to symbolise unyielding firmness, the quality of immovability, permanence, and energy made manifest.

sundial – an artistic symbol representing time, both in the sense of an instant passing, and also the weight of history and static time already passed.

swastika – originally a Hindu solar symbol of luck, good fortune, the cycle of life, death and rebirth, the path of life itself, the entirety of creation, the four Noble Aims of human life, and prosperity and benefit in general. The symbol's use by

the Nazi Party has stained its associations significantly, for now at least.
sword – Freudian symbol for an erect penis.

T

ten – the number of wholeness, maximum quality and satisfaction.
tent – symbolises temporary space, a portable sacred zone kept away from reality, and therefore can become a sacred place of power in which to contact the divine.
thirteen – the number of bad luck, defeat and death.
thorn – early society, virgin soil and, by extension, virginity in general; also, because many hot-climate plants bear thorns, associated with the element of fire.
three – the number of completion, sexual union, manifestation, energy, resolution, magic and divinity.
thunderbolt – Greek symbol of a jagged lightning bolt representing death, destruction, ruin and righteous vengeance.
tie – item of clothing that symbolically declares the wearer is owned, like a slave.
train entering tunnel – Freudian symbol of sex.
tree of life – Jewish symbol representing both the act and the entirety of creation, the process of converting God's will into matter, the path to enlightenment, the creative process and the structure of systems in general.
triquetra – European knot symbol representing eternity and infinity and, by extension, the realm of heaven and the power of the gods.
triregnum – the pope's three-layered crown, representing his authority over church, state and populace.
tudor rose – British symbol representing unification and healing after the civil war known as the Wars of the Roses.
twelve – the number of measurement, cycles and complete sets.
twenty-three – symbolic of the positive chaotic forces of creation.
two – the number of perception, duality, opposition, deviance, corruption, stability, reflection, balance and creation.

U

udgitha – the sacred om, symbol of the unreality of the world, the enlightenment of the self and the true nature of the infinite divine.

V

valley – landscape representing fertility, shelter, hospitality, peace, plenty and safety.
vampire – Jungian archetype symbolising parasitic behaviour.
vase of treasure – Buddhist symbol representing financial wealth, material possessions, long life and good health.
venus figurine – symbolic representation of female fertility.

violet – the colour of spirituality and divinity.
violin – artistic symbol of technical expertise in the musical arts.

W

wand – a variant of the staff; the magickal weapon of the element of fire, representing energy and force applied.
water – symbol of the unconscious mind, pregnancy and birth, life itself, psychic ability, higher consciousness, and the quality of being proof against all magic.
west – the direction of death, darkness, evil, old age, illness, lawlessness, frontiers, exploration and purgatory.
wheel of Dharma – Buddhist symbol representing the circular process of learning and understanding, particularly as applied to Buddhism itself.
white – the colour of purity, perfection, innocence, truth, sincerity, joy, glory, sterility, coldness, arrogance, cruelty, extremism, insanity and royalty.
White House, the – building symbolizing American power and self-determination, the pinnacle of ambition, and the American Dream.
wood – symbolic of suppleness and flexibility, natural matter, the quality of supernatural knowledge and wisdom, potential, and the awakening of love.
wreath – symbolic of victory and the honours accrued by winning; also military token of rank.

X

x – mathematical symbol for an unknown quantity, and by extension, anything mysterious, enigmatic or unknown.

Y

yahrzeit – Jewish symbol of the soul and its journey after death to the kingdoms of heaven.
yellow – the colour of cheer, hope, harmony, idealism, stimulation, creativity, wisdom, personal power, communication, attention and peacefulness.
yin-yang – balance, perfect harmony, completion, eternity, and the way of Taoism.

Z

zero – the number of absence, loss, irrelevance, unimportance and void.

The publishers would like to thank the following sources for their kind permission to reproduce the pictures in this book.

Adelaide City Council: 88

AKG-Images: 29 tl, 30 b, 51, 57, /British Library: 76, 85, 140 b, /Cameraphoto: 22 b, 38, /Peter Connolly: 31 t, /Erich Lessing: 47 tr 103 t,

Alamy Images: /ArkReligion.com: 110, /Christine Osborne Pictures: 126, 145 t, /David Crausby: 104, /Robert Fried: 136, /Jack Cox - Travel Pic Pro: 103 b, /Fiona Jeffrey: 130 b, /Maurice Joseph: 129 t, /Mikael Karlsson: 101, /Bob Watkins Photofusion Picture Library: 89 tl, /Malie Rich-Griffith/Infocus Photos: 72/73, / Robert Harding Picture Library Ltd: 145 b, /Janine Wiedel Photolibrary: 90

Ancient Art & Architecture: 142 bl

Bandiana Museum: 95tr, cr, bl, bc &br

The Bridgeman Art Library: Bildarchiv Steffens - Happiness and Love, from 'The Never-ending Knot of Life' 131 b / Birmingham Museums and Art Gallery - Beata Beatrix by Dante Gabriel Rossetti 52 tr / Private Collection - Gathering Wood, engraved by R. M. Meadows : 29 b / Moby Dick by Jonathan Barry: 30 t / Plan of the Road from the City of Destruction to the Celestail City from the Pilgrims Progress: 33 / Members of the SS Nationalist Party with Heinrich Himmler: 89 b / General William H. Harrison at the Battle of Tippecanoe 92 / Imperial War Museum - Congressional Medal of Honor 94 r,/ Walker Art Gallery, National Museums, Liverpool - Queen Elizabeth IThe Pelican Portrait by Nicholas Hilliard: 82, /Brooklyn Museum of Art, New York, USA, Charles Edwin Wilbour Fund - The Goddess Anuket by Jean-Francois Champollion 31 b, /Lauros/Giraudon/Louvre, Paris, FranceThe Medici Cycle by Peter Paul Rubens 8, /The Virgin and Child with SS Anne and J: 43, /Palazzo del Te, Mantua, Itlay –Venus by Giulio Romano 10 br, /Canadian Museum of Civilisation, Ottawa, Canada - View of the museum complex 69

Corbis: 135 t, /Alinari Archives: 64 t, /Andy Clark/Reuters: 114, /Araldo de Luca: 45 t, 142 tl, /Archivio Iconografico, S.A.: 10 tr, 32 bl, 34, 36, 39, 41 b, 41 t, 50 b, /Arte & Immagini srl: 40, /Dave Bartruff: 108, 138 b, /Nathan Benn: 111 br, /Bettmann: 37, 79, 80, 84, 133 b, /Christie's Images: 14 t, /Lorenzo Ciniglio / Corbis / Sygma: 115 t, /Darama: 99 b, /Darren Staples/Reuters: 112, /David Samuel Robbins: 131, /David Turnley: 15 t, /Ed Quinn: 93 b, /Emely/zefa: 25 tl, /Greg English /Corbis Sygma: 102 t, /Francis G. Mayer: 46, /Robert Garvey: 115 c, /Gianni Dagli Orti: 47 tl, 47 b, /Farrell Grehan: 74, /Gunter Marx Photography: 144, /Historical Picture Archive: 67 b, /Andrew Holbroke: 98 , /Hulton-Deutsch Collection: 139, /James P. Blair: 62 t, /John & Lisa Merrill: 93 t, /Joseph Sohm; Visions of America: 60, /Daniel Laine: 102 b, /Lecocq Alain/Corbis Sygma: 78, /David Lees: 83, /Matthew Eye Ubiquitous: 115 b, /Wally McNamee: 140 t, /NASA/JPL/Cornell/Zuma: 10 tl, /Nathan Benn: 94 l, /Owaki-Kulla: 13 tr, /Barbara Peacock: 25 tr, /Peter Russell/ Military Picture Library: 95tl, /Petr Josek: 14 b, /Carl & Ann Purcell: 111 bl, /Rebecca McEntee-Scoggin / Corbis Sygma: 105, /Roger Ressmeyer: 67 t, /Lew Robertson: 111 br, /Galen Rowell: 26, /Royalty Free: 20 t, 65, 109 t, /Royalty- Free: 116, 120, /Royalty-Free: 10 bl, 19t, 109b, 122, 125, 135 t, 137 /Rypka/ Bettmann: 107, /Paul A. Souders: 91, /Ted Spiegel: 44, /Michael St. Maur Sheil: 143 r, /Summerfield Press: 42, 48, /Homer Sykes: 64 b, /William Whitehurst: 21 t, /Eric K. K.Yu: 89 tr

Empics: Matthew Ashton: 16 bl

Getty Images: 58, 62 b, /AFP/Thomas Coex: 86, /Chuck Nacke/ Timepix/Time Life Pictures: 96 , 100, /Graeme Robertson: 106, /Headhunters / DigitalVision: 17, /Ronald Martinez: 113, /Paul & Lindamarie Ambrose: 16 br

Instant Art ©: 119, 120t, 121, 122, 123b, 124

Lonely Planet Images: Phil Weymouth: 75

Mary Evans Picture Library: 13 tl

Masterengraver: 104t

Photos12.com: ARJ: 22 t, 49, 53, /Collection Cinema: 32 br, /Institut Ramses: 143 bl, /Oronoz: 19 b, 29 tr, 45 b, 50 t, 70, /Succession Picasso / DACS 2006: 54 & 55

Picture Desk: Egyptian Museum Cairo / Dagli Orti: 142 r, /Lucas Film / 20th Century Fox: 18, /Private Collection: 111 t, /Warner Bros: 13 b

Rex Features: Mimmo Frassineti: 21 b, /Andy Paradise: 12 t, / Dave Penman: 68, /Sky Magazine: 12 b

Science Photo Library: Space Imaging: 61

The University of Reading: Otto & Marie Neurath Isotype Collection: 118

Tim Graham: 87

Topfoto.co.uk: 25 b, 66, 130 t, 132, 133 t, 138 t, 141, 142 tl, 146, 147, /Collection Roger-Viollet: 23, / The Image Works: 15 b (David Frazier), 24, 63, 99t (Peter Hvizdak), /Fortean: 28, 134, /PAL: 16 t, /Private Collection: 20 b,

Trip and Art Directors: Peter Barker: 128, /Tibor Bognar: 129 b

Werner Forman Archive: Statens Historiska Museet, Stockholm: 135 b

Every effort has been made to acknowledge correctly and contact the source and/or copyright holder of each picture and Carlton Books Limited apologises for any unintentional errors or omissions which will be corrected in future editions of this book.